HOW TO
EATALY

ITALY
IS
EATALY

YOU ARE
WHAT YOU
EATALY.

EATALY

VINO

HOW TO
EATALY

A Guide to Buying, Cooking, and Eating
ITALIAN FOOD

INTRODUCTION BY
OSCAR FARINETTI, FOUNDER

FOREWORDS BY
JOE BASTIANICH, LIDIA BASTIANICH, MARIO BATALI, AND
ADAM & ALEX SAPER

WRITTEN WITH NATALIE DANFORD
PHOTOGRAPHS BY FRANCESCO SAPIENZA

RIZZOLI
NEW YORK

New York Paris London Milan

GRAZIE MILLE to Marco Ausenda, Christopher Steighner, Natalie Danford, Francesco Sapienza, Alison Lew, Tricia Levi, and Maeve Sheridan for your unwavering patience and direction. We know we sometimes had too many cooks in the kitchen.

GRAZIE INFINITE to Dino Borri and Cristina Flores for supervising the editorial production of this book at every stage, as well as to Alex Pilas, Fitz Tallon, Katia Delogu, Dan Amatuzzi, Tracey Bachman, Alicia Walter, John Wersan, Simona Picco, Peter Mutino, Peter Molinari, Greg Blais, Lara Beggin, Olivia Butrick, Kristen Boidy, Abigail Grueskin, Nick Coleman, Andrew Marcelli, Cristina Villa, Noemi Ferro, and Fred Avila for helping us capture our market, restaurants, and cooking school between the two covers of this book.

GRAZIE DI CUORE to the entire Eataly team whose dedication, hard work, and talent is unequivocally unsurpassed.

"Life is a combination of magic and pasta."
—*Federico Fellini*

First published in the United States of America in 2014
by Rizzoli International Publications, Inc.
300 Park Avenue South
New York, NY 10010
www.rizzoliusa.com

© 2014 Rizzoli International Publications, Inc.

Text by Natalie Danford
Photographs by Francesco Sapienza
FrancescoSapienza.com
Photo page 3 by Virginia Mae Rollison
Design by Vertigo NYC
Illustrations by Zachary Hewitt

2014 2015 2016 2017 / 10 9 8 7 6 5 4 3 2 1

Distributed in the U.S. trade by Random House, New York
Printed in China
ISBN-13: 978-0-8478-4335-0
Library of Congress Catalog Control Number: 2014941649

CONTENTS

INTRODUCTION
BY OSCAR FARINETTI

I opened the first Eataly in Turin in 2007 with the idea that it would be much more than a store—it would be a school, a market, a place to gather and to eat, but also a place to learn about food and, through food, about life. Eataly stores are large—they are often referred to in the press as "mega-stores"—but each one comprises hundreds of stories of small producers. And Eataly is not simply a place—or these days, a series of places located around the world—but an experience. It has met and even exceeded my expectations. Yes, you can visit Eataly and buy a few tomatoes, a piece of cheese, and a bread and make yourself a delicious dinner, but you can (and I hope you will) learn how those tomatoes were grown, explore the history of an Italian region through that cheese, and stop to appreciate the smell of baking bread made with natural yeast.

Similarly, the book you hold in your hands is more than just a cookbook. Of course, if you want to know how to make an excellent tagliatelle alla Bolognese, you will find a recipe here. (On page 56, to be exact.) But I hope that you will delve into these pages and find so much more: information about the products that make Italian food great, descriptions of my country's regional classics, informal instructions for making hundreds of Italian home-style dishes, profiles of many of the small producers who are a great strength of Eataly, and instructions for living the way Italians do, with enjoyment, style, and an appreciation for the small delights that make life worthwhile.

Forgive me if this all sounds serious. At Eataly, we want to challenge you to look at your food (and drink) in a different way, but we don't want to make it seem like dreary homework. We love high-quality food and drink, and we're endlessly fascinated by the stories of the people who produce it and the places where it is made and grown. Food brings people together, and eating is the one thing that unites us all, everywhere in the world. We hope that you'll agree with us that eating mindfully, with education and knowledge, and satisfying your curiosity is even more fulfilling than simply nourishing yourself because you're hungry. We're passionate about food, but equally passionate about enjoying it and deriving happiness from it. We hope you'll feel the same, and that you'll return to this book again and again to learn, to practice, and to feed not just your stomach, but your mind and your heart.

FOREWORDS

Joe Bastianich

I believe that wine is food. Wine should be an integral part of every meal and every menu, not just an afterthought. Italian wine is as diverse and interesting as Italian food, and the two have a natural affinity for each other—as they say, if it grows together, it goes together. Wine can be intimidating for some, but keep an open mind and an open palate. Have the confidence to trust what tastes good to you, and you'll find that determining which wines you like is no more difficult than determining which foods you like. There is a specific section dedicated to wine in this book, but it's not solely segregated to one place—wine is a fundamental part of what makes up Italian cuisine, and subsequently can be found throughout all parts of this book. Eataly is designed to stimulate all of your senses. When you visit Eataly, you don't simply taste things—you also smell the food cooking and touch vegetables to test their ripeness. You look around and take in the contemporary style of the stores, and you listen and learn from our knowledgeable staff members and sometimes from your fellow customers, who may recommend some of their favorites that become your favorites, too. Eataly—the stores and this book—forms a kind of community, and you should rely on that community, but also be an active member of it through exploration, of wine, food, and everything else that Italy has to offer.

Lidia Bastianich

Every Italian—from Sicilia up to Piemonte—thinks that the food his or her mother made was the best ever. It's no accident that we associate eating Italian food with gathering around a table with friends and family—that truly is how we Italians eat.

Step back for a moment and look at the larger picture. Italian food is strongly regional. Italy has twenty regions, and each has its own specialties. A region's cuisine is a reflection of many things: its history, its geography, its climate. That's why many of the recipes in this book are marked as belonging to specific regions. But if you drill down further, each town in Italy (most of which were originally city-states with their own currency, language, and ruler) within those regions has its own traditions. Pan in a little closer, and you'll see that each neighborhood in those towns has its rituals, and then, at the most granular level, enter any home kitchen and you'll find that each family has its specific way of doing things, handed down over the generations.

With the recipes and the information in this book, you'll be able to prepare delicious food for your own friends and family and discover the pleasure of feeding them. But don't be afraid to put your own twist on a classic, using the ingredients that are fresh and available in your area—nothing could be more Italian than that.

Mario Batali

If I had to summarize what Eataly does—in the stores, in this book, and elsewhere—I'd say that it heightens awareness of what makes Italian food great. And if I had to summarize what it is that makes Italian food great, I'd say it's simplicity. Almost every first-time visitor to Italy has this experience: you get there, and you taste something you've eaten before in your home country— say spaghetti al pomodoro. But in Italy, you can't believe how delicious it is. That's because they're using the right kind of spaghetti, the right kind of tomatoes, the right kind of olive oil, the right kind of salt. Everything is in balance. The ingredients aren't arranged in some fancy new way, or cooked employing a complicated technique that takes years to master. They're handled with respect, and they're used properly. Seasonal ingredients are not just in season, they are grown not far from where you're eating. (And each Eataly store, whether in Chicago or Tokyo or Rome, sells products from local producers.) But you have to start with the best ingredients, or your dish will go nowhere. When you're blown away in Italy, it's almost always a moment of discovering that less is more. In these pages, you'll discover the same.

Adam & Alex Saper

Eataly is more than a store; it's a lifestyle. Just as an Italian starts his or her day by visiting a bar for an espresso and a quick glance at the newspaper, visits a fruttivendolo and a macellaio later in the day to buy food for lunch or dinner, and stops at a gelateria for a cone or a cup of something sweet, you can visit the various areas in Eataly throughout the day for different reasons, or you can dip into this book and use it as a guide for engaging in that Italian lifestyle. Want to know the proper way to indulge in a digestivo after a meal? See page 287. Facing a plate of spaghetti and unsure how to enjoy it without splattering yourself? See page 57. Want to hold an olive oil tasting for your friends? That's on page 15. But really this entire book is meant to help you understand that there's a whole world of pleasure out there that's yours for the taking. A lot of it is related to food and drink, but much of it is related to a broader concept: relaxing and enjoying life. Slow your pace a bit, and no matter where you find yourself, inject a little of that Italian approach into your day.

HOW TO
EATALY

DAL MERCATO

The secret to quality of life?
Quality products.

OLIO EXTRA VERGINE D'OLIVA

Olives are a fruit, and olive oil is a fresh fruit juice—and a pretty delicious one. Every year in the fall, olives are harvested across Italy. Then the olives are pressed using a time-honored process. (Like wine, olive oil has a vintage—the harvest date should appear on the bottle.) Extra-virgin olive oil is the highest quality—the term indicates that an oil is from the first pressing, which means it's lower in acidity. Locate an olive oil that you enjoy—whether it be grassy, mild, peppery, or sweet—and stock up on it. But don't buy more than you can use over the course of a few months and expect it to last infinitely. Time, light, heat, and air are the enemies of olive oil. We store our bottles away from the windows in our stores, and you should do the same at home—and don't store the oil near your stove or other sources of heat, either.

Olive oil is very versatile: It can be used for cooking, dressing salads, or drizzled *crudo,* or raw, on a finished dish. Indeed, it would be easier to count the dishes in this book where we don't call for olive oil than where we do—it's an essential ingredient throughout. Additionally, Italians preserve a wide array of produce—chili peppers, eggplants, mushrooms, and more—in olive oil. Truly, olive oil's rewards are endless; it is even used to make skin-care products.

Fine olive oil is expensive, but for good reason—many of the olives for high-quality oils are handpicked and then cold-pressed within hours of the harvest. This results in an oil that captures the taste and aroma of the fruit—an oil that truly tastes of olives. And olive oil is like wine, in the sense that you shouldn't cook with an olive oil you wouldn't happily consume in its raw state. We've seen the advice over the years to cook with lesser quality olive oil, but as Italians, we shudder at that idea. Most Italian food—pasta, beans—is incredibly inexpensive. Splurge on the olive oil, and use it with a free hand. When you think you've added enough, drizzle on just a touch more.

SIGNS OF QUALITY

Almost every Italian dish benefits from being finished with a drizzle of extra-virgin olive oil.

Olive oil has been used as a preserving agent for eons. Try olives, vegetables, and other Italian specialties preserved in quality extra-virgin olive oils.

ANATOMY OF AN OLIVE OIL BOTTLE

HARVEST DATE A bottle of olive oil should bear a *harvest date;* the freshest oils are best. Unlike wine, olive oil does not need to be aged.

CULTIVAR High-quality olive oil always indicates the type of olives, or *cultivar,* used.

REGION OF ORIGIN High-quality Italian olive oil will name the *region of origin* and not just say "Product of Italy." Bottles labeled with the country in general may contain oil that was simply bottled in Italy but came from olives grown elsewhere.

OLIVE OIL VOCABULARY

The three basic categories to consider for olive oil are fruitiness, pungency, and bitterness. Here are some other flavors and qualities you may discern in olive oil:

almond	apple	artichoke	banana	buttery	cherry
creamy	floral	grassy	green tomato	herbaceous	nutty
peppery	pine	pine nuts	stone fruit	sweet	

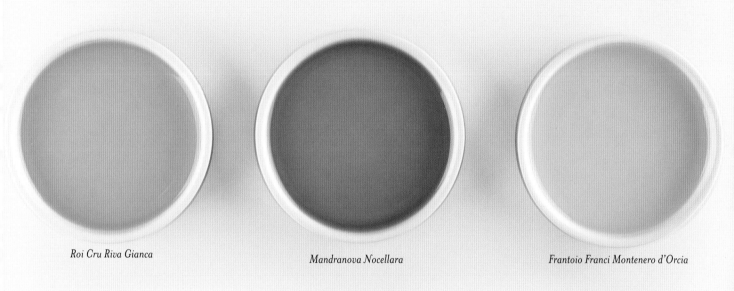

Roi Cru Riva Gianca

Mandranova Nocellara

Frantoio Franci Montenero d'Orcia

How to TASTE OLIVE OIL

OLIVE OIL TASTING IS SIMILAR TO WINE TASTING, and just like wines, olive oils have a very wide variety of tastes and aromas. A tasting can both sharpen your palate and allow you to identify what kind of oil you prefer. Stage a home tasting of at least three and no more than five oils as a prelude to your next dinner party—it's a fun way to get the evening started and pique both appetites and curiosity.

1. Pour a tablespoon or two of olive oil into a stemless wineglass. (The pros use special blue glasses that are intended to disguise the color of the oil, which says little about the flavor but might unconsciously affect judgment.)

2. Cup the glass in your hands and swirl the oil gently to release aromas.

3. Stick your nose in the glass and inhale deeply.

4. Slurp a mouthful of oil while inhaling noisily, just as your mother taught you not to eat soup. Drawing air in heightens the flavor. Then breathe out through your nose.

5. Swallow while concentrating on the flavor.

6. Between oils, cleanse your palate with a thin slice of Granny Smith apple or a cube of plain bread.

BAGNA CAUDA
GARLIC AND ANCHOVY SAUCE WITH CRUDITÉS

Serves 8 to 10 as an appetizer   *Piemonte*

6 cups seasonal vegetables (see suggestions page 17)

Fine sea salt to taste

Freshly ground black pepper to taste

½ cup extra-virgin olive oil

2 tablespoons butter (optional)

6 cloves garlic, thinly sliced

6 anchovy fillets, minced

Bagna cauda, which literally means "hot bath," is a flavorful sauce first devised by ancient Piemontese winemakers. Traditionally, diners gather around the bagna cauda, which is served warm in a special earthenware pot, and dip in their raw vegetables (kind of our version of crudités and onion dip). That's a fun, communal way to start a dinner (and if you've got a fondue pot around, you can give it a try), but tossing the vegetables with the warm sauce is a more convenient way to serve the dish. This pungent and highly addictive sauce tastes good with almost anything—the suggestions for seasonal vegetables are simply that, suggestions. Use whatever you find in the market that is wonderfully fresh, cut it into manageable pieces, and you can't go wrong. The secret is to cook the mixture over a very low flame and only until it is a light golden color—stir it very frequently to keep it cooking low and slow. A burnt bagna cauda will be bitter and difficult to digest. If you have an immersion blender, it works perfectly for pureeing this sauce. This is an ideal opportunity to use Eataly's vegetable butcher and save yourself the trouble of cutting up all the vegetables.

IN a large bowl, toss the vegetables with salt and pepper. (Remember that the anchovies will be salty.)

PLACE 3 tablespoons of the olive oil and the butter, if using, in a heavy-bottomed pot (preferably earthenware) over very low heat. Add the garlic and cook, stirring very frequently, just until the garlic begins to color, about 30 minutes. Add the anchovies and continue to cook over low heat, stirring constantly, until the anchovies dissolve, about 5 additional minutes. Remove from the heat and stir in the remaining 5 tablespoons olive oil. Process until smooth with an immersion blender or beat vigorously with a wooden spoon to combine.

IMMEDIATELY pour 6 tablespoons of the anchovy mixture over the vegetables. Toss, taste, adjust seasoning, and add more anchovy mixture if desired, then serve immediately. Any leftover anchovy mixture will keep covered in the refrigerator for 3 to 4 days. Warm over the lowest heat possible before using again.

ROI

In 1900, Giuseppe Boeri signed a two-year lease on a municipal olive oil mill in the hills of Badalucco in Liguria. More than a hundred years and four generations later, the Boeri family (led by Franco, Giuseppe's great-grandson) still uses a traditional stone press to produce its superb, sustainable oil using local Taggiasca olives.

The family accumulated land over the years in Valle Argentina, near Sanremo, so that it now owns about four thousand Taggiasca olive trees. The olive grove sits at about 1,150 to 1,650 feet above sea level and is surrounded by Mediterranean scrub and chestnut trees. Because of the proximity to the sea and the herbs that grow wild all around, the air in this area is wonderfully aromatic, and the oil made there is impregnated with those same irresistible aromas. ROI's olives were certified organic in 2002.

The techniques for processing the olives into oil are designed to wield as little impact on the olives and the resulting oil as possible. For example, ROI uses a traditional stone olive mill to cold-press the olives and keeps their temperature low, as heat alters and dims the flavor of oil. The result is an award-winning series of extremely smooth oils that elevate any dish they touch. ROI olive oil is even used in beauty products such as soap and moisturizer. It benefits the body inside and out.

SEASONAL VEGETABLES FOR BAGNA CAUDA

SPRING	SUMMER	FALL	WINTER
ASPARAGUS, thinly sliced at an angle	BELL PEPPERS, cored and cut into thin strips	BEETS, peeled and thinly sliced	BROCCOLINI, cut into thin stalks
CELERY, thinly sliced at an angle	GREEN BEANS, cut into 1-inch pieces at an angle	CELERY ROOT, peeled and thinly sliced	CARROTS, peeled and cut into matchsticks
RADISHES, cut into eighths	SUMMER SQUASH, thinly sliced	FENNEL, thinly sliced	CAULIFLOWER, cut into small florets
			WINTER SQUASH, peeled and thinly sliced

SALE E PRODOTTI SOTTO SALE

Salt is a key ingredient in every cuisine on earth; Italian food is no exception. Italians cook with sea salt, which is available in fino and grosso (fine and large-grain, or rock salt) versions. Too much salt can overwhelm a dish, but too little salt can also do irreparable damage. The key is to taste constantly, and to keep in mind that dishes with saltier ingredients, such as salumi, may call for a little more restraint on the part of the cook. The best way to get accustomed to using salt instinctively is to keep it in a small jar on the counter, so that you pinch the amount of salt you need rather than pouring it out of a spout. (You'll notice in our stores that Italian salt is packaged in bags and jars, because it's meant to be used this way.) Finally, taste early and often during cooking to ensure that you are striking the right balance. It's almost impossible to correct a lack of salt at the table.

Salt is used not just for seasoning food, but for preserving it as well—salt preservation made it possible to keep seasonal items available year-round long before refrigeration was widely introduced. Italians make great use of these punchy salt-preserved items—olives, capers, and the like—to this day. Almost any savory dish that feels anemic, lacking in that quality the Japanese would call umami, can be perked up with a sprinkling of capers or olives.

capers

Cerignola olives

Castelvetrano olives

Ligurian olives

Taggiasca olives

coarse sea salt

black truffle salt

orange and lavender salt

The Italian Way with SALT RUBS

AT EATALY, MEAT AND POULTRY ARE SEASONED THE NIGHT BEFORE THEY ARE TO BE COOKED. This gives the salt time to penetrate and keeps the meat and poultry moist when they are cooked. Using a salt rub doesn't require much more effort, and it adds flavor to the dish.

The addition of a little sugar to a salt rub helps the surface of the meat brown and sear. This is a kind of light version of the curing process used to make salumi, and you can add all kinds of flavorings to the salt you use.

When working with cut-up meat or poultry, we find it useful to spread out the pieces in a single layer on a sheet pan to season it evenly and thoroughly. Simply sprinkle on a liberal amount of the salt rub and pat it gently into the meat, then turn and sprinkle on the other side. Cover and refrigerate.

For one of our favorite salt rubs, see the recipe for Costine di Manzo ai Porcini con Aceto Balsamico on page 202, or add one of these combinations to a mixture of 3 parts salt and 1 part sugar:

minced fresh rosemary and sage leaves

crushed red pepper flakes and freshly ground black pepper

grated lemon zest and torn mint leaves

minced fresh parsley leaves and toasted ground fennel seeds

grated orange zest and lavender

How to
SALT PASTA COOKING WATER

NO PASTA IS EVER COOKED IN UNSALTED WATER. There is no making up for bland pasta after it is cooked—the only way your finished pasta dish will taste good is if you salt the pasta cooking water sufficiently.

1. Never salt the water until it boils. When the water is boiling, remove the lid.

2. Add a handful of coarse sea salt to the water. This looks like a lot of salt, but most of the salt washes away when you drain the pasta. You want the water to be "just slightly less salty than the sea," according to Alex Pilas, executive chef at Eataly New York.

3. When the water returns to a boil, add the pasta.

SPAGHETTI ALLA PUTTANESCA
SPICY SPAGHETTI WITH OLIVES, CAPERS, AND TOMATOES

Serves 4 as a first course   *Campania*

1 tablespoon extra-virgin olive oil, plus more for drizzling

2 cloves garlic, minced

¼ teaspoon crushed red pepper flakes

¼ cup salted capers, soaked and drained

¼ cup black olives, pitted and chopped

2 anchovy fillets, rinsed and chopped

1 (16-ounce) can whole peeled tomatoes

Coarse sea salt for pasta cooking water

1 pound dried spaghetti

No one is certain how this dish got its name, which translates as "prostitute-style." It may refer to the hot pepper in the sauce, or the fact that it can be thrown together quickly with ingredients that most people have on hand, so that the ladies of the night making it could get back out on the street. This is just one of the dozens of recipes that draw on a well-stocked pantry. With a few choice ingredients and pasta on hand, you will never go hungry.

BRING a large pot of water to a boil.

PLACE the olive oil in a large pan over medium heat. Add the garlic and red pepper flakes and cook, stirring frequently, until the garlic is golden, about 5 minutes. Add the capers, olives, and anchovies and cook. Squeeze the tomatoes into the pan, leaving most of their liquid behind in the can. Cook over medium heat, stirring frequently, until the tomatoes have thickened somewhat, about 5 minutes more.

MEANWHILE, when the water in the large pot boils, salt the water, add the spaghetti, and cook, stirring frequently with a long-handled fork, until al dente. (See page 74 for more detailed instructions on the proper cooking technique for long dried pasta.)

WHEN the pasta is cooked, drain it in a colander and transfer it to the pan with the sauce. Toss vigorously over medium heat until combined, about 2 minutes. Drizzle with additional olive oil and serve immediately.

How to PREPARE GARLIC

GARLIC IS AN INTEGRAL PART OF ITALIAN COOKING, though it is employed with restraint. Garlic is incorporated in different forms. One thing no self-respecting Italian uses, however, is a garlic press. It's unnecessary, not to mention impossible to clean.

1. Separate a clove of garlic from the head.

2. To peel garlic, crush it lightly with the side of a chef's knife. The papery skin should detach easily.

3. Once peeled, garlic may be chopped, minced, sliced, or firmly crushed with the side of a chef's knife.

CAPONATA DI MELANZANE
EGGPLANT CAPONATA

Makes 4 cups, serves 8 as an appetizer   *Sicilia*

2 unpeeled eggplants, cut into ½-inch dice

Fine sea salt to taste

½ cup plus 3 tablespoons red wine vinegar

2 tablespoons golden raisins

5 stalks celery, cut into 1-inch pieces

Extra-virgin olive oil, preferably Sicilian, for cooking the vegetables

1 large red onion, cut into ½-inch dice

2 red bell peppers, cut into ½-inch dice

4 cloves garlic, thinly sliced

2 fresh chili peppers, thinly sliced

5 salted anchovy fillets, rinsed and minced

3 tablespoons sugar

½ cup sun-dried tomatoes in oil, drained and chopped

¼ cup pitted Sicilian green olives, such as Nocellara olives

2 tablespoons pine nuts, lightly toasted

Caponata is a classic sweet-and-sour vegetable relish served as an appetizer (sometimes also served as a side dish) in Sicilia, where eggplants are abundant and flavorful. The trick to a great caponata is to cook the vegetables separately and then combine them at the end; otherwise, their flavors grow muddled. While this is slightly fussy, it is offset by the fact that caponata actually benefits from being prepared in advance and allowed to sit, and the fact that you can use the same pan to prepare each of the vegetables, simply wiping it out in between. The amount of oil required will depend on the size and shape of your pan. If a substantial amount of oil remains in the pan after cooking the celery and onions, pour it off, strain it, and reserve it for another use where its strong onion- and celery-infused flavor will work well. A proper caponata glistens with a fair amount of olive oil—this is a dish lavish with healthy fat.

PLACE the eggplants in a colander and toss with a generous amount of salt. Set aside to drain for 30 minutes.

PLACE ½ cup vinegar in a small bowl. Soak the raisins in the vinegar until plump, about 20 minutes.

HEAT a large sauté pan over high heat. Add the celery to the pan and then add enough olive oil to cover the celery halfway. Cook the celery, stirring often, until it is light golden brown, about 5 minutes. Use a slotted spoon to remove the celery from the pan and let cool in one layer on paper towels.

WIPE out the sauté pan. Reheat it over high heat. Add the onion to the pan and then enough oil to cover the onion halfway. Cook the onion, stirring often, until light golden brown, about 5 minutes. Remove the onion and let it cool in one layer on paper towels.

WIPE out the sauté pan. Gently squeeze excess water out of the eggplant. Heat the sauté pan over medium-high heat. Add just enough oil to coat the bottom of the pan and add the eggplant. Sauté the eggplant, stirring frequently, until golden brown and just cooked through, about 5 minutes. Remove the eggplant from the pan and let it cool in one layer on paper towels.

WIPE out the sauté pan and sauté the bell peppers until soft, about 5 minutes. Remove to cool.

PLACE the garlic and chili peppers in a small sauté pan, season lightly with salt, and add enough oil just to cover. Heat gradually over low heat

until the garlic is soft. Stir in the anchovies, then remove the pan from the heat and allow the mixture to cool.

COMBINE the remaining 3 tablespoons vinegar and the sugar in a small pot. Place over low heat and cook, stirring constantly, until the sugar has dissolved. Set aside to cool.

IN a large bowl, combine the cooked eggplant, celery, and onion with the chopped bell peppers, sun-dried tomatoes, olives, and pine nuts. Drain the raisins and add them to the bowl. Pour the garlic and anchovy mixture on top. Finally, add the sugar and vinegar sauce and mix to combine thoroughly. Season with salt to taste. Add enough additional oil to coat the mixture generously. Store in the refrigerator for at least 3 hours and up to 3 days, but bring to room temperature before serving.

ACETO

Vinegar is a versatile condiment that comes from fermented alcohol. It can be made with red or white wine, beer, cider, or sweet fruit. Prized for its acidic quality, it comes in a range of flavors and viscosities. Before the days of refrigeration, vinegar—like olive oil—was used as a preserving agent in Italy. It is a key component in *agrodolce*, a traditional sweet-and-sour sauce, as well as in dishes such as Pesce in Saor (page 224).

The Italian Way with
VINEGAR AND ITS COUSINS

Balsamic vinegar gets much of the glory, but Italy is home to many other equally good vinegars that are worth exploring. Here are a few of our favorites:

ACETO DI BAROLO *Barolo Vinegar*	full-bodied and rich, this vinegar made from Piemonte's signature wine is delicious drizzled on a risotto
ACETO DI MELE *Apple Cider Vinegar*	possessing thin flavor with a hint of sweetness, this vinegar is perfect for any kind of *agrodolce* preparation
GLASSA DI ACETO BALSAMICO *Balsamic Glaze*	made by reducing balsamic vinegar with sugar; brush on grilled meats
SABA *Cooked Grape Must*	saba is made using the same procedure as for balsamic vinegar, but the must is cooked for a longer period, so that the result is extremely thick; drizzle a little saba on ice cream for a tangy treat

Vinegar isn't just for salad dressing; it's a versatile condiment that ranges in flavor and viscosity.

balsamico di Modena

apple cider vinegar

Pinot Grigio white wine vinegar

saba

red wine vinegar

INSALATA TRICOLORE
THREE-COLOR SALAD

Serves 4 as a side dish   *Emilia-Romagna*

1 bunch arugula

1 head radicchio

1 head endive

¼ cup extra-virgin olive oil

1 tablespoon balsamic vinegar

Fine sea salt to taste

4 ounces Parmigiano Reggiano or Grana Padano

The three colors of this classic salad are those of the Italian flag: red radicchio, white endive, and green arugula. Don't be tempted simply to add the oil and vinegar to the salad and toss—the extra step of emulsifying a vinaigrette in a small bowl and then tossing it with the greens highlights the flavor of both the oil and the vinegar. You can use this dressing on almost any salad or vegetable preparation—it is the only "salad dressing" Italians ever make. Red wine vinegar can be used in place of the balsamic vinegar for a more astringent flavor and is actually a more common choice in Italy for dressing salads.

TEAR the arugula and radicchio into bite-size pieces. Chop the endive. Place the salad greens in a large bowl.

IN a small bowl, whisk together the olive oil and vinegar with a pinch of salt. Drizzle the vinaigrette over the greens and toss, either by hand or with a large spoon and fork.

DIVIDE the salad among individual serving plates. Use a vegetable peeler to shave the cheese over the top.

The Italian Way with
BALSAMIC VINEGAR

Sweet balsamic vinegar—native to Modena, where it has been produced for almost one thousand years—is made by slowly boiling grape must, crushed grape juice made from local Trebbiano and Lambrusco grapes, until it reaches half of its original volume. It is then aged in a series of wood casks. The longer a balsamic vinegar ages, the more syrupy its texture.

There are two official designations for balsamic vinegar: IGP (*Indicazione Geografica Protetta*) balsamic vinegar is aged for at least three years, while DOP (*Denominazione di Origine Protetta*) balsamic vinegar is aged for at least twelve years. Both are made only in the province of Modena.

Balsamic vinegar should never be heated, and though it is technically a vinegar, Italians don't use pricey long-aged balsamic vinegar to dress salads—it is a very precious condiment suitable for use by the drop to accent flavor. Try it any of the following ways:	Drizzle on sliced macerated strawberries and/or whole raspberries.
	Brush on grilled meats.
	Sprinkle a few drops on slices of cheese on a cheese plate.
	Drip a little on vanilla ice cream.
	Toss with roasted onions or other roasted vegetables after they have cooled to room temperature.

POMODORI

Hard to believe that tomatoes—so closely identified with Italian cuisine—are not native to Italy, or even to Europe. Tomatoes were among the many plants brought back to Europe from the New World. But no matter where they started out, they have found their greatest welcome in the Italian kitchen, where they are served fresh in summer, and then canned and jarred in numerous guises for use year-round. Each area of Italy has its own preferred variety of tomato, including the famous San Marzano tomatoes of Naples and the Pachino tomatoes grown in Sicily—look for place of origin on the container if you would like to match the type of tomato to a regional dish you are preparing. By the way, the idea of the long-cooked tomato sauce that burbles on a stovetop for hours is an antiquated one. High-quality canned tomatoes taste bright and fresh and need to be cooked only briefly. They are not second-best to fresh tomatoes, but equally tasty items with different uses.

The Italian Way with
TOMATO PRODUCTS

POMODORI PELATI *Whole Peeeled Tomatoes*	crushed to make chunky tomato sauce and added to soups
PASSATA DI POMODORO *Tomato Puree*	used to make smooth tomato sauce and also for soups and risotto—anywhere a smooth texture is desired
CONCENTRATO DI POMODORO *Tomato Paste*	a strong concentrate used in small amounts, almost always thinned in a little liquid and often in conjunction with other tomato products
POMODORI SECCHI *Sun-dried Tomatoes and* *Semi-dried Tomatoes*	stored in olive oil, with a piquant salty flavor; drained, minced, and added to room-temperature salads, with the oil drizzled on to finish

tomato paste

tomato puree

whole peeled cherry tomatoes

whole peeled tomatoes

sun-dried tomatoes

semi-dried tomatoes

SPAGHETTI AL POMODORO
SPAGHETTI WITH TOMATO SAUCE

Serves 4 as a first course   *Campania*

¼ cup extra-virgin olive oil, plus more for finishing

2 cloves garlic

1 pinch crushed red pepper flakes (optional)

1 (16-ounce) can whole peeled tomatoes in their juices

Fine sea salt to taste

3 to 4 sprigs fresh basil

Coarse sea salt for pasta cooking water

1 pound dried spaghetti

If in a culinary Rorschach test someone said the words "Italian food" to you and then asked what image sprang to mind, you would likely be picturing a bowl of spaghetti with tomato sauce. This is perhaps the most famous Italian dish, and it is not only simple and delicious, but can be made with ingredients that you probably have on hand most of the time. The quality of the tomatoes is front and center here, so it really matters—use only Italian tomatoes that truly taste of the Mediterranean sun. When finished, the tomato sauce should be a rich red color. If it is brick red, it's too thick and needs to be thinned with water.

HEAT the olive oil in a large saucepan over medium heat. Crush the garlic cloves with the heel of your hand. Add the crushed cloves to the oil and cook, stirring occasionally, until the garlic is golden brown, about 5 minutes.

ONCE the garlic is brown, add the red pepper flakes, if using, and then immediately add the tomatoes, crushing them between your fingers and letting them fall into the saucepan. Add the tomato juices as well. Season with salt to taste.

SIMMER the tomato sauce over low heat until slightly thickened, about 20 minutes. Add the basil sprigs to the sauce and set aside.

BRING a large pot of water to a boil for cooking the pasta. When the water is boiling, salt the water (see page 20), add the spaghetti, and cook, stirring frequently with a long-handled fork, until al dente. (See page 74 for more detailed instructions on the proper cooking technique for long dried pasta such as spaghetti.) Drain in a colander. If the tomato sauce has cooled completely, heat it gently.

REMOVE the basil sprigs from the tomato sauce and discard. Transfer the spaghetti from the colander to the pan. Toss over medium heat to combine. Add a drizzle of olive oil and serve immediately.

How to
CRUSH WHOLE PEELED CANNED TOMATOES

THERE'S NO NEED TO PUREE WHOLE PEELED TOMATOES before adding them to the pan when making a sauce. Your hands are the best tools you have.

1. Place a pan on the stove.

2. With your hand, lift a tomato out of the juice in the can. Let most of the juice drip back into the can.

3. Squeeze the tomato between your fingers and let the pieces drop into the pan. If you like less chunky tomatoes, break them down further with a wooden spoon while they are cooking.

BRANZINO CON POMODORI E OLIVE
BRANZINO WITH TOMATOES AND OLIVES

Serves 4 as a main course   *Campania*

2 tablespoons extra-virgin olive oil

1 clove garlic, thinly sliced

1 (16-ounce) can whole peeled cherry tomatoes

¼ cup small black olives, pitted

4 branzino fillets (about 5 ounces each), with or without skin

Fine sea salt to taste

Freshly ground black pepper to taste

1 tablespoon fresh oregano leaves

This dish will work with almost any kind of fillet—adjust the cooking time to the thickness of the fish—and even whole fish or other types of seafood. If you can't locate canned cherry tomatoes, substitute larger peeled whole tomatoes, but crush them between your fingers as you add them to the pan, or in season substitute fresh tomatoes. Accompany this with lots of crusty bread for soaking up the juices.

PREHEAT the oven to 425°F.

IN a bowl, combine the olive oil, garlic, tomatoes, and olives. Spread a thin layer of the mixture in the bottom of an ovenproof skillet or baking dish large enough to hold the fillets in a single layer. Season the fillets with salt and pepper. Place the fillets in the dish. Spoon the remaining tomato mixture around the fillets.

BAKE the fillets until just opaque, about 12 minutes. Garnish with the fresh oregano leaves.

What grows together goes together: Try to match the olive oil you're using with the region where the dish originated.

LEGUMI SECCHI

Dried beans and lentils are the thrifty cook's best friend—as filling, tasty, and nutritious as they are economical. They are one of the stars of Italy's *cucina magra,* basically meatless food that sustained most Italians—who could afford to eat meat only on Sundays and holidays—for centuries.

The Italian Way with
DRIED BEANS AND LENTILS

Lentils can be cooked without soaking, but larger dried beans should be soaked overnight in cold water to cover. First, place the beans in a sieve and give them a quick rinse. Transfer the rinsed beans to a bowl and add enough cold water to cover by 2 inches. If any skins or broken beans float to the top, skim them off and discard. Soak the beans for about 8 hours, then drain them and discard the soaking water. Place the beans or rinsed lentils in a pot and add enough cold water to cover by 2 inches. Place over high heat and bring to a boil, then turn down to a simmer and cook until the beans are soft enough that you can crush them easily against the side of the pot with a wooden spoon. Cooking time can vary from 30 minutes for small lentils to more than 2 hours for chickpeas. Never salt beans until they are finished cooking—it toughens the skins and may add to their cooking time.

SUGO AI BORLOTTI *Tomato Sauce with Cranberry Beans*	Sauté minced carrot, onion, and celery in olive oil, then add cooked cranberry beans; sauté briefly to flavor, then add a splash of tomato puree and cook until slightly thickened. Serve over pasta or polenta.
CANNELLINI E TONNO *Cannellini Beans and Canned Tuna*	Toss cooked cannellini beans with drained, flaked tuna canned in olive oil. Add minced scallion, diced hard-boiled egg, and a generous grinding of fresh black pepper.
PASTA E CECI *Pasta with Chickpeas*	Sauté minced carrot, celery, onion, garlic, fresh rosemary, and pancetta in olive oil; add cooked chickpeas and water to cover by a couple inches and simmer about 5 minutes to combine flavors. Puree about one-third of the resulting chickpea mixture. Return the mixture to a boil. Add small pasta such as small shells and cook until the pasta is al dente. Serve with a drizzle of olive oil on top.
PURÈ DI FAVE E CICORIA ALLA PUGLIESE *Puglia-Style Fava Bean Puree with Chicory*	Soak dried fava beans (use above method). Place the soaked and drained beans in a pot with a whole onion and a bay leaf. Cook as instructed above until the beans are very soft. Remove and discard the bay leaf and onion. Puree the mixture in a food mill, then return it to the pot and beat with a spoon while drizzling in olive oil. While the beans are cooking, cook chicory greens in boiling salted water, then chop the cooked greens and sauté them in olive oil with garlic. Serve puree and greens side by side, drizzled with a generous amount of olive oil.
LENTICCHIE E RISO *Lentils with Rice*	Place cooked lentils in a pot with a generous amount of water. Bring to a boil, season with salt, and stir in short-grain Italian rice (see page 142). Cook, stirring frequently, until the rice is tender, about 15 minutes. Serve with grated Parmigiano Reggiano or Grana Padano.

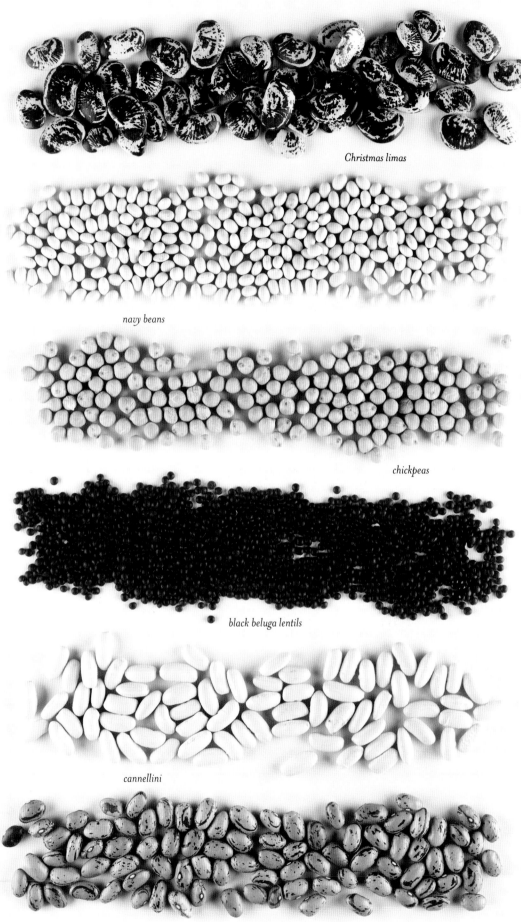

Christmas limas

navy beans

chickpeas

black beluga lentils

cannellini

cranberry beans

ZUPPA DI LENTICCHIE CON POLPETTINE
LENTIL SOUP WITH MEATBALLS

Serves 4 as a main course   *Umbria*

---

2 tablespoons extra-virgin olive oil

1 carrot, diced

2 stalks celery, diced

1 yellow onion, diced

Fine sea salt to taste

Freshly ground black pepper to taste

2 cups small lentils, preferably Castelluccio lentils, rinsed

1 (14½-ounce) can whole peeled tomatoes

2 links sweet Italian sausage, casings removed

The region of Umbria is famous for pork sausages and lentils (as well as truffles), especially the small and extra-tasty lentils from the town of Castelluccio. As we often say at Eataly, what grows together goes together, and this duo is no exception. Castelluccio lentils cook quickly—a larger variety may require more time. This earthy soup can be prepared year-round, but it is especially satisfying on a chilly evening.

IN a medium saucepan, heat the olive oil over medium-high heat. Add the carrot, celery, and onion. Season with salt and pepper. Cook the vegetables, stirring frequently to keep them from browning, until soft, about 10 minutes. Add the lentils. Crush the tomatoes by hand, letting them drop into the pan. Add enough water to cover the lentils by 2 inches. Cook, covered, until the lentils are soft, about 30 minutes.

MEANWHILE, using your hands, roll the sausage meat into 1-inch meatballs.

WHEN the lentils are cooked, add the meatballs to the pan and push them down so that they are submerged. Simmer, stirring occasionally, until the meatballs are cooked through, 2 to 3 minutes. Serve immediately placing a few meatballs and some of the soup in individual serving bowls.

SIGNS OF QUALITY

Even dried items such as beans don't last forever. It's best to use them within one year of purchase.

FAGIOLI ALL'UCCELLETTO
BEANS IN TOMATO SAUCE

Serves 8 as a side dish   *Toscana*

---

1 pound (about 2 cups) dried cannellini beans, soaked overnight (see page 34)

2 cloves garlic, sliced

¼ cup extra-virgin olive oil, preferably Tuscan

1 cup canned whole peeled tomatoes, including their juices

8 fresh sage leaves, chopped

Fine sea salt to taste

Freshly ground black pepper to taste

This dish—a Florentine classic—could not be simpler, or better. The name translates as "beans in the style of small birds," though there's no poultry involved. Presumably, the use of sage—which is often used when roasting small game birds—is what's being referenced. These beans are often served as a side dish alongside roasted meats and stews, but they also make a hearty vegetarian main course on their own. Feel free to drizzle on a little additional olive oil and season with a generous grinding of additional pepper before serving.

DRAIN the beans and place them in a medium saucepan. Add enough cold water to cover the beans by 2 inches. Bring the beans to a boil, reduce the heat to a simmer and cook, covered, until tender, 45 minutes to 1 hour. Reserve 1 cup cooking liquid and drain the beans in a colander.

IN a Dutch oven or other heavy pot, cook the garlic in the olive oil over moderate heat, stirring frequently, until softened. Add the reserved cooking liquid, the beans, the tomatoes with their juices (crushing them with your hands as described on page 31), and the sage. Season to taste with salt and pepper. Bring to a boil, reduce the heat to a simmer, and cook, stirring occasionally, until thickened, about 25 minutes. Serve hot.

How to
DETERMINE WHETHER
A BEAN IS COOKED

ALWAYS CHECK A FEW BEANS, as their cooking times may vary.

1. A properly cooked bean will be crushed easily when you press it against the side of the pot with a wooden spoon.

2. Alternatively, rinse a few beans in cool water and taste them. They should crush easily when you press them against your palate with your tongue.

3. If you're still not sure, remove a few beans with a slotted spoon and cut them in half. When they are fully cooked, they will be the same color and consistency throughout. If the center is chalky and light in color, keep cooking and testing.

FARINATA
CHICKPEA FLOUR PANCAKE

Serves 8 as an appetizer or snack   *Liguria*

1 cup chickpea flour

1 teaspoon fine sea salt

2 tablespoons extra-virgin olive oil, plus more for sautéing and finishing

½ small yellow onion, thinly sliced (optional)

1 tablespoon chopped fresh rosemary (optional)

Freshly ground black pepper to taste

This rustic, blistered pancake showered with fresh black pepper is served up and down the coast of Liguria, as well as in the south of France. As with crepe batter, this batter needs to sit before being used. One hour is the minimum, but you can make the batter up to twelve hours in advance—the longer it sits the better. Be sure to use Italian chickpea flour and not the Indian type, which is actually made from chana dal and is toasted. Farinata is delicious paired with a crisp white wine and a few chunks of aged cheese.

IN a mixing bowl, whisk together the chickpea flour and 1¾ cups water. Whisk in the salt and 2 tablespoons olive oil. Cover and set aside at room temperature for at least 1 hour and up to 12 hours.

WHEN you're ready to prepare the pancake, preheat the oven to 400°F.

IF using the onion, sauté it in olive oil over low heat until soft and translucent but not brown, about 7 minutes. Stir in the rosemary and cook for an additional 30 seconds, then remove the pan from the heat. Stir the onion into the batter.

HEAT a few teaspoons of olive oil in a 12-inch ovenproof skillet (cast iron is ideal) over medium-high heat. When the oil is hot, add the batter. Tilt the skillet if necessary to cover the surface. Bake the pancake in the oven until it is completely set and a paring knife inserted in the center comes out clean, 20 to 30 minutes. If the top has not browned, place the pancake under the broiler for 1 to 2 minutes until it is flecked with brown spots.

REMOVE the pancake from the oven and let it cool in the pan for 1 to 2 minutes. Carefully transfer the pancake to a cutting board. Cut into wedges, drizzle with your best extra-virgin olive oil, and top with a very generous amount of pepper. Serve warm.

CONSERVE DI PESCE

Just as Italians have long excelled at capturing the taste of vegetables, they are also champions of preserving various types of fish and seafood. Canned or jarred tuna, for example, is native to Sicilia, and several companies on the island produce wonderful tuna in olive oil. Italian canned tuna is chunky and moist; *ventresca,* or tuna belly, is especially prized. Italians also preserve fish through salting, as with anchovies and baccalà, or salted codfish. Stoccafisso, or stockfish, is very similar to baccalà, but it is dried without being salted. Baccalà and stoccafisso were first developed for sailors, who could bring them on long journeys—from ships they migrated to the tables of maritime republics such as Venice and Genoa. Bottarga—native to Sardegna, Sicilia, and coastal areas of other regions—is made from either mullet or tuna roe. The eggs are compressed into a kind of lobe that is then dried for about five months so that it is firm and dry and can be either grated or shaved. It has the salty tang of caviar with a pleasant fishiness.

The Italian Way with
COLATURA

Colatura is amber-colored fermented anchovy liquid, a relative of the *garum* of the ancient Romans and somewhat similar in flavor (and pungency) to the fish sauce of southeast Asia. A secret weapon of Italian cooking, colatura adds a unique savory flavor to dishes. Colatura is native to Cetara in the Campania region and is made from the anchovies fished in the Gulf of Salerno between March and early July. The anchovies are cleaned by hand, salted, and layered in wooden tubs. After several months, the colatura drips through small holes in the tubs. Here are just a few uses for delicious colatura, which should always be employed with a light hand:

drizzle on cooked linguine just before serving
brush lightly on toasted bread and top with minced fresh parsley
place a few drops on a cooked pizza; scatter on a little minced fresh chili pepper
brush lightly on grilled eggplant slices
whisk a drop or two into a vinaigrette

salted anchovies

baccalà

colatura

tuna roe sauce

anchovy fillets

jarred tuna

bottarga

The Italian Way with
BACCALÀ AND STOCCAFISSO

Baccalà and stoccafisso are nearly hard as a rock and must be rehydrated before being used in cooking. The two are virtually indistinguishable from each other, except that you may need to salt recipes using stoccafisso more than you need to salt those using baccalà. Confusing the matter is the fact that what the people of Venice—where dried cod is a major ingredient—refer to as "baccalà" is actually stoccafisso. No matter, since they differ very little from each other in taste and in preparation. Three days before you plan to prepare the baccalà or stoccafisso, rinse it and place it in a bowl. Add cold water to cover by a couple of inches, cover the bowl with a plate, and soak in the refrigerator, changing the water every 8 hours or so. The fish will smell a little funky—that's normal. When the fish is pliable, remove it from the soaking water, discarding the water, and cut the fish into large chunks. Run your hands over the surface to check for bones. Use fish tweezers to remove any bones you find.

BACCALÀ FRITTO *Fried Dried Cod*	Cut soaked baccalà or stoccafisso into chunks. If using baccalà, taste a little piece to determine how salty it is. Squeeze the fish dry with a clean flat-weave dishtowel. Dredge the pieces in a small amount of flour. Deep-fry a few pieces at a time in olive oil that is about 350°F—it should take about 4 minutes for a piece of fish to be browned and crisp. Remove fried pieces to paper towels to drain briefly, sprinkle with salt (just a touch if you determined that the baccalà you used was plenty salty), and serve hot.
BACCALÀ ALLA LIVORNESE *Livorno-Style Dried Cod*	Squeeze soaked baccalà or stoccafisso and pat dry. Dredge large chunks in flour, then brown in olive oil in a skillet. Blot the cooked baccalà and simmer with tomato sauce made from fresh tomatoes and a handful of capers. Serve hot or at room temperature.
BACCALÀ MANTECATO *Whipped Dried Cod*	Place soaked baccalà or stoccafisso chunks in a pot and add cold water to cover. Bring to a boil, skim off any foam on the surface, turn down to a brisk simmer, and cook until tender, 20 to 30 minutes. Drain the fish, check again for bones, and place the pieces in a bowl or the work bowl of a food processor fitted with the metal blade, along with a clove of garlic. Beat the fish with a wooden spoon or process it while steadily adding a stream of olive oil through the feed tube until you have a creamy, fluffy mixture. (Doing this by hand may take up to 30 minutes of energetic activity.) Taste and adjust salt and season with freshly ground black pepper if desired. You can also garnish with minced parsley. This classic Venetian *cicheto,* or bar snack, is traditionally served with grilled pieces of polenta (see page 147).
BACCALÀ ALLA VICENTINA *Vicenza-Style Dried Cod*	As with all traditional recipes, variations abound, but this is the way that the Confraternita del Baccalà alla Vicentina (the Brotherhood of Vicenza-Style Baccalà) recommends preparing the dish: Thinly slice a yellow onion and sauté it in a generous amount of olive oil. Add chopped salted sardines (previously rinsed and filleted) and sauté briefly. Remove from the heat and stir in minced parsley. Dredge the soaked fish chunks in flour. Spread about half the onion mixture over the bottom of a Dutch oven. Place the dredged fish on top and scatter the remaining onion mixture on top of the fish. Sprinkle on grated grana cheese (see page 104), salt, and pepper. Add enough milk to leave just the top of the fish exposed, and then enough olive oil to cover the fish completely. Cook over very low heat until the fish is tender, about 4½ hours, rotating the pot every once in a while (clockwise or counter-clockwise) but never stirring. The dish benefits from resting 12 to 24 hours before serving. Serve over polenta and garnish with chopped parsley.

SPAGHETTI CON LA BOTTARGA
SPAGHETTI WITH BOTTARGA

Serves 4 as a first course   *Calabria, Sardegna, Sicilia, Toscana*

¼ cup extra-virgin olive oil

1 clove garlic

¼ teaspoon crushed red pepper flakes (optional)

½ cup fine breadcrumbs (see page 134)

2 tablespoons grated bottarga

Coarse sea salt for pasta cooking water

1 pound dried spaghetti

¼ cup minced fresh parsley

This is yet another recipe that is more than the sum of its simple parts, so that the highest quality ingredients are required. Always purchase bottarga—pressed fish roe—in a whole piece and grate it yourself for best results. You may use either tuna bottarga or mullet bottarga. Mullet bottarga has a more mild flavor; it hails from Sardegna and the coast of Toscana. Tuna bottarga, which is more assertive and darker in color, is native to Sicilia and parts of Calabria. Bottarga will keep for about one year in the refrigerator after its vacuum packaging is opened (or its beeswax coating is removed). It has an outer membrane that needs to be removed before grating—simply peel back the membrane of the size chunk you think you'll need and leave the rest covered.

BRING a large pot of water to a boil.

HEAT the olive oil in a large pan over medium-low heat. Add the garlic and red pepper flakes, if using, and cook, stirring frequently, until the garlic is golden. Remove and discard the garlic. Add the breadcrumbs to the pan and cook, stirring constantly to keep them from burning, until they are golden, about 3 minutes. Remove from the heat. Stir in the bottarga.

MEANWHILE, when the water in the large pot boils, add salt (see page 20 but keep in mind that the bottarga will be salty), and then add the spaghetti. Cook, stirring frequently with a long-handled fork, until spaghetti is al dente. (See page 74 for more on the proper cooking technique for long dried pasta.)

WHEN the pasta is cooked, reserve about 1 cup cooking water, then drain the pasta in a colander. Transfer the pasta to the pan with the breadcrumb mixture. Toss vigorously over medium heat until combined, about 2 minutes. If the pasta looks dry, add some of the cooking water, 1 to 2 tablespoons at a time, and toss between additions until it looks moist. Garnish with the minced parsley and serve immediately.

BUCATINI AL TONNO
BUCATINI WITH TUNA

Serves 4 as a first course   *Sicilia, Calabria*

2 tablespoons plus 1 teaspoon extra-virgin olive oil

1 yellow onion, minced

1 clove garlic, sliced

1 Calabrese chili pepper in olive oil or fresh red chili pepper, drained and minced

1 (7-ounce) jar Italian tuna preserved in olive oil, drained

2 tablespoons salted capers, rinsed and drained

Grated zest of 1 lemon

¼ cup breadcrumbs

Coarse sea salt for pasta cooking water

1 pound bucatini

If you have a couple of slices of stale bread, you can make crispy croutons for this dish rather than using breadcrumbs. Just back away from the grated cheese—we Italians never serve grated cheese on pasta with fish. Calabrese chili peppers are small red chili peppers similar to cayenne peppers that are sold preserved in olive oil. Tuna also makes a delicious addition to tomato sauce. Just flake the drained contents of a can of Italian tuna into the tomato sauce on page 30 and simmer for a few minutes.

BRING a large pot of water to a boil.

PLACE the 2 tablespoons olive oil in a large pan over medium-low heat. Add the onion, garlic, and chili pepper and cook, stirring frequently, until the onion and the garlic are golden. Flake the tuna into the pan and cook until tuna is heated through, about 2 minutes. Stir in the capers and the lemon zest and remove from the heat.

TOSS the breadcrumbs with the remaining teaspoon olive oil and toast in a toaster oven or in a cast-iron skillet over medium heat until crisp.

MEANWHILE, when the water in the large pot boils, add salt, and then add the bucatini. Cook, stirring frequently with a long-handled fork, until the bucatini is al dente. (See page 74 for more on the proper cooking technique for long dried pasta.)

WHEN the pasta is cooked, reserve about 1 cup cooking water, then drain the pasta in a colander. Transfer the pasta to the pan with the tuna. Toss vigorously over medium heat until combined, about 2 minutes. If the pasta looks dry, add some of the cooking water, 1 to 2 tablespoons at a time, and toss between additions until it looks moist. Garnish with the toasted breadcrumbs and serve immediately.

MARMELLATA E MIELE

Honeys and jams are for more than just spreading on bread or drizzling on yogurt—not that we're against either of those things! Both honeys and jams and their close relatives, which include fruit in syrup, gelatins, and mostarde—Italy's answer to chutney—can add a little dose of interesting flavor when served alongside cheese or even braised or roasted meats. We carry an almost limitless supply of these items at Eataly, including tomato jam and spreads made from Sicily's prickly pear cactus. We're particularly fond of *cognà*, from the Langhe area in the Piemonte region—it's a mixture of grapes and other fruit reduced to a spreadable consistency. *Marmellata* (jam), *confettura* (preserves), and *gelatina* (gelatin) are labeled "extra" if they contain at least 45 percent fruit. A *composta di frutta* is a fruit spread that contains less sugar and at least 65 percent fruit. Like canned and jarred tomato products, jams and preserves are not a less desirable version of fruit—they are simply used differently. Indeed, the fruit used in Italian jams and preserves is always picked at peak ripeness.

TYPES OF HONEY

TYPE	SEASON	COLOR	FLAVORS
ACACIA *Acacia*	May	light, straw-yellow	sugared almond and vanilla
CASTAGNO *Chestnut*	late June to mid-July	amber	herbal and pungent with a slightly bitter and tannic aftertaste
EUCALIPTO *Eucalyptus*	July	amber or light hazelnut brown	licoricelike and smoky with woodsy balsamic flavor notes
FIORI DELLE ALPI *Flowers from the Alps*	July and August	amber	mountain flowers and cooked artichoke
MELATA DI BOSCO *Forest Honeydew*	July and August	dark amber ranging from red to brown	spices, carob, rhubarb, and licorice with a melted brown sugar aftertaste
MILLEFIORI *Thousand Flowers*	spring and summer	inconsistent characteristics unique to each beekeeper	flowers, candied fruit, peach syrup
SULLA *French Honeysuckle*	July and August	dark amber sometimes with greenish hues	resin and balsamic with malt and caramel tones
TIGLIO *Linden Blossom*	late June	golden yellow to amber	menthol, fresh spices, walnuts

The Italian Way with HONEY

At Eataly, we use honey, or *miele*, frequently. Try any of these, using a light hand, and experience for yourself the extra dimension that honey can add:

COMBINE 8 parts honey to 1 part amaretto liqueur and warm in the top of a double boiler, then stir in toasted slivered almonds; serve with cheese

WHISK a few drops of honey into a vinaigrette

BLEND honey with room temperature *lardo* or ricotta until smooth and serve as a spread with toasted bread

BRUSH a small amount of a dark, savory honey such as fiori delle alpi on meat before roasting to create a caramelized crust

REPLACE some of the sugar in your favorite baked goods with honey

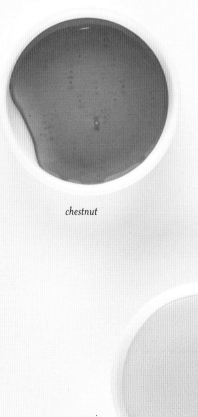

forest honeydew

French honeysuckle

chestnut

orange blossom

acacia

linden blossom

CROSTATA ALLA MARMELLATA
JAM TART

Makes one 8-inch round, 9-inch round, or 8-inch square tart, about 12 servings

---

1 cup unbleached all-purpose flour, plus more for rolling dough

¼ cup sugar

1 pinch fine sea salt

6 tablespoons (¾ stick) unsalted butter, cold and cut into pieces, plus more for buttering pan

1 egg yolk

2 cups jam or preserves, any flavor

¼ cup apricot jam for glaze (optional)

Jam tarts are an Italian home-baking classic and a wonderful way to highlight fruity jams and preserves. The pastry dough here is *pasta frolla*, a versatile short-crust pastry that can be baked blind or with a filling and can also be rolled and cut into cookies. Pasta frolla is not hard to make, but it shouldn't be overhandled. Always chill pasta frolla before rolling it out. It also freezes nicely either in a ball and wrapped in plastic, already rolled out and placed in a tart pan, or baked blind. You can easily double this recipe and bake a larger tart in an 11-by-8-inch pan. If you are using a berry jam for the tart, try adding a little grated lemon zest to the crust.

PLACE the flour, sugar, and salt in a bowl and mix with a fork to combine. Scatter the butter on top and, with a pastry cutter or your fingers, pinch the butter until the mixture resembles coarse meal. Add the egg yolk and stir with the fork again until thoroughly combined. (You may need to switch to kneading briefly by hand.)

TO make the crust with a food processor, place the dry ingredients in the bowl fitted with the metal blade. Pulse to combine, then add the butter and pulse 4 to 6 times until the mixture resembles coarse meal. Add the egg yolk and process just until the dough forms a ball.

SHAPE the dough into a fat disk, wrap it in plastic wrap, and refrigerate for at least 1 hour and up to 1 day.

WHEN you are ready to bake the tart, preheat the oven to 350°F.

BUTTER an 8- or 9-inch tart pan with a removable bottom, or an 8- or 9-inch springform pan, or an 8-by-8-inch square pan and set aside.

PLACE the dough on a lightly floured work surface. Cut off about one-third of the dough, rewrap it in plastic, and set aside. (Refrigerate if your kitchen is warm.) Roll the two-thirds of the dough ¼ to ½ inch thick in a circle or square about 1 inch larger than your pan. (If the dough resists, let it relax for a few minutes and come back to it.) Wrap the rolled dough around the rolling pin, transfer it to the pan, and unfold it into the pan. Press it against the bottom and sides of the pan.

CUT off a small piece of dough from the remaining piece and, with your hands, roll it into a ½-inch rope on the work surface. Place the rope around the perimeter of the pan, on top of the rolled dough. Return the remaining dough, wrapped in plastic, to the refrigerator.

LINE the crust with foil, fill with dried beans or pie weights, and bake until the crust is set and matte, about 15 minutes.

ramasin plum compote

apricot preserves

lemon marmalade

onion mostarda

Lambrusco Montavano jelly

black fig jam

pepper compote

mandarin extra marmalade

REMOVE the crust from the oven and allow it to cool slightly. Increase the heat to 400°F.

WHEN the crust is cool enough to handle, spread the 2 cups jam in it in an even layer. Lightly flour the work surface and roll out the remaining dough to the shape of the pan but about 1 inch larger all around. It should be between ¼ and ½ inch thick. Cut this disk or square into ½-inch- to 1-inch-wide strips. Place alternating strips on top of the tart, attaching the ends to the rope of dough you created earlier. Arrange the remaining strips at an angle to the first strips, again attaching them to the rope of dough to create a lattice.

BAKE until the lattice strips are golden and dry, 15 to 20 minutes.

IF using the glaze, while the tart is baking, combine the apricot jam with 2 tablespoons water in a small pot. Heat over low heat and whisk to combine, then strain out any chunks of fruit. While the tart is still warm, brush the lattice strips with the glaze. Cool completely on a rack and serve at room temperature.

PASTA

*One of the things that makes pasta
so perfect is how simple it is.*

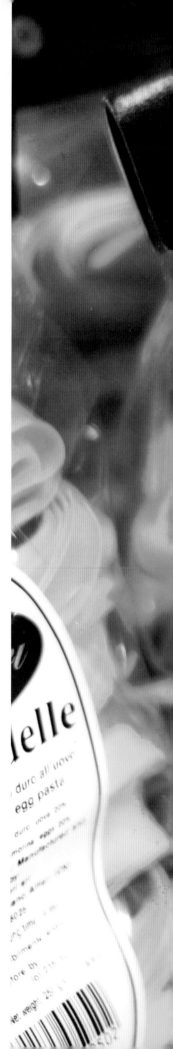

SIGNS OF QUALITY

The best dried pasta adheres to simple principles of artisan production: It is extruded through a bronze mold and air-dried for 24 to 48 hours to ensure pasta of the perfect consistency to stick to sauce.

Fresh pasta is not inherently "better" than dried pasta; the two are simply different and generally paired with different sauces.

Italians enjoy small portions of pasta as a *primo*, or first course. It is rarely eaten as a meal in and of itself.

Pasta is served in low, wide ceramic bowls (both the larger size for serving and smaller individual bowls). It's always a good idea to warm the pasta bowls before serving. To do this, ladle a small amount of the boiling water that will be used to cook the pasta into a bowl, swish it around, and discard it.

PASTA FRESCA

Tender fresh pasta—whether egg noodles, one of the fresh flour and water pastas made in the south, pillowy gnocchi, or some other delight—offers a satisfying yet soft texture and mellow flavor. Almost every region of the country has at least one signature fresh pasta.

The Italian Way with EGG PASTA

NAME	TYPE OF PASTA	SIZE	CLASSIC PAIRING
CANNELLONI	large Piemontese noodles for filling and baking	about 4 inches square	To make ricotta-filled cannelloni, see the recipe on page 98.
FETTUCCINE	noodles from a sheet of dough rolled out slightly thicker than usual	⅛ inch wide	Roman noodles often paired with cream- and oil-based sauces.
MALTAGLIATI/ STRACCI	uneven pieces, usually rough rhombus shapes	about ½ inch wide	Delicious in bean purees; cook them directly in soup.
PAPPARDELLE	noodles, sometimes cut from an open sheet of dough with a pastry wheel for a fluted edge	⅝ inch wide	Serve with game-based sauces.
QUADRETTI	little confettilike squares	½ inch to ¾ inch	Either cut an extended sheet of dough in a grid or roll the dough, cut it into noodles, and then unfurl the noodles and cut them into squares; cook in broth.
TAGLIATELLE	ribbonlike noodles	¼ inch wide	The pride of Bologna and the perfect foil to the city's famous ragù (page 56).
TAJARIN	noodles	1/16 inch wide	Tajarin are the same as the noodles known as tagliolini or taglierini elsewhere, but they are made with extra egg yolk; replace every other egg in a batch of tajarin with 2 egg yolks, so, for example, pasta for four people would be made with approximately 4 cups of flour, 2 whole eggs, and 4 egg yolks.

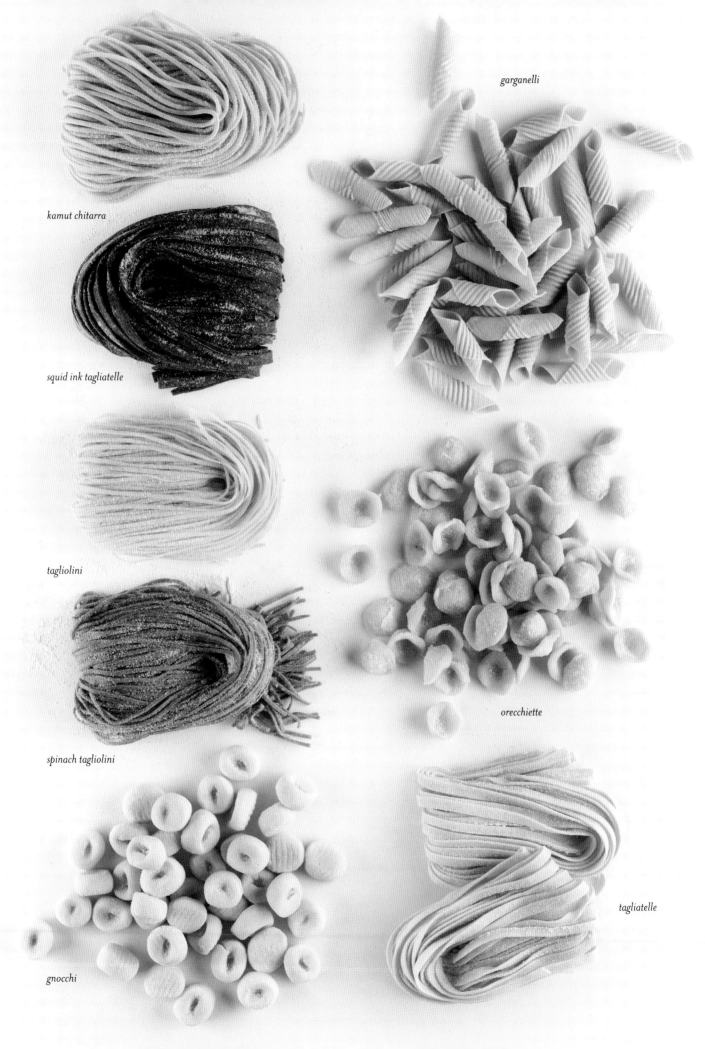

garganelli

kamut chitarra

squid ink tagliatelle

tagliolini

orecchiette

spinach tagliolini

gnocchi

tagliatelle

How to MAKE EGG PASTA

EGG PASTA IS THE MOST COMMON FORM OF FRESH PASTA IN ITALY and is eaten throughout central and northern Italy. Egg pasta is not difficult to make, and it uses only two ingredients, which you likely already have on hand: unbleached all-purpose flour and eggs.

You will need 1 large egg and about 1 cup flour per portion. If you are new to making pasta, start with ¾ cup flour for each egg and then add as you go along. You will need a large wooden work surface (in Italy, most home kitchens are equipped with a board that has a lip that hangs over the side of the counter to hold it in place), a bench scraper, and a straight dowel rolling pin if you are rolling out the dough by hand (preferable, but it takes practice) or a crank pasta machine. Egg pasta is also used to make stuffed pasta and *pasta al forno*, or baked pasta.

1. Form the flour into a well on the work surface or in a bowl. (In a bowl is easier and recommended the first few times you try this.) Crack the eggs into the well, and with the index and middle finger of one hand or with a small fork, whisk the eggs. Gradually draw in flour from the sides of the well until the egg has been absorbed by the flour. With a bench scraper, set the dough off to the side.

2. Clean off your hands, adding any dough scraps to the dough, and wash your hands. Clean the work surface, first by scraping it with the bench scraper, and then by wiping it with a damp cloth or sponge. (If you began by kneading the dough in a bowl, you don't need to perform this step.) Lightly flour the work surface.

3. Transfer the dough to the lightly floured part of the work surface. Knead the dough. The weather, the age of your flour, the size of your eggs, and numerous other factors can influence the dough's texture. If the dough is dry and crumbly, sprinkle it with lukewarm water until it becomes pliable. If it is so wet that it is unwieldy, add flour, about a tablespoon at a time, until you can handle it. Continue kneading the dough until smooth, about 10 minutes. When you cut through the dough with a knife, you should see a consistent color and texture, not whorls of flour and/or egg.

4. Clean off the work surface with a bench scraper. Set the dough to the side on the work surface, cover with an overturned bowl (if you used a bowl above, just rinse it out and use it here), and allow to rest for 30 minutes. This is probably the most important step in making egg pasta dough—don't try to skip it.

5. Cut off a piece of pasta dough the size of an egg. Leave the remaining dough covered under the overturned bowl.

6. *To roll by hand,* shape the dough into a rough circle. Lightly flour the clean work surface. Begin rolling the dough as you would a pastry crust, starting in the center and rolling away from you to the outer edge. Turn the ball of dough a quarter-turn and repeat all the way around, then continue rolling, turning the dough about one-eighth of the way around, until the sheet of dough is ⅛ inch thin or less. Scatter a small amount of flour on the dough any time it threatens to stick to the surface or the rolling pin. Finish thinning the sheet of dough by wrapping three-quarters of the sheet around the rolling pin toward you, then rapidly unrolling it while running your hands across the sheet of dough, from the center of the rolling pin to the ends. Press out and away from you with the rolling pin. Continue to do this, turning the dough between rolls, until the sheet is extremely thin (see Note).

   To roll pasta dough using a crank machine, pass the piece of dough between the smooth rollers on the widest setting. Fold the piece of dough in half and pass it through again, fold it, and pass it through a third time. It should be smooth. Proceed to thin the pasta dough through the smooth rollers by decreasing the setting between rolls. In other words, if 10 is the widest setting on your machine, now decrease the setting to 9 and pass the piece of dough through. This time, do not fold it, but decrease the setting step-by-step until you have thinned the dough to the desired thickness, usually the thinnest setting, but see below for some exceptions. Set the thinned pasta dough aside for about 10 minutes while you repeat with the remaining dough.

Arrange the sheet of dough on a table or counter so that about one-third is hanging over the edge while you repeat with the remaining dough.

7. *To cut hand-rolled pasta dough into noodles,* clean and very lightly flour the work surface. Spread out a clean flat-weave dishtowel on the counter and set aside. Gently roll the first sheet of dough around the rolling pin and slip it off the rolling pin and onto the work surface. (It should be a flat roll.) Cut the roll of dough into strips the desired width, then gently lift them in the air and let them drop onto the dishtowel to separate them. Repeat with remaining sheets of dough. (Flour the cut noodles lightly if they threaten to stick, though by now they should be fairly dry.)

To cut machine-rolled pasta dough into noodles, proceed as follows: The surface of the sheets of dough should feel very dry and matte. Flour them lightly and pass the dough through the notched rollers for noodles, or cut it by hand into the desired shape.

NOTE: *Tradition dictates that the sheet of dough should be transparent enough that if you lay it over a newspaper, you can read the newsprint through it. Since that's not a very sanitary practice, to determine whether or not the sheet of dough is thin enough slide your hand underneath and check whether you can see it.*

VARIATIONS

We've seen egg pasta colored and flavored with all kinds of things over the years, but in Italy there are really only two options besides golden egg noodles:

FOR GREEN SPINACH PASTA: Cook spinach as described on page 168 and chop it as finely as you can. Add it to the flour well with the eggs in step 1 and proceed. The pasta dough may need a little extra flour to balance out the moisture from the spinach. Use about ¼ pound of fresh spinach per egg/portion. Most common shapes: lasagne, tagliatelle. Serve with meat sauces, such as the ragù on page 56. You can also combine egg and spinach tagliatelle for *paglia e fieno,* or straw and hay—delicious with a sauce of peas and cubes of prosciutto.

FOR BLACK SQUID INK PASTA: Add squid ink to the flour well with the eggs in step 1 and proceed. Use about 1 tablespoon squid ink per egg/portion. Most common shapes: tagliatelle, tagliolini. Serve with any seafood sauce.

A WORD ON COOKING FRESH EGG PASTA: Fresh egg pasta cooks in a flash. As soon as it rises to the surface of the pasta cooking water, it is likely ready. (Always taste, of course.) It may be cooked in as little as 5 or 10 seconds, so always be ready with all the other elements before dropping the pasta into the cooking water.

TAGLIATELLE ALLA BOLOGNESE
TAGLIATELLE WITH BOLOGNESE RAGÙ

Serves 4 as a first course   *Emilia–Romagna*

2 tablespoons unsalted butter

2 tablespoons extra-virgin olive oil

1 small yellow onion, minced

1 small carrot, minced

1 rib celery, minced

1 tablespoon minced garlic

4 ounces ground veal

4 ounces ground pork

4 ounces ground beef

Fine sea salt to taste

¼ cup white wine

¼ cup tomato paste

Freshly ground black pepper to taste

¼ cup chicken or beef stock

Coarse sea salt for pasta cooking water

Fresh tagliatelle made with approximately 4 cups unbleached all-purpose flour and 4 large eggs (see page 54)

Grated grana cheese (see page 104) for serving

A good ragù is a thing of beauty, but it is often misunderstood. Ragù is not a tomato sauce. Rather, it is a sauce of ground meat that is very lightly flavored with canned tomatoes or tomato paste. The predominant taste should be of the meat, and the meat should be cooked slowly—hurriedly browning it will dry it out. Ragù served over silken fresh egg tagliatelle is one of the signature dishes of the city of Bologna, and indeed this type of ragù is so closely associated with Bologna that any dish described as Bolognese, or Bologna-style, will be cloaked in it.

IN a heavy Dutch oven or large heavy-bottomed pot over medium heat, melt the butter with the olive oil. Add the onion and cook, stirring frequently, until the onion is translucent, about 5 minutes. Add the carrot, celery, and garlic and cook, stirring frequently, until softened and fragrant, about 2 minutes more.

CRUMBLE the veal, pork, and beef into the pot. Season with fine sea salt. Reduce the heat to low and cook, stirring frequently, until the meat has rendered most of its fat and is just beginning to brown, about 5 minutes. Spoon out and discard some of the rendered fat, but leave enough to cover the bottom of the pan. (This will depend on the meat you're using—there may not be an excessive amount of fat.)

ADD the wine and increase the heat to medium. Cook, stirring occasionally, until the wine has evaporated, about 6 minutes.

DECREASE the heat to low, add the tomato paste, stir to combine, and cook, stirring frequently, for 20 minutes. Season to taste with salt and pepper. Add the stock and adjust the heat if necessary to reach a gentle simmer. Simmer until the stock has reduced but the sauce is still moist, about 45 minutes longer. Taste the sauce, adjust the seasoning if necessary, and remove from the heat.

BRING a large pot of water to a boil for the pasta. When the water is boiling, salt it with coarse salt (see page 20) and add the pasta. Cook until the pasta rises to the surface of the water (see page 55).

SMEAR a small amount of the sauce on the bottom of a warmed pasta serving bowl.

WHEN the pasta is cooked, drain it in a colander, then transfer it immediately to the serving bowl. Top with the remaining sauce and toss vigorously to combine. Serve immediately with grated cheese on the side.

TAJARIN CON BURRO AL TARTUFO
TAJARIN WITH TRUFFLE BUTTER

Serves 4 as a first course   *Piemonte*

Coarse sea salt for pasta cooking water

Fresh tajarin made with approximately 4 cups unbleached all-purpose flour, 2 whole eggs, and 4 egg yolks (see page 54)

1 tablespoon white truffle butter

Tajarin is the Piemontese dialect word for thin egg noodles known as taglierini elsewhere in Italy. You can make this with black instead of white truffle butter if you prefer.

BRING a large pot of water to a boil for the pasta. When the water is boiling, salt it (see page 20) and add the pasta. Cook until the pasta rises to the surface of the water, probably no more than 2 minutes (see page 55).

MEANWHILE, heat the truffle butter over very low heat in a saucepan large enough to hold the pasta. Remove from the heat as soon as the butter is melted.

DRAIN the pasta, reserving about 1 cup cooking water, and add the pasta to the pan with the truffle butter. Toss over high heat to coat the pasta. Add small amounts of pasta cooking water, if necessary, to keep the sauce from getting too dense. Divide equally among 4 heated pasta bowls and serve immediately.

How to EAT LONG PASTA

IN ITS EARLIEST DAYS, LONG PASTA WAS ACTUALLY CONSIDERED A FINGER FOOD. It was served plain and dangled into one's mouth by hand. Doing that today would cause you to present a truly *brutta figura*, but there's no need to be intimidated by spaghetti or linguine, and there's no need to use the bowl of a soupspoon to handle the strands. Instead, proceed as follows:

1. Insert a fork into the tangle of spaghetti, tilting it at a 45-degree angle toward the side of the bowl.

2. Twirl slightly while pulling upward toward the rim of the bowl.

3. Bolster your courage, lift the fork quickly, and lean in to eat the pasta.

LASAGNE PRIMAVERA
LASAGNE WITH SPRING VEGETABLES

Serves 6 as a first course   *Emilia–Romagna*

2 cups whole milk

1 bay leaf

4 to 5 whole black peppercorns

4 tablespoons (½ stick) unsalted butter

3 tablespoons unbleached all-purpose flour

Fine sea salt to taste

Pinch grated nutmeg

1 clove garlic

Leaves of 1 bunch fresh basil (about 2 loosely packed cups)

2 tablespoons pine nuts, plus more for garnish

½ cup extra-virgin olive oil, plus more for oiling pan

¾ cup grated pecorino Romano

About 24 fresh 4-by-10-inch egg pasta noodles made with approximately 3 cups unbleached all-purpose flour and 3 large eggs (see page 54)

Coarse sea salt for pasta cooking water

1 pound asparagus, cut in half lengthwise if thick

1 cup fresh shelled or frozen peas

Traditional Bolognese lasagne (note that *lasagne* is the plural form of the noodles, a *lasagna* would be a single noodle—not a very satisfying portion!) is made with béchamel and Bolognese ragù (page 56), but there are lots of interesting variations on baked pasta that you can make with fresh egg noodles once you've got the hang of them. This dish is popular in spring, but you can swap different seasonal vegetables for the asparagus and peas. If you are using fresh peas and shelling them yourself, you will need approximately ¾ pound.

PLACE the milk in a small saucepan with the bay leaf and the peppercorns and warm over low heat. Strain out and discard the bay leaf and peppercorns. In another small saucepan, melt the butter. Whisk in the flour and cook, whisking constantly, over low heat for 2 minutes. Add the warm milk 2 tablespoons at a time, stirring to combine between additions. Add fine sea salt to taste and cook, stirring, until the mixture has the consistency of sour cream and has no hint of raw-flour flavor, about 15 minutes. Stir in the nutmeg and set aside.

PLACE the garlic and a generous pinch of fine sea salt in a large mortar and grind against the sides until crushed into a paste. Reserve a few basil leaves for garnish, and add about a quarter of the remaining basil leaves to the mortar and grind until broken down. Continue to add the basil a little at a time, breaking down all the leaves before adding more. Add the 2 tablespoons pine nuts and grind until crushed. Add the oil and grind until the pesto is creamy. Finally, add ½ cup pecorino Romano cheese and grind until creamy and thoroughly combined.

BRING a large pot of water to a boil for cooking the pasta. Spread a clean flat-weave dishtowel on a work surface and set a bowl of ice water nearby. When the water is boiling, salt it with the coarse salt (see page 20) and add 4 of the noodles. Cook until the noodles rise to the surface, about 30 seconds (see page 55), then remove with a skimmer, dip briefly in the cold water, and spread them on the dishtowel in a single layer. Repeat with the remaining noodles. Gently blot the noodles dry.

(continued)

PLACE the asparagus in a skillet in one layer. Add water just to cover, salt, and simmer over medium heat until just tender, 3 to 5 minutes. Remove with a slotted spoon, shock in ice water, drain, and chop into ½-inch lengths. Meanwhile, add the peas to the same skillet. Add a little more water to cover if necessary and simmer over medium heat until just tender, 5 minutes for fresh peas, less for frozen peas. Drain and set aside.

PREHEAT the oven to 450°F. Lightly oil a 13-by-9-inch baking pan. Divide the béchamel loosely into fifths and the pesto loosely into quarters (no need to be exact). Cover the bottom of the pan with a layer of noodles, cutting them to fit if necessary. (You will make 9 layers of noodles in all, but this is the only layer that should fit tightly in the pan. With the rest, you have more leeway.) Spread about one-fifth of the béchamel on top of the noodles. Top with another layer of noodles. Spread about one-quarter of the pesto on top of the noodles, then one-fifth of the béchamel. Sprinkle on 2 tablespoons of grated pecorino Romano. Sprinkle about one-third of the chopped asparagus and peas in an even layer. Top the vegetables with one-fifth of the béchamel, then another layer of noodles.

CONTINUE assembling by topping the layer of noodles with one-quarter of the pesto, another layer of noodles, and another one-third of the vegetables. Add another layer of noodles, another one-quarter of the pesto, another layer of noodles, and the remaining vegetables. Top these with another layer of noodles, the remaining pesto, another layer of noodles, one-fifth of the béchamel, and the remaining noodles. Spread the remaining béchamel on top, sprinkle on the remaining 2 tablespoons of pecorino Romano, and bake until a crust forms and the top is browned, about 10 minutes. If the top has not browned after 10 minutes, place under the broiler until it does, about 4 minutes.

To experience the true flavors of your pasta (those delicious grains), enjoy it al dente.

ORECCHIETTE CON CIME DI RAPA E PECORINO

ORECCHIETTE WITH BROCCOLI RABE AND PECORINO

Serves 4 as a first course   *Puglia*

1 cup durum semolina flour

1½ cups unbleached all-purpose flour, plus more for flouring work surface and hands

Coarse sea salt for cooking water

1 bunch broccoli rabe, any fibrous stems trimmed

¼ cup extra-virgin olive oil, plus more for drizzling

1 clove garlic

¼ cup grated aged pecorino, preferably from Puglia

Crushed red pepper flakes to taste

Puglia's signature pasta, orecchiette, is wonderfully chewy due to a healthy dose of harder flour. Orecchiette are shaped by being dragged across a wooden work surface rather than being rolled out, so the dough does not need to rest before shaping. Because orecchiette contain no egg, they keep very well. You can prepare orecchiette and let them dry completely on the baking sheets, then store them in tightly sealed jars or other containers up to two months, or you can use them immediately. In the latter case, they will cook quickly. You can substitute packaged orecchiette in this recipe, but because orecchiette are relatively simple to produce at home and can be stored at length, you owe it to yourself to try making them at least once.

IN a medium bowl, use a whisk to combine the flours completely. Mound the flour on a work surface and make a well in the center.

PLACE about 2 tablespoons room-temperature (not cold) water in the well. With two fingers, stir in some of the flour off the walls and into the center. When the water has been absorbed, repeat with more water, always adding small amounts, until you have a soft dough. (You will probably need between ⅔ cup and 1 cup water. If necessary, reshape the mound of flour between additions.)

KNEAD the dough until it is smooth and soft, about 10 minutes. If it crumbles while you are kneading, wet your hands a few times to incorporate a small amount of additional liquid.

LIGHTLY flour a baking sheet and set aside. Cut off a piece of dough about the size of a golf ball and put the remaining dough under an overturned bowl to keep it from drying out. On the work surface, roll the piece of dough into a rope about ½ inch wide.

USE a knife to slice off a disk about 1⅛ inch wide and pull the disk away from the rope of dough, pressing it against the work surface. Then lift up the disk and invert it over a fingertip. It should be shaped like a little hat with a rolled "brim" all around the perimeter. Transfer the shaped pasta to the prepared baking sheet. Repeat with the remaining rope of dough, then with the remaining pasta dough.

(continued)

BRING a large pot of water to a boil. When the water boils, add salt and cook the broccoli rabe until tender, 3 to 5 minutes.

REMOVE the broccoli rabe with a slotted spoon and run under cold water. Squeeze as much water as possible out of the broccoli rabe and chop roughly. Set aside.

LET the water return to a boil, then add the orecchiette and cook until al dente, about 5 minutes if freshly made and 12 minutes for orecchiette that you have made and allowed to dry completely (the time will vary depending on how dry the pasta is and how thick or thin it is). Taste a few pieces to account for variation.

HEAT 2 tablespoons oil in a large pan. Peel and crush the garlic clove, sauté it until browned, then remove it from the pan with a slotted spoon and discard.

WHEN the pasta is cooked, drain it and add it to the pan along with the remaining olive oil and the chopped broccoli rabe. Toss over medium heat until combined, about 2 minutes. Remove the pan from the heat, sprinkle on the grated cheese and some crushed red pepper flakes, and toss to combine. Finish with a drizzle of olive oil and serve immediately.

GNOCCHI AL POMODORO PICCANTE
POTATO GNOCCHI WITH SPICY TOMATO SAUCE

Serves 6 as a first course   *Veneto*

4 russet potatoes (about 1½ pounds total)

2 cups coarse sea salt, plus more for salting the pasta cooking water

3 cups unbleached all-purpose flour, plus more for dusting

1 tablespoon fine sea salt, plus more for seasoning the sauce

¼ cup extra-virgin olive oil, plus more for finishing

2 cloves garlic, crushed

Pinch crushed red pepper flakes

1 (16-ounce) can whole peeled tomatoes

Pillowy potato gnocchi are the perfect mildly flavored canvas for a tomato sauce with a hit of *peperoncino*. They are also delicious matched with sharply flavored piccante Gorgonzola cheese (see page 94). We like to roast the potatoes for our gnocchi rather than boiling them, as it keeps them from getting soggy. Gnocchi are some of the easiest fresh pasta to make. The only tricky part is not going overboard with the flour—add it gradually, as you may not need all 3 cups.

PREHEAT the oven to 350°F. Line a baking sheet with parchment paper and set aside.

SPRINKLE about ½ cup of the coarse salt in the bottom of a baking dish just large enough to hold the potatoes. Place the potatoes on the salt, then cover them with the remaining coarse salt. Bake in the preheated oven until easily pierced with a paring knife, about 40 minutes. Set aside to cool. (Discard the salt.)

ONCE the potatoes are cool enough to handle, peel them and mash them with a potato ricer. (You can use a fork, just be sure to crush them fairly thoroughly and not leave any large chunks.) On a work surface, spread the potatoes into a square about 10 by 10 inches.

IN a bowl, combine 2 cups flour and the 1 tablespoon fine sea salt. Sprinkle the flour mixture evenly over the potatoes.

KNEAD the potato mixture (use a bench scraper to help you get started, if necessary) until the mixture is uniform and forms a soft, still slightly sticky dough. If the dough is too sticky, add the remaining 1 cup flour in small amounts, but the less flour you manage to add, the lighter your gnocchi will be.

WITH a knife, cut the dough into equal-size pieces roughly the size of an egg. Working one at a time, roll the pieces into ropes about ¾ inch wide. Cut the ropes into 1-inch pieces.

PICK UP one piece of the dough, roll it over the back of a fork, and let it drop onto the prepared baking sheet. Repeat with the remaining pieces of dough. The resulting gnocchi should be slightly curved with grooves that will capture the sauce. Dust the gnocchi lightly with flour and set aside.

PLACE the olive oil, garlic, and red pepper flakes in a saucepan and cook over medium heat until the garlic is fragrant and just light brown. Add the tomato juices and the tomatoes to the pan, crushing them by hand as you do (see page 31). Season to taste with salt. Simmer the sauce until slightly thickened, about 20 minutes.

BRING a large pot of water to a boil for the gnocchi. When the water is boiling, salt it (see page 20), then add the gnocchi. Cook the gnocchi until they rise to the top of the water, about 1 minute. As they are finished cooking, remove them to a colander with a slotted spoon.

SPREAD a small amount of the tomato sauce on the bottom of a serving dish. Add the drained gnocchi, then spoon the remaining sauce on top. Toss to combine. Drizzle with a little olive oil and serve immediately.

PASTA FRESCA RIPIENA

Tortellini, cappelletti, agnolotti, and other small types of stuffed pasta are generally holiday fare in Italy, and they bring back wonderful memories for us of "helping" in the kitchen. Indeed, kids with their nimble little fingers are often recruited in Italy to assist in folding small pieces of pasta. Larger stuffed pasta such as cannelloni (see page 98 for a recipe) are less labor-intensive and equally delicious. Always have the filling ready to go before you start rolling out the pasta.

The Italian Way with
STUFFED PASTA

Stuffed pasta is made with the same egg pasta dough described on page 54. Add a tablespoon of milk to the dough for added elasticity, and take special care not to go overboard with the flour—the dough for stuffed pasta should be especially supple, as you will be manipulating it more. For that reason, rather than letting one sheet dry as you roll out the others, you should proceed to filling the dough right away and leave the unrolled dough under the overturned bowl. Always use small amounts of filling or the pasta will tear when it is cooking.

NAME	SHAPE	FILLING	CLASSIC PAIRING
CAPPELLACCI	larger cappelletti from Ferrara	winter squash and grated cheese	butter and sage or Bolognese ragù (page 56)
CAPPELLETTI	literally "little hats," very similar to tortellini but made by folding squares rather than circles and attaching two of the corners, so that they resemble tricorner hats	meat and/or cheese, often with a bit of mortadella or prosciutto; or made with a fish-based filling along the coast	cooked and served in broth
CASUNZIEI	half-moons from Cortina d'Ampezzo in the Veneto	beets and a small amount of cheese (there are also casunziei verdi, or green casunziei, filled with greens)	butter and poppy seeds
RAVIOLI	squares made by folding a strip of dough in half over the filling, then cutting in between; dough may be sealed by pressing with the tines of a small fork around the perimeter	greens and ricotta	butter and sage

cappelletti

ravioli cacio e pepe

pansotti

ravioli di zucca

ravioli quadrati

agnolotti del plin

AGNOLOTTI DEL PLIN CON BURRO FUSO

AGNOLOTTI DEL PLIN IN MELTED BUTTER

Serves 4 as a first course   *Piemonte*

8 ounces spinach

5 tablespoons unsalted butter

1 small yellow onion, minced

1 clove garlic, thinly sliced

1 pound ground beef or veal
or a combination of the two

Fine sea salt to taste

½ cup grated grana
cheese (see page 104)

Pinch grated nutmeg

Pasta dough made with
approximately 3 cups
unbleached all-purpose flour
and 3 large eggs, cut into strips
1 inch wide (see page 54)

Coarse sea salt for pasta
cooking water

4 fresh sage leaves, minced

The pride of Piemonte, agnolotti del plin are little squares of meat-filled pasta like miniature ravioli that are served in a butter sauce or the juices from roasted meat. They are typical of the region's cuisine: luxurious, yet lacking in artifice. *Plin* is dialect for "pinch," which refers to the way these are sealed. If you prefer, you can cut the pasta into squares first and then fill each square with the meat mixture; we think the method described below is a little quicker and easier.

STEAM the spinach as described on page 168. Squeeze dry and set aside.

MELT 1 tablespoon butter in a large skillet over medium heat. Add the onion and cook, stirring frequently, until the onion is translucent, about 5 minutes. Add the garlic and cook until it begins to brown, about 5 minutes more. Add the meat to the pan, crumbling it in with a fork. Brown the meat. Season the mixture with salt and remove from the heat; let cool slightly.

MINCE the meat mixture and the spinach together. (Do this by hand—a food processor or blender will make it mushy.) Stir in the grated cheese and the nutmeg.

ARRANGE one strip of pasta dough on a work surface. Place ¼ teaspoon of the meat mixture 1 inch apart down one long side of the strip. Fold the other (empty) half of the strip over the side with filling. With your fingers, gently press between the small mounds of filling to seal the two halves together. With a serrated pastry wheel, trim the long (unfolded side) of the dough, then cut between the small mounds of filling with the pastry wheel. You should have 1-by-½-inch agnolotti. Repeat with the remaining dough and filling.

BRING a large pot of water to a boil for the pasta. When the water is boiling, salt it (see page 20) and add the pasta. Cook until the pasta rises to the surface of the water (see page 55), probably no more than 3 minutes.

MEANWHILE, heat the remaining 4 tablespoons butter in a saucepan large enough to hold the pasta over very low heat. Remove from the heat as soon as the butter is melted.

DRAIN the pasta and add the pasta to the pan with the butter. Toss to coat the pasta. Stir in the minced sage. Divide equally among 4 heated pasta bowls and serve immediately.

PANSOTTI CON SALSA DI NOCI
PANSOTTI IN WALNUT SAUCE

Serves 4   *Liguria*

---

8 ounces spinach

¾ cup ricotta, drained if necessary

1 cup plus 2 tablespoons grated grana cheese (see page 104), plus more for serving

2 teaspoons fine sea salt

Pasta dough made with approximately 3 cups unbleached all-purpose flour and 3 large eggs, cut into strips 3½ to 4 inches wide (see page 54)

2 cups walnuts

2 cloves garlic

6 tablespoons extra-virgin olive oil

3 tablespoons chopped fresh flat-leaf parsley

Freshly ground black pepper to taste

Coarse sea salt for pasta cooking water

3 tablespoons unsalted butter, cut into pieces

Pansotti (the Ligurian dialect word for "belly," sometimes spelled *pansòti* or *pansòtti*) are half-moon or triangular ravioli filled with greens and ricotta that are traditionally served in a walnut sauce. We also like to serve them with a simple sauce of melted butter and lemon zest with a handful of pistachios scattered on top. If the ricotta you purchase for your pansotti filling has a large quantity of liquid, drain it in a fine-mesh strainer for an hour or so. You want it to be fairly dry, so that when you pinch a bit of the filling and roll it between your fingertips it forms a ball.

COOK spinach as described on page 168, squeeze as dry as possible, and mince by hand. Combine the spinach, ricotta, ¾ cup grated cheese, and 1 teaspoon salt and mix to combine. Taste and adjust the salt.

USING a cookie cutter (we use a fluted cutter at Eataly, which is pretty, but a plain border will taste just as good) or the rim of a juice glass, stamp out circles with a 3½- to 4-inch diameter from the strips of pasta. Reroll scraps and cut out additional circles. (You will always end up with a few odd scraps of dough, but we usually roll those last few scraps into rough circles and use them anyway.)

PLACE about 1 tablespoon of the cheese and spinach mixture slightly off center on each circle of dough. Fill a small bowl with lukewarm water. Lightly moisten a fingertip and run it around the perimeter of one circle, then fold the circle in half, pressing the edges together to seal. Set aside and repeat with the remaining circles of dough.

WHEN all the pasta is ready, make the sauce. Toast the walnuts either dry in a skillet or in a 350°F oven or toaster oven until fragrant, about 5 minutes in the skillet and 8 to 10 minutes in the oven or toaster oven.

WITH a mortar and pestle or a food processor fitted with the metal blade, process the walnuts and the garlic until they are finely chopped but not ground into a powder. With a spatula, scrape the nut and garlic mixture into a bowl. Stir in the olive oil, 6 tablespoons grated cheese, the parsley, and 1 teaspoon salt until thoroughly blended. Taste and season with pepper and additional salt if needed.

BRING a large pot of water to a boil for the pasta. When the water is boiling, salt it (see page 20) and add the pasta. Cook until the pasta rises to the surface of the water, probably no more than 3 minutes (see page 55).

USE a strainer to scoop the pasta out of the cooking water and into a warmed serving bowl; reserve about 1 cup cooking water. Scatter the butter on top of the pasta and toss to melt the butter and to combine. If the walnut sauce seems thick, thin it with a few tablespoons of the pasta cooking water, then add the walnut sauce to the pasta and toss to combine. Again, if the sauce is chunky and doesn't adhere to the pasta, add a little of the pasta cooking water, about 1 tablespoon at a time, until the pasta is nicely coated. Serve immediately with additional grated cheese on the side.

TORTELLINI IN BRODO
TORTELLINI IN BROTH

Serves 8 to 10 as a first course   *Emilia-Romagna*

2 pounds beef on the bone

2 pounds capon

2 ribs celery, chopped

2 carrots, chopped

1 large yellow onion, peeled and chopped

1 bay leaf

1 sprig parsley

2 cloves garlic

1 tablespoon whole black peppercorns

2 tablespoons unsalted butter

8 ounces pork loin, chopped

2 fresh sage leaves

4 ounces prosciutto crudo

4 ounces mortadella

½ cup grated Parmigiano Reggiano

Pinch freshly grated nutmeg

Fine sea salt to taste

Freshly ground black pepper to taste

1 large egg, lightly beaten

Pasta dough made with approximately 3 cups unbleached all-purpose flour and 3 large eggs (see page 54)

Tortellini are little circles that are folded and formed into rings. Legend has it that the shape was created as an homage to the belly button of Venus, as glimpsed through a keyhole by an innkeeper. Purchase prosciutto and mortadella in a chunk (not sliced) to make the filling. You can replace up to half of the pork with veal or a combination of veal and turkey, but pork is always the hallmark of tortellini. Tortellini that have already been stuffed and shaped freeze nicely. Spread them out in a single layer on a pan in the freezer for about 45 minutes, then once they're frozen, toss them into a zippered storage bag. They can go right from the freezer into the cooking water or broth without thawing. For the broth, use any beef cuts suitable for long cooking—shank, ribs, and so on. Traditionally, a capon is used in the broth, but you can replace the capon with turkey or with some additional beef. This recipe is a bit of a project, but each component (with the exception of the pasta dough) can be made in advance.

COMBINE the beef and capon in a large stock pot. Add enough water to cover by about 4 inches and bring to a boil. Skim off any foam and add the celery, carrots, onion, bay leaf, parsley, garlic, and peppercorns. Bring to a boil, then reduce the heat to a simmer and cook at a low simmer, partially covered, for 3 hours. Strain the broth into a large bowl (save the meat for another use) and let it cool, then refrigerate until the fat hardens on the surface. Remove almost all of the fat (leave about 1 teaspoon behind for flavor) and discard. Refrigerate the broth until you're ready to use.

MELT the butter in a large skillet over medium heat. Add the pork and sage leaves and cook over medium heat until the meat begins to brown, then reduce the heat to low and cook until the pork is cooked through, about 15 minutes more. Remove and discard the sage. Allow to cool slightly.

IN a food processor fitted with the metal blade or a meat grinder, grind the cooked pork and its juices with the prosciutto and mortadella, then add the cheese and nutmeg. The mixture should form a ball when you grab a bit with your hand, but it should still have a bit of texture to it. Season with salt and pepper. Mix in the egg and set the filling aside to cool, or refrigerate up to 8 hours.

ROLL a portion of pasta dough into a very thin sheet (see pages 54–55 for specific instruction). Leave the remaining dough covered. Arrange the sheet of pasta dough on a work surface. Use a cookie cutter to cut out disks of pasta dough about 1½ to 2 inches in diameter, as close together as possible. Save the scraps and reroll them, or cut them into small squares and serve them in soup. (You can freeze them in a zippered storage bag.)

PUT about ¼ teaspoon of the filling on one of the disks. Fold in half to form a semicircle, pressing to seal. (If the pasta is dry and the edges won't stick together, brush the edges with a little water.) Press the two ends of the flat side of the semicircle together around your index finger to form a ring. The flat side should fold up to form a kind of cuff. Seal the two ends together, overlapping them slightly. Repeat with the remaining dough and filling.

PLACE the broth in a large pot and bring to a boil. Salt the broth and taste to be sure it is properly salted. Add the tortellini a few at a time. About 1 minute after they rise to the surface (this should happen fairly quickly, in about 3 minutes or less, see page 55) remove them with a slotted spoon and transfer to soup bowls. Ladle broth over the cooked tortellini and serve.

PASTA SECCA

Dried pasta made with water and semolina flour is a great boon to the home cook. It can be stored for months, it's relatively inexpensive, and it is filling and satisfying. While egg pasta hails largely from central and northern Italy, dried semolina pasta has deep roots in the Campania region and specifically in the town of Gragnano, outside of Naples, where modernized production of dried pasta was born. At Eataly, we sell dried pasta that is made in Gragnano using bronze molds. These molds create a microscopically rough surface that grips sauce; lesser quality pasta is made in Teflon molds that create a perfectly smooth surface.

To cook dried pasta, bring a large pot of water to a boil, salt it (see page 20), wait for it to return to a boil, and add the pasta. Stir the pasta immediately, and continue to stir it occasionally during cooking. If you are cooking long pasta, such as spaghetti, wait a moment for the portion of the pasta immersed in water to soften, then push the remainder of the pasta into the water using a wooden spoon. *Do not break spaghetti and other long pasta to get it into the pot.* Stir long pasta with a long-handled fork if you have one. Stir all pasta frequently while it is cooking. Cook the pasta until al dente. Begin testing 1 to 2 minutes before the cooking time on the package.

The Italian Way with
MATCHING DRIED PASTA WITH SAUCE

The shapes of pasta are almost infinite; no one has ever been able to perform an accurate census because there are so many, and often the same shape has several different names. That said, pasta can be roughly classified as long versus short, or as cup-shaped versus tubular. And it's not a free-for-all when it comes to matching pasta with sauce; certain pairings are simply inappropriate. Here are the rules to keep in mind:

TYPE OF PASTA	EXAMPLES	MATCHING SAUCES
LONG AND THIN	spaghetti, bucatini, linguine	oil-based sauces, smooth tomato sauces, seafood sauces
CUP-SHAPED	conchiglie (shells)	sauces with peas or small bits of meat or vegetables, which get trapped in the cups to delicious effect
SHORT AND TUBULAR	penne, rigatoni	meat sauces such as ragù
COMPLEX SHAPES	fusilli, rotelle	cream sauces, sauces with peas or small bits of meat or vegetables

calamari

tajarin

ditalini

filei

vesuvio

linguini

whole wheat casarecce

How to
DETERMINE PASTA IS COOKED AL DENTE

PASTA COOKING TIMES CAN VARY WIDELY. Test early, and test often. You can taste a piece, but the method below is a little more reliable.

1. Cut a piece of pasta in half.

2. If there is still a rather large chalky white area in the center, it's not ready yet.

3. When it is al dente, the center will remain slightly lighter in color, but most of the pasta will be the same color.

AFELTRA

Pastificio Giuseppe Afeltra is located in Gragnano in the Campania region—the birthplace of dried pasta making. Afeltra has made dried semolina pasta in the same location since 1848. Afeltra also uses the classic techniques and tools of dried pasta. Pasta is made using bronze dies that give each piece a slightly roughened surface, and each shape is dried on a specific schedule timed to bring out the best in it. Drying is never rushed—it can take as long as two days for pasta to dry properly before it is packaged. Afeltra creates numerous different shapes, but some of its most popular are the classics: long thin spaghetti, squiggly fusilli, ruffled mafalde, and ridged rigatoni. The pasta is made with semolina flour and locally sourced spring water. The company also makes olive oil, panettone, and DOP red wine.

VESUVIO AL RAGÙ DI SALSICCIA E SCAROLA

VESUVIO PASTA WITH SAUSAGE RAGÙ AND ESCAROLE

Serves 6 as a first course   *Campania*

12 ounces sweet sausage

1 tablespoon red wine

1 cup tomato puree

½ cup chicken or beef stock

3 cups shredded escarole

Fine sea salt to taste

Coarse sea salt for pasta cooking water

1 pound Vesuvio pasta or other short pasta, preferably with a complex shape

3 tablespoons extra-virgin olive oil

Grated grana cheese (see page 104) for serving

Vesuvio (named for the still-active volcano on whose slopes the city of Naples was built) is a short curly pasta that looks like a tangled ball of yarn. Each piece has numerous nooks and crannies that make it a great match for a chunky sauce like this one, which is a Neapolitan-style ragù rather than the Bolognese-style ragù served over tagliatelle on page 56. Just be sure to use plain sausage for this pasta, not the type with fennel or hot pepper in it, which would overwhelm the other flavors. As with the Bolognese ragù, you want to cook the meat very gently rather than browning it.

REMOVE the sausage casings and crumble the meat into a small bowl. Sprinkle the wine over the meat and massage the wine into the meat by hand until it is soft and elastic, about 2 minutes.

PLACE the meat in a cold skillet with high sides. Place the skillet over low heat and slowly cook the meat until it is no longer raw looking, about 2 minutes. Do not brown the meat.

ADD the tomato puree and stir to combine. Increase the heat until the tomato puree is simmering gently.

ADD the stock, stir once, and decrease the heat until the ragù is at a very gentle simmer, with a bubble just occasionally breaking the surface. Simmer, uncovered, without stirring for 2 hours. The meat should poach in the liquid and turn very soft.

WHEN the sauce is cooked, carefully spoon off and discard any liquid remaining on the top. Stir in the escarole and cook until just wilted, about 2 minutes. Season to taste with fine sea salt. Remove from the heat.

BRING a large pot of water to a boil for the pasta. When the water is boiling, salt it with coarse sea salt (see page 20) and add the pasta. Cook the pasta until al dente (see page 74).

SMEAR a small amount of the sauce on the bottom of a warmed pasta serving bowl.

WHEN the pasta is cooked, drain it in a colander, then transfer it immediately to the serving bowl. Top with the remaining sauce and toss vigorously to combine. Drizzle on the olive oil and toss again. Serve immediately with grated cheese on the side.

PACCHERI CON SUGO DI MARE
PACCHERI WITH SEAFOOD SAUCE

Serves 4 as a first course   *Campania*

3 cups extra-virgin olive oil, plus more for drizzling

Zest of 1 lemon in wide strips

8 ounces fresh tuna belly

Fine sea salt to taste

Freshly ground black pepper to taste

20 medium shrimp, shelled and deveined

20 mussels

½ cup dry white wine

Coarse sea salt for pasta cooking water

1 pound paccheri pasta

1 clove garlic

Pinch crushed red pepper flakes

½ cup tomato puree

2 tablespoons chopped fresh flat-leaf parsley

Paccheri are wide tubes of pasta with lots of room for capturing bits of seafood in this tasty, savory sauce. Paccheri are also sometimes cooked and filled like cannelloni.

IN a small saucepan, combine the olive oil and strips of lemon zest. Place over low heat and, using a thermometer, bring the oil to about 130°F. Season the tuna with fine sea salt and pepper, add it to the saucepan, and poach the tuna in the oil until it is medium rare, about 7 minutes. Remove the tuna from the oil and set aside. Strain the oil and discard the lemon zest. Reserve the oil. (You won't use all of it in this recipe, but it can be used in other dishes.)

CHOP the shrimp into ¼-inch pieces. Thinly slice the poached tuna.

PLACE the mussels in a medium pot set over medium heat. Add the wine and cover with a tight-fitting lid. Remove the mussels from the pot as they open. Strain any liquid left in the bottom of the pot through a coffee filter or cheesecloth and set aside in a bowl. Remove the mussels from their shells and set aside in the bowl with the strained liquid.

BRING a large pot of water to a boil for the pasta. When the water is boiling, salt it (see page 20) and add the pasta. Cook until al dente (see page 74).

IN a large pan, heat about 3 tablespoons of the oil from poaching the tuna. Crush and peel the garlic clove and add it to the pan with the red pepper flakes. Sauté until the garlic is golden, then remove and discard the garlic. Add the tomato puree and cook until slightly reduced, about 5 minutes. Add the shrimp to the pan and toss until cooked, about 1 minute. Add the sliced tuna.

WHEN the pasta is cooked, drain it in a colander, then transfer it immediately to the pan with the seafood. Toss a few times, then add the mussels and their cooking liquid. Toss vigorously over medium heat until the pasta and seafood are combined, about 1 minute. Drizzle with a generous amount of olive oil, sprinkle on the parsley, and serve immediately.

SPAGHETTONI CACIO E PEPE
THICK SPAGHETTI WITH CRUSHED
BLACK PEPPER AND PECORINO

Serves 6 as a first course   *Lazio*

---

2 tablespoons unsalted butter

2 tablespoons whole black peppercorns, or more to taste

Coarse sea salt for pasta cooking water

1 pound spaghettoni

1½ cups freshly grated pecorino Romano, or more to taste

This pasta is anything but shy and retiring. It uses a generous amount of coarsely ground pepper and grated cheese, and while it may seem simple, when made properly it is a truly memorable start to a meal.

BRING a large pot of water to a boil.

HEAT the butter in a large saucepan over medium heat. Grind the peppercorns very coarsely and add them to the butter.

WARM up a large pasta serving bowl. (The easiest way to do this is to add some of the boiling water for the pasta and swish it around in the bowl, then discard it.)

WHEN the water is boiling, salt it (see page 20) and add the pasta. Cook until al dente (see page 74).

QUICKLY lift the pasta from the pot with tongs, letting it drain for an instant, then drop it directly into the saucepan. Mix the pasta with the sauce until well coated.

REMOVE the pan from the heat and immediately scatter 1 cup of the grated cheese over the pasta, tossing in quickly. As you mix, sprinkle over a spoonful of hot water from the cooking pot to moisten and unify the pasta and sauce. Taste and add more pepper and/or cheese as desired.

SERVE immediately, while the spaghettoni is very hot.

SALUMI E FORMAGGI

When you demand quality products, you support the local farmers, fishermen, butchers, bakers, and cheesemakers who produce them and create a better environment—for eating and beyond.

SALUMI

Salumi—cured meats—are one of Italy's great gifts to the world. Whether made from pork or beef, whether salt-cured or air-dried, thin-sliced Italian salumi are delicious on their own and equally irresistible when incorporated into dishes, where they provide a hit of savory flavor.

The Italian Way with REGIONAL SALUMI

REGION	TYPE	DESCRIPTION
FRIULI–VENEZIA GIULIA, EMILIA-ROMAGNA	prosciutto crudo	Salted pork thigh that slices into dark pink sheets with a ring of white fat around the perimeter. Sweet prosciutto di Parma from Emilia-Romagna and slightly gamier prosciutto di San Daniele from Friuli–Venezia Giulia are both DOP products, strictly regulated.
VENETO, VALLE D'AOSTA	lardo	Pork fat flavored with pepper, garlic, and herbs, and then salted and aged. Lardo has a slightly sweet edge despite the salting.
TRENTINO–ALTO ADIGE	speck	Lean pork leg that's salted and seasoned with juniper, bay leaves, and rosemary, then dry-cured, smoked, and briefly aged. Speck is strongly flavored—a little goes a long way.
LOMBARDIA	salame Milano	Fine-grained brick-red pork and beef salami with very small white dots (said to look like grains of rice) evenly distributed throughout.
LOMBARDIA, TRENTINO–ALTO ADIGE	bresaola	Dark red air-dried beef that is sliced paper thin.
LIGURIA, TOSCANA, PUGLIA, BASILICATA, CALABRIA	soppressata, also known as testa in cassetta	Dried pork salami that includes all the parts of the head, roughly chopped so that slices of the finished salami resemble a mosaic; the southern Italian versions may be spicy.
TOSCANA	finocchiona	Pork belly and shoulder salami with fennel seeds.
EMILIA-ROMAGNA, UMBRIA, MARCHE, CALABRIA	coppa, also known as capocollo	Salami made from a specific section of the pig's neck; tongue and ear cartilage form the white web visible when the salami is sliced. The most sought-after is the coppa from Piacenza (a DOP product). Calabrian coppa is spicy, while Umbrian coppa contains lemon zest, and the coppa from the Marche is laced with ground cinnamon.
EMILIA-ROMAGNA	culatello di Zibello	Made from a large muscle mass from a pig's back leg stuffed into a pig's bladder and aged in special cellars according to DOP standards. It's similar to prosciutto crudo but drier.
EMILIA-ROMAGNA	prosciutto cotto	Cooked ham with a delicate flavor and moist texture.
EMILIA-ROMAGNA	mortadella	Bologna's rosy pink specialty, made from minced lean pork with cubes of fat (and sometimes pistachios) stuffed into a casing so that when sliced it has a pebbled appearance; sometimes called bologna in other parts of the world.
LAZIO	guanciale	Cured pork jowl, similar to unsmoked bacon.
ALL	pancetta	Cured pork belly (pancetta literally means "little belly"), dates back to ancient Rome; may be a rectangular slab or rolled into a cylinder.

speck

prosciutto crudo

finocchiona

lardo

mortadella

bresaola

There are two ways to buy cured
meats—either have them sliced for
you to order, or opt for presliced
selections in special packaging
designed to keep them fresh.

guanciale

fino finocchiona

culatello

coppa

wild boar cacciatorini

How to PUT TOGETHER
AN ANTIPASTO PLATTER

THERE IS NO MEAL THAT IS NOT IMPROVED by having a delicious antipasto platter at the start to whet diners' appetites.

1. Choose one or two thinly sliced cured meats—about 2 ounces per person should be adequate. There is one exception: If you are serving prosciutto crudo, all bets are off. It is our experience that people will consume as much as you put out.

2. Choose a soft cheese and an aged cheese, 2 to 3 ounces per person. Set out the cheeses with knives and cut a few pieces to give people a hint of how to cut them.

3. Choose a preserved veggie (olives, semi-dried tomatoes, eggplant). Arrange it in one or more ramekins.

4. Choose a bread and slice thinly.

PROSCIUTTO E MELONE
PROSCIUTTO AND MELON

Serves 6 as an appetizer

1 ripe cantaloupe

8 ounces thinly sliced prosciutto crudo, preferably prosciutto di Parma

Freshly ground black pepper to taste

This classic dish is magic. You don't have to turn on the stove. It requires only three ingredients. And everybody loves it. The hardest thing about it is finding a ripe melon.

CUT the cantaloupe in half lengthwise. Scoop out and discard the seeds. Cut the melon halves into quarters. Slice off the melon peel and discard. Trim any green flesh and discard. Slice each quarter into crescents about ½ inch thick.

ARRANGE the slices of melon in a single layer on a serving platter. Arrange the prosciutto on top in a single layer. Season to taste with pepper. (The prosciutto is salty enough—you don't need more.)

SERVE at room temperature.

Variations: You can substitute almost any kind of seasonal fruit, as the saltiness of the prosciutto works beautifully with various sweet flavors. Try any other type of melon, halved or quartered fresh figs (especially good with prosciutto di San Daniele), half rings of juicy pineapple, pitted and quartered apricots, peeled and cored pears cut into eighths, or pitted, peeled, and sliced white or yellow peaches in place of the cantaloupe.

PROSCIUTTO DI PARMA E SAN DANIELE

Certified by a consortium created in 1963, prosciutto di Parma is one of Italy's most famous and most delectable products. Ham hocks have been dried in and around Parma in the Emilia-Romagna region since at least 100 B.C. Only prosciutto crafted in a specific geographical area between the Enza and Stirone rivers can be called prosciutto di Parma and branded with the consortium's crown symbol. Prosciutto di Parma is made from specially bred Large White, Landrance, and Duroc breed pigs whose carefully managed diet includes whey from the production of Parmigiano Reggiano cheese. The rear haunches are cured in sea salt—just enough to preserve them without covering up the naturally sweet taste of the meat. During the curing process, a prosciutto loses more than one quarter of its weight through evaporation. Pork and salt are the sole ingredients in this delicately flavored savory prosciutto crudo, which enjoys DOP status.

Prosciutto di San Daniele, made in Friuli–Venezia Giulia, is also a DOP prosciutto crudo and has its own consortium (and its own logo—a hock with the letters SD in the center). This prosciutto is sweeter than its cousin from Parma, and usually a little bit larger in size. When sliced thinly, prosciutto di San Daniele is so soft that it seems to melt in your mouth. Prosciutto di San Daniele is produced on the banks of the Tagliamento, an Alpine river. The production area enjoys breezes from both the mountains and the Adriatic Sea (just over twenty miles away) that result in ideal humidity levels for curing meats. The natural drying process is gradual and measured, lasting a minimum of thirteen months. Longer aging times will result in a more strongly flavored prosciutto. Like prosciutto di Parma, prosciutto di San Daniele is made only of meat and sea salt.

SALTIMBOCCA ALLA ROMANA
VEAL WITH PROSCIUTTO AND SAGE

Serves 6 as a main course   *Lazio*

**6 veal scaloppine (about
4 ounces each)**

Fine sea salt to taste

**Freshly ground black
pepper to taste**

6 thin slices prosciutto crudo

**12 fresh sage leaves, plus
a few more for garnish**

**Unbleached all-purpose
flour for dredging**

2 tablespoons extra-virgin olive oil

4 tablespoons unsalted butter

½ cup white wine

These little bundles are irresistible—you may want to make extra, especially if you are having guests. Indeed, *saltimbocca* literally means "jumps into your mouth."

POUND the scaloppine about ⅛ inch thick. Season with salt and pepper (remember that the prosciutto is salty). Place 1 slice of prosciutto on top of each. Place 2 sage leaves on top of each as well, then use toothpicks to attach the sage leaves and prosciutto to the meat. Dredge each piece lightly in flour and set aside.

HEAT the oil and 2 tablespoons of the butter in a large pan over medium heat. Add the veal to the pan, prosciutto side down, in a single layer. (Work in batches if all the veal won't fit at once.) Cook until browned and crispy, about 1 minute, then turn and cook the other side. Transfer to a platter to keep warm.

ADD the wine to the pan and deglaze, scraping any browned bits of meat from the bottom. Cook, stirring constantly, until the mixture thickens into a sauce, 1 to 2 minutes. Melt the remaining 2 tablespoons butter in a small pan and quickly fry the sage leaves for garnish until crispy.

REMOVE the toothpicks from the veal. Pour the sauce over the veal, garnish with fried sage leaves, and serve immediately.

BRESAOLA E RUCOLA
BRESAOLA AND ARUGULA SALAD

Serves 4 as an appetizer or light main course   *Lombardia*

4 ounces thinly sliced bresaola

1 lemon

**4 cups loosely packed
arugula leaves**

**2 tablespoons extra-virgin
olive oil**

Fine sea salt to taste

**Freshly ground black
pepper to taste**

**2 ounces Parmigiano Reggiano
or Grana Padano cheese**

Though bresaola originated in the Lombardia region, this refreshing bresaola salad has become a mainstay across Italy. Try it with one of the lighter red wines from the Valtellina area of Lombardia.

ARRANGE the bresaola in a single layer on a serving plate or on 4 individual salad plates.

GRATE a small amount of lemon zest from the lemon, then halve the lemon and juice it. Strain out and discard any seeds.

PULL off any rough stems on the arugula and discard them. Place the arugula in a large bowl. Combine the lemon juice, lemon zest, and olive oil. Season with salt and pepper, and whisk to combine. Pour the olive oil dressing over the arugula and toss to combine. Taste and adjust seasoning.

MOUND the arugula on top of the bresaola in the center of each plate.

WITH a vegetable peeler, shave the cheese over the arugula. Serve immediately.

FUSILLI CON SPECK E RADICCHIO
FUSILLI WITH SPECK AND RADICCHIO

Serves 4 as a first course   *Trentino—Alto Adige*

1 small head radicchio

2 ounces speck

1 shallot

1 tablespoon extra-virgin olive oil

Fine sea salt to taste

¾ cup heavy cream

Coarse sea salt for pasta cooking water

1 pound fusilli

Freshly ground black pepper to taste

Purchase the speck for this dish in a single slab and then cut it into cubes at home. When radicchio cooks, it loses much of its bitterness and turns slightly sweet, a flavor that plays off the smokiness of the speck very well. This is the perfect dish to throw together when unexpected guests knock at your door. It can be made with egg noodles (see page 54) for a somewhat more substantial dish, and it would be fabulous with fresh garganelli, a quill-shaped egg pasta. You can also serve grated grana cheese (see page 104) on the side if you like. Any variety of radicchio will work here.

BRING a large pot of water to a boil for the pasta.

CUT the radicchio into ribbons. Chop the speck into ¼-inch cubes. Mince the shallot.

IN a skillet large enough to hold the pasta comfortably, heat the olive oil over medium heat. Add the shallot and speck and cook, stirring frequently, until the shallot is translucent, about 3 minutes.

ADD the radicchio and stir to combine. Season lightly with fine sea salt. (Remember that the speck is somewhat salty.) Turn the heat to low and cook, covered, until the radicchio is very wilted and has turned dark purple, about 7 minutes. (If the radicchio starts to stick to the pan before it is cooked, add 1 to 2 tablespoons water.) Add the cream to the pan, stir, and cook until just slightly reduced and clinging to the radicchio, about 3 minutes.

MEANWHILE, when the water in the large pot boils, add coarse salt (see page 20) and then add the fusilli. Cook, stirring frequently with a wooden spoon, until the pasta is al dente. (See page 74 for more on the proper cooking technique for dried pasta.)

WHEN the pasta is al dente, drain in a colander and then transfer to the pan with the sauce. Toss over medium heat until the pasta is coated in sauce. Season with a generous amount of fresh pepper and serve immediately.

VERDURE INVERNALI CON PANCETTA E UOVA

WINTER GREENS WITH PANCETTA AND EGG

Serves 4 as an appetizer or side dish

2 ounces pancetta, in 1 chunk

¾ cup plus 1 tablespoon
extra-virgin olive oil

Juice of 1 large lemon
(about ¼ cup)

2 tablespoons acacia honey

Fine sea salt to taste

Freshly ground black
pepper to taste

6 cups winter greens, such
as radicchio, frisée, escarole,
endive, and spinach

4 slices rustic bread

4 large eggs

Winter greens are delicious, but they can also be a little tougher than the more tender shoots available in spring. What to do when you're craving a salad in cooler weather? This dish solves the problem by making a savory salad with winter greens that wilt from the heat of a warm poached egg. Encourage your guests to toss vigorously as they are served—the results are sublime.

CUT the pancetta into matchsticks. Line a plate with paper towels.

PLACE a sauté pan over medium-high heat. When the pan is hot, add the 1 tablespoon olive oil. Add the pancetta in a single layer and cook, stirring occasionally and keeping it in a single layer, until crispy, about 4 minutes. When the pancetta is crispy, use a slotted spoon to remove it from the pan and transfer it to the paper towel–lined plate. Reserve the fat in the pan.

WHISK together the lemon juice and honey in a small bowl. Season with salt and pepper. Whisking continuously, drizzle in the remaining ¾ cup olive oil. Taste and adjust the seasoning, adding more honey and/or salt if necessary.

PLACE the greens in a large bowl and season with salt and pepper. Toss the greens (the salt should wilt them just a little), then dress the greens with the vinaigrette. (You may not need all of the vinaigrette.) Distribute the greens among 4 individual serving bowls.

TOAST the bread. Reheat the reserved pancetta fat if it has cooled and brush it onto the toasted bread. Set a piece of bread on each serving of greens.

POACH the eggs by bringing 4 inches of water to a boil in a saucepan over high heat. Lightly salt the water. Crack 1 egg into a small bowl. Reduce the heat so that the water is at a low boil. Stir the water counterclockwise to create a vortex in the pan. Gently pour the egg into the center of the vortex. The whites will wrap around the yolk. Repeat with the remaining eggs, always pouring them out of a small bowl and creating a vortex in the water. Poach the eggs until the whites are set, about 4 minutes. Scoop out 1 egg with a slotted spoon. Hold it over the saucepan for a few seconds to drain, then gently place it on top of the toast. Repeat with the remaining eggs.

SEASON the eggs with salt and pepper. Sprinkle the pancetta matchsticks over the individual dishes and serve immediately.

FORMAGGI

There are dozens of different families of cheese in Italy, and then each of those is varied. For example, there are hundreds of different types of robiola. Below is just a sampling of the major families of cheese Italy has to offer.

The Italian Way with
AGED REGIONAL CHEESES

REGION	FAMILY	DESCRIPTION
VALLE D'AOSTA	fontina	Semi-firm creamy cow's milk cheese with a hint of mushroom flavor; the star of fonduta (page 107).
PIEMONTE	robiola	Soft cheese made with cow's milk, goat's milk, sheep's milk, or a combination; tangy and spreadable.
LOMBARDIA	Gorgonzola	Pungent veined blue cheese from the town of Gorgonzola outside Milan, where this DOP product dates back to the ninth century; Gorgonzola is generally divided into Gorgonzola dolce, or sweet Gorgonzola, and Gorgonzola piccante, or spicy Gorgonzola.
LOMBARDIA	Taleggio	Named after a valley near Italy's border with Switzerland, this cow's milk cheese is shaped into a square and often covered in an orange rind.
VENETO	Asiago	Pale yellow, firm, smooth-textured DOP cow's milk cheese aged three to eighteen months; Asiago originated in the town of the same name in the Vicenza province.
VENETO	Piave	Made along the Piave river and aged in large wheels; Piave vecchio (aged) and stravecchio (super-aged) are dense and grainy.
VENETO	ubriaco	Literally "drunk," this cow's milk cheese from the Treviso area is washed in wine, which gives it a unique flavor and a deep purple rind.
TOSCANA, MARCHE, ABRUZZO, SARDEGNA	pecorino	Catch-all word for sheep's milk cheese (*pecora* is "sheep" in Italian); these are anywhere from semi-soft to aged until hard for grating.
PUGLIA	canestrato	Straw-yellow, fairly sharp sheep's cheese aged in rush baskets (the name means "placed in a basket").
BASILICATA, CALABRIA, CAMPANIA, MOLISE, PUGLIA	caciocavallo	Drawn curd cheese made in the southern Apennines; formed into shapes like water balloons and tied together in pairs with rope to be hung for aging (or to be transported on the back of a donkey or horse, as the name indicates).
CAMPANIA, PUGLIA	scamorza	White stretched-curd cow's milk cheese (sometimes made from water buffalo's milk in Campania); often smoked, which gives it a thin brown rind.

fontina

ricotta salata

aged asiago

blue Lanzo

piacentinu di Enna

robiola oro

robiola di capra

Taleggio crudo

burrata

caprino

ricotta

bocconcini

mascarpone

mozzarella

The Italian Way with
FRESH REGIONAL CHEESES

REGION	FAMILY	DESCRIPTION
LOMBARDIA	mascarpone	Double- or triple-cream mild spreadable cow's milk cheese sometimes likened to cream cheese; sold in tubs, it is the key ingredient in tiramisù (page 291)
LOMBARDIA	stracchino	Acidic spreadable white cheese that is not aged.
PUGLIA	burrata	Luxurious liquid cream contained in an edible purse of curds from the Murge area of Puglia.
CAMPANIA	mozzarella di bufala	Extra-creamy DOP mozzarella made from water buffalo's milk and eaten very fresh.

SIGNS OF QUALITY

Cheesemongers and salumi cutters don't mind making suggestions and offering samples—in fact, that's their job! Ask lots of questions.

We're always happy to grate your cheese for you at Eataly, though, of course, you can grate it at home just before using.

CANNELLONI ALLA RICOTTA CON MELANZANE E POMODORI

RICOTTA CANNELLONI WITH EGGPLANT AND TOMATO SAUCE

Serves 6 to 8 as a first course   *Piemonte*

1 pound plum tomatoes

1 tablespoon extra-virgin olive oil

Fine sea salt to taste

Freshly ground black
pepper to taste

2 sprigs fresh thyme

4 medium eggplants
(about 6 pounds total)

½ teaspoon crushed
red pepper flakes

1 (16-ounce) can whole
peeled tomatoes

1 tablespoon red wine vinegar

2 cups loosely packed
fresh basil leaves

1¼ cups grated grana
cheese (see page 104)

Coarse sea salt for pasta
cooking water

About 36 fresh 4-by-4-inch
egg pasta noodles made
with approximately 3 cups
unbleached all-purpose flour
and 3 large eggs (see page 54)

3 cups ricotta, drained
in a cheesecloth-lined
sieve if very liquid

Freshly ground white
pepper to taste

1 large egg, beaten

The ricotta for cannelloni should be on the dry side so that liquid doesn't leak out into the pan while the pasta is baking. If you make your own ricotta for this recipe (page 99), let it drain until fairly firm.

PREHEAT the oven to 400°F. Line 2 large baking sheets with foil and set aside.

CUT the plum tomatoes in half lengthwise and toss with the olive oil. Season with salt and black pepper. Place the thyme sprigs on one of the lined baking sheets and arrange the tomatoes on the pan, cut side down. Place the eggplants (whole) on the second baking sheet. Roast both until the tomato skins turn dark and puff, and the eggplant skins look dark and tear easily and the eggplant pulp is completely tender, about 15 minutes. (The tomatoes and eggplant may be done at different times.) Cool both slightly, remove the skins and seed sacks from the eggplants, and chop the roasted tomatoes and eggplants coarsely. Turn the oven to 425°F.

PLACE the roasted tomatoes, eggplants, and red pepper flakes into a large saucepan. Lift the canned tomatoes out of their juices and crush them by hand (see page 31) into the pot. Cook over medium heat for 5 minutes, then add the red wine vinegar and adjust salt to taste. Continue cooking until the mixture tastes homogenous, about 5 additional minutes. Tear in the basil and stir in 2 tablespoons of the grated grana.

MEANWHILE, bring a large pot of water to a boil for cooking the pasta. Spread a clean flat-weave dishtowel on a work surface and set a bowl of ice water nearby. When the water is boiling, salt it with the coarse salt (see page 20) and add 4 of the noodles. Cook until the noodles rise to the surface, about 30 seconds, then remove with a skimmer, dip briefly in the cold water, and spread them on the dishtowel in a single layer. Repeat with the remaining noodles. Gently blot the noodles dry.

COMBINE the ricotta and 1 cup of the grated grana in a bowl. Season to taste with salt and white pepper. Stir in the egg.

LINE the bottom of a large baking dish with about ¾ cup of the egg-plant and tomato sauce.

SPOON about ⅓ cup of the ricotta mixture along the edge of one of the pasta squares, leaving a ½-inch margin. Roll up into a tube, pressing and evening out the tube as you roll. Don't roll so tightly that you squeeze out the filling. Set the filled noodle in the prepared baking dish, seam side down, and repeat with the remaining noodles and filling, tucking them in next to one another. (You may have leftover filling or noodles.) Cover the cannelloni with the remaining eggplant and tomato sauce and sprinkle the remaining 2 tablespoons grana over the top. Bake until the cannelloni are browned and bubbling, about 25 minutes. Remove and let stand 5 minutes before serving.

How to MAKE RICOTTA

RICOTTA IS TECHNICALLY NOT A CHEESE—it is a by-product of the cheesemaking process. This type of ricotta (created with milk rather than the whey used by large cheesemaking operations) is easy to make at home. You can skip the heavy cream and make this with just milk if you like, but not skim milk—the resulting ricotta will be too grainy and watery. One gallon of milk will yield about 4 cups of ricotta.

1. Rinse out a large pot with cold water to prevent scorching. Place 1 gallon whole or reduced-fat milk or a combination of the two and ¾ cup to 1 cup heavy cream in the pot.

2. Heat, stirring occasionally, to somewhere between 185°F and 195°F without bringing the milk mixture to a boil. If you don't have a thermometer, don't sweat it—just heat the milk until it is simmering actively but not boiling.

3. Remove from the heat and stir in $1/3$ cup apple cider vinegar and 1 tablespoon fine sea salt. Stir constantly for 1 minute, then let the mixture cool untouched and uncovered for 10 minutes. Curds will form.

4. Line a fine-mesh sieve with damp cheesecloth and set the sieve over a bowl. Using a slotted spoon, transfer the ricotta to the lined strainer. (Pouring it will disturb the curd and may cause the bowl to overflow with liquid.) Refrigerate the ricotta until it has drained to the desired consistency—about 30 minutes for very smooth and creamy ricotta, and 2 to 3 hours for drier ricotta. Serve immediately or store in the refrigerator, in a covered container, for up to 5 days.

POMODORO E MOZZARELLA
TOMATO AND MOZZARELLA SALAD

Serves 4 as an appetizer or 2 as a light main course   *Campania*

1 ball mozzarella (about 1 pound)

2 large, perfectly ripe tomatoes

3 tablespoons extra-virgin olive oil

Freshly ground black pepper to taste

Fine sea salt to taste

½ cup loosely packed fresh basil leaves

Our housemade mozzarella is so good that it should always be paired with good ingredients, as in the perfectly ripe tomatoes in this salad. Other options include serving it with freshly sliced prosciutto or using it in a great panino made on our Pane Rustico (page 119)—or just pair it with nothing but more mozzarella.

SLICE the mozzarella into ¼-inch-thick slices. Slice the tomatoes into ¼-inch-thick slices.

ARRANGE the tomato and mozzarella slices on a serving platter, over-lapping slightly.

DRIZZLE on the olive oil. Season with pepper and salt. Scatter the fresh basil leaves (torn if large) over the top. Serve at room temperature. (Never refrigerate.)

How to MAKE OUR MOZZARELLA

WE MAKE FRESH MOZZARELLA ALL DAY LONG.

1. Start with local milk. Eataly's fresh curd is made every day with local whole milk. Our resident mozzarella makers start their days at 10 a.m. to begin production for our restaurants and our customers.

2. Separate the curd. The fresh curd is pushed through a *chitarra*, an instrument shaped like a guitar, to separate the solids.

3. Add hot water. Very hot, salted water is added to the curd to bring the cheese to a warmer temperature.

4. Stretch it! The mixture is then stirred and stretched by hand to ensure that it has melted evenly and no bits of curd are left in the cheese.

5. Fresh mozzarella for all! The cheese is then broken off into pieces and given to the Eataly restaurants that are serving it that day. The rest of the fresh product is displayed inches from where it's made.

We've learned from the best: We visited Caseificio Olanda in Andria, Puglia, to learn the art of making fresh **fior di latte** *(cow's milk) mozzarella. Our fresh mozzarella counters follow in their footsteps to make 100% Italian mozzarella using 100% local milk.*

FRICO FRIABILE
CRISPY FRICO

Makes about 16 crisps, serves 8 as an appetizer   *Friuli–Venezia Giulia*

1 cup grated Montasio cheese

Crispy frico has only one ingredient: Montasio cheese. The fresh, semi-aged, and aged varieties will all work. The disks will be flexible when warm but will crisp as they cool. If you'd like to get fancy, you can shape them into tubes or little cups or baskets when they are warm and they will maintain the shape. You can flavor crispy frico with all kinds of herbs or minced pancetta or prosciutto. Making frico is a lesson in transforming humble ingredients into something special.

HEAT a griddle or cast-iron pan (or coat another pan very lightly with olive oil) and sprinkle about 1 tablespoon grated Montasio in a thin circle.

COOK until crisp and golden, then flip and cook the other side as well, about 5 minutes total. Repeat with remaining cheese.

FIORI DI ZUCCHINA RIPIENI
STUFFED ZUCCHINI BLOSSOMS

Serves 6 as an appetizer   *Lazio*

12 zucchini blossoms

1 cup fresh buffalo or cow's milk ricotta (see Note)

1 large egg

2 scallions, thinly sliced

1 anchovy fillet, rinsed and minced

¼ teaspoon freshly grated nutmeg

Fine sea salt to taste

Freshly ground black pepper to taste

1 cup rice flour

¾ cup cold sparkling water

½ cup extra-virgin olive oil

Orange zucchini blossoms are a beautiful early summer treat. Male blossoms grow on stems and are slightly larger (and therefore easier to handle) than female blossoms, which grow atop zucchini. Both have a delicate, vegetal taste and can be stuffed and fried or served raw. They make a lovely decorative topping for a frittata and add brilliant color to salads. Always use zucchini blossoms the same day you purchase them (or snip them from your garden if you're lucky enough to have them)—they fade quickly. To clean the blossoms, do a quick check for any insects or stray dirt and brush gently with a damp paper towel. They're too fragile to be rinsed under running water.

TO prepare the zucchini blossoms, gently tease open the petals and pinch off the fuzzy-looking stamens in the center. Discard the stamens. (There's nothing wrong with them per se, but they can impart a bitter aftertaste.)

IN a medium bowl, combine the ricotta, egg, scallions, minced anchovy, nutmeg, salt, and pepper. Using a measuring spoon or demitasse spoon, stuff each zucchini blossom with 1½ teaspoons of the filling and set aside.

PLACE the rice flour in a bowl. Pour the sparkling water over the rice flour and whisk until thoroughly combined and smooth.

IN a 10- or 12-inch sauté pan, heat the olive oil over high heat until smoking. Dip 4 of the stuffed zucchini blossoms in the batter and coat well.

PLACE the battered blossoms in the pan and cook until golden brown, turning once with a slotted spatula, about 3 minutes total. Remove to butcher paper or paper towels to drain and sprinkle lightly with salt. Repeat with the remaining blossoms. Serve hot.

NOTE: *Buffalo ricotta is especially light and creamy, but cow's milk ricotta will still taste great in these blossoms. As always, the fresher the better—if you follow the instructions on page 99 for making ricotta, freshness is guaranteed.*

The Italian Way with GRANA

GRANA IS THE ITALIAN WORD FOR AN AGED CHEESE MADE IN A LARGE WHEEL. Grana has a somewhat crunchy texture due to crystals that form as it ages. The two best-known types of grana are Parmigiano Reggiano and Grana Padano. Grana has been made for more than a millennium. Try one of these classic uses for grana:

1. Chip off chunks of grana using the traditional spade-shaped knife and serve with ripe pears.

2. Use a vegetable peeler to shave grana over almost any type of salad.

3. Grate grana finely and sprinkle over pasta, soup, or risotto, or incorporate grated grana into a frittata (page 191).

4. When you've finished all of the delicious cheese, simmer the rind from a piece of grana in soup for added flavor; remove and discard the rind before serving.

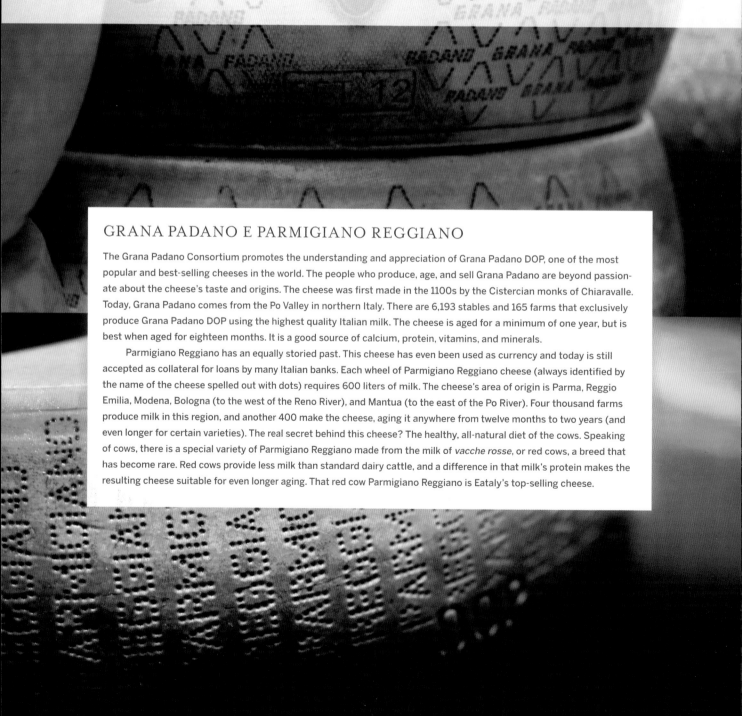

GRANA PADANO E PARMIGIANO REGGIANO

The Grana Padano Consortium promotes the understanding and appreciation of Grana Padano DOP, one of the most popular and best-selling cheeses in the world. The people who produce, age, and sell Grana Padano are beyond passionate about the cheese's taste and origins. The cheese was first made in the 1100s by the Cistercian monks of Chiaravalle. Today, Grana Padano comes from the Po Valley in northern Italy. There are 6,193 stables and 165 farms that exclusively produce Grana Padano DOP using the highest quality Italian milk. The cheese is aged for a minimum of one year, but is best when aged for eighteen months. It is a good source of calcium, protein, vitamins, and minerals.

Parmigiano Reggiano has an equally storied past. This cheese has even been used as currency and today is still accepted as collateral for loans by many Italian banks. Each wheel of Parmigiano Reggiano cheese (always identified by the name of the cheese spelled out with dots) requires 600 liters of milk. The cheese's area of origin is Parma, Reggio Emilia, Modena, Bologna (to the west of the Reno River), and Mantua (to the east of the Po River). Four thousand farms produce milk in this region, and another 400 make the cheese, aging it anywhere from twelve months to two years (and even longer for certain varieties). The real secret behind this cheese? The healthy, all-natural diet of the cows. Speaking of cows, there is a special variety of Parmigiano Reggiano made from the milk of *vacche rosse*, or red cows, a breed that has become rare. Red cows provide less milk than standard dairy cattle, and a difference in that milk's protein makes the resulting cheese suitable for even longer aging. That red cow Parmigiano Reggiano is Eataly's top-selling cheese.

shaved Grana Padano

Grana Padano

coarsely grated Grana Padano

Parmigiano Reggiano

Parmigiano Reggiano chunks

finely grated Parmigiano Reggiano

PASTA ALLA NORMA
PASTA WITH EGGPLANT

Serves 4 as a first course   *Sicilia*

**2 medium eggplants
(about 3 pounds total)**

Fine sea salt to taste

2 tablespoons extra-virgin olive oil

1 clove garlic, minced

1 medium red onion, diced

1 cup tomato puree

**Coarse sea salt for pasta
cooking water**

**1-pound package penne or
other short dried pasta**

5 ounces ricotta salata, cubed

Leaves of 1 sprig fresh basil

Pasta alla Norma showcases Sicilia's flavorful eggplant, along with aged ricotta salata cheese. The name is an homage to the much-lauded opera *Norma* by Vincenzo Bellini, himself a native of Catania, Sicilia. Legend has it that upon tasting the dish in the 1800s, Sicilian playwright Nino Martoglio was so impressed that he compared it to the bel canto classic. You can fry the eggplant if you like, but we find it tastier when roasted, and it doesn't make a mess that way. Ricotta salata is ricotta that has been pressed, salted, and dried. We like to cut it into cubes for a pretty presentation, but if you'd rather, you can shred it and sprinkle it on.

CUT the eggplants into ¾-inch cubes. Place in a colander, sprinkle with fine sea salt, and toss to combine, then set the colander over a bowl (or directly in a sink) and allow the eggplants to drain for 1 hour.

PREHEAT the oven to 350°F.

PAT the eggplant cubes dry and toss them with 1 tablespoon olive oil. Season with salt, keeping in mind that you've already salted the eggplant once. Spread the eggplant on a baking sheet (lined with foil for easy cleanup, if you like) and roast in the preheated oven for 15 minutes without disturbing them. Turn the eggplant once—the undersides should be nicely browned, and continue roasting until the pieces are golden brown and soft, 15 to 20 minutes longer. Set the eggplant aside.

BRING a large pot of water to a boil for cooking the pasta.

IN a large skillet, heat the remaining tablespoon of olive oil over medium heat and add the garlic and onion. Cook until the onion is translucent and the garlic is fragrant, about 3 minutes, then add the tomato puree and season with salt. Decrease the heat and simmer until thickened, about 10 minutes.

MEANWHILE, when the water in the large pot boils, add coarse salt (see page 20) and then add the penne. Cook, stirring frequently with a wooden spoon, until the penne is al dente. (See page 74 for more on the proper cooking technique for dried pasta.)

WHEN the pasta is al dente, drain it in a colander. Add the eggplant to the skillet with the tomato and toss to combine, then transfer the drained pasta to the pan. Toss to combine over medium heat. Remove from the heat and add the cubes of cheese. Toss to combine, then scatter the basil leaves on top (tear if large) and serve immediately.

FONDUTA VALDOSTANA
VALLE D'AOSTA FONDUE

Serves 4 as a main course   *Valle d'Aosta*

12 ounces fontina cheese

2 cups whole milk

8 (1½-inch-thick) slices Pane Rustico (page 119) or other country-style bread

3 tablespoons unsalted butter

4 egg yolks

Fine sea salt to taste

4 fresh white truffle shavings or 1 teaspoon white truffle puree

Cheesy fondue from the north of Italy is a one-dish meal. It is a cousin to Swiss fondue, but it doesn't include wine or garlic and it does incorporate egg yolks. In addition to or in place of the cubes of bread, you can serve lightly steamed vegetables such as cauliflower florets for dipping. You can also pour it over cooked vegetables or a vegetable flan as if it were a sauce.

REMOVE the rind from the cheese and slice the cheese thinly. Place the cheese in the top of a stovetop-safe fondue set if you have one, the top of a double boiler, or a bowl that will sit on top of a saucepan of water.

POUR the milk over the cheese and refrigerate for at least 1 hour and up to 3 hours to allow the cheese to infuse the milk.

PREHEAT the oven or toaster oven to 350°F.

CUT the bread into 1½-inch cubes. Spread the cubes on a baking sheet and bake, turning once or twice, until golden, about 20 minutes. Set aside.

STRAIN the cheese out of the milk, reserving the milk. Return the cheese to the top of the double boiler and add the butter. Fill the bottom of the double boiler with water, bring to a boil, reduce the heat to a brisk simmer, then set the top of the double boiler containing the cheese and butter over the boiling water. Cook, whisking constantly, until the cheese and butter have melted and are smoothly combined, about 10 minutes. (At first the mixture will look gloppy—just keep whisking.)

WHISK in the egg yolks one at a time, whisking smooth between additions. Slowly add the reserved milk in a thin stream, whisking constantly, until the mixture is creamy and pourable. (You may not need all the milk.) Whisk until the milk is heated through and the mixture is very smooth, about 10 minutes more. Taste and season with salt.

IF you are using a fondue pot, transfer the fonduta in the double boiler into the pot; set the pot over the flame, keeping the flame low. If not, rinse out 4 individual serving bowls with hot water to heat them, then divide the fonduta among them. Top each with a truffle shaving or ¼ teaspoon puree. Serve immediately with the bread cubes for dipping.

CROXETTI AL PESTO GENOVESE
CROXETTI PASTA WITH PESTO

Serves 6 as a first course   *Liguria*

Coarse sea salt for cooking water

8 ounces green beans

2 small Yukon gold potatoes, peeled
and sliced about ¾ inch thick

1-pound package croxetti pasta

1 clove garlic

Fine sea salt to taste

Leaves of 1 bunch fresh basil
(about 2 loosely packed cups)

2 tablespoons pine nuts

½ cup extra-virgin olive oil

½ cup grated pecorino Romano

The cuisine of Liguria is famed for its herb-heavy dishes, chief among them pesto. A proper pesto hits your nose with the scent of basil, which can only be described as intensely green. A pesto is literally a paste and is never cooked. Pesto Genovese is the best-known example. Croxetti are coin-shaped disks of pasta produced with special stamps that often imprint the disks with symbols. You can use another type of dried pasta in this recipe, and pesto is also delicious with fresh egg noodles.

BRING a large pot of water to a boil.

WHEN the water is boiling, add coarse salt. Add the green beans and cook until tender, about 5 minutes. Remove with a slotted spoon. Add the potato slices and cook until tender enough to be pierced easily with a paring knife but not falling apart, about 8 minutes. Remove with a slotted spoon to a warmed large serving bowl.

ADD the pasta to the pot, and cook, stirring frequently with a wooden spoon, until the croxetti are cooked. (See page 74 for more on the proper cooking technique for dried pasta.)

WHILE the pasta is cooking, cut the green beans into 1-inch pieces and add to the serving bowl with the potatoes.

PLACE the garlic and a generous pinch of fine sea salt in a large mortar and grind against the sides until crushed into a paste. Add about a quarter of the basil leaves and grind until broken down. Continue to add the basil a little at a time, breaking down all the leaves before adding more. Add the pine nuts and grind until crushed. Add the oil and grind until the pesto is creamy. Finally, add the cheese and grind until creamy and thoroughly combined.

STIR about 2 tablespoons of the pasta cooking water into the pesto. Add a little of the pesto to the serving bowl and toss with the potatoes and green beans.

WHEN the pasta is cooked, drain it and add it to the serving bowl. Top with the remaining pesto, toss to combine thoroughly, and serve hot.

PANE E
CEREALI

Bread is a serious thing.

PANE

Italy is a country made up of culinary micro-regions with thousands of recipes for any food item you can name, and bread is no exception. Each region, indeed each town and village, in Italy has its own traditional bread. It would be impossible to replicate those various types of bread without the local flour, techniques, and even water. (Yes, water has a big impact on bread. Any Neapolitan worth his salt will tell you that pizza never tastes the same outside of Naples because the water used to make the dough isn't the same, and many serious bread bakers opt for bottled water from the place where the loaves they are producing originated, much as a wine from a certain area will inevitably pair well with the local cuisine.)

So, at Eataly, we created our own "local" bread. It's not the bread from any particular region, although you will find similar rough-hewn, rustic loaves in many places in Italy. Instead, in each store, we use organic stone-ground flour from a nearby producer. Eataly stores in the United States use flours milled in that country; Eataly stores in Italy use Mulino Marino flour. (If you are accustomed to purchasing flour at a mainstream grocery store, you will be amazed at the flavor and texture imparted to baked goods using "fresh" flour that was recently milled.) We share the same *lievito madre,* a mother or natural yeast. Ours is more than thirty-five years old. When we open a store, we transport a bit of that starter to the new location. (See page 121 for information on creating your own natural starter.) Our bread is baked fresh in a wood-burning oven crafted in Italy. This means you won't find a pale imitation of the bread you've eaten in Italy on our shelves. Instead, you'll find bread that reproduces what is important about that Italian bread: It's fresh and flavorful—baked within the preceding twenty-four hours—with a springy interior and a crisp crust that make it the ideal accompaniment to any meal. Properly made bread cooked in a wood-burning oven is a piece of edible Italian art.

SIGNS OF QUALITY

Breadmaking is an ancient art and the key is the highest-quality ingredients: stone-ground flour and natural yeast.

Whole grain flours and whole grains such as polenta and farro contain oils that can turn rancid and should be stored tightly sealed in the freezer. There's no need to thaw them before using.

The Italian Way with REGIONAL BREADS

CIABATTA *Slipper*	Lombardia	A flat, oval bread with large holes in the exceptionally light crumb due to its very liquid dough.
COPPIA FERRARESE *Ferrara Couple*	Emilia-Romagna	A roll made from oil-based dough with a golden matte crust and cottony crumb; two cylinders of dough are entwined to form an X.
GRISSINI *Breadsticks*	Piemonte	Long, crisp breadsticks.
PANE DI ALTAMURA *Altamura Bread*	Puglia	A DOP-certified bread made with durum flour derived from specific local strains of hard wheat; bread labeled "pane tipo Altamura" (Altamura-style bread) is made in similar fashion but not certified.
PANE DI BOLZANO *Bolzano Bread*	Trentino–Alto Adige	A dense-crumbed rye bread.
PANE PUGLIESE *Pugliese Bread*	Puglia	A large, round loaf with a very airy, moist crumb and a dimpled, dark, cracked crust.
PANE TOSCANO *Tuscan Bread*	Toscana	Very plain rustic bread that is made without salt.
ROSETTA *Rosette*	Lombardia	A roll with petals that come up around the sides, a small circle of dough at the top, and a largely hollow center.

bread with walnuts

ciabatta

thin breadsticks

multigrain bread

semolina with sesame seeds

bread with candied orange peel

bread with olives

kamut wheat breadsticks

The Italian Way with
CROSTINI AND BRUSCHETTE

Crostini and bruschetta are versatile and simple appetizers—basically toasted or grilled bread with a topping. Crostini are best made with a fine-crumbed bread such as a filone, sliced about ¾ inch thick and toasted in a toaster or oven until crisp. Bruschetta tends to be more rustic and the bread is often grilled and rubbed with a garlic clove for extra flavor; Eataly's signature Rustico bread (page 119) is perfect. Cut it about 1 inch thick and use about 1 tablespoon of any topping for each slice. You can also use the Paté di Fegatini di Pollo on page 221 for classic Tuscan crostini.

CROSTINI AI CANNELLINI *Cannellini Bean Crostini*	By hand, roughly mash cooked white beans with plenty of freshly ground black pepper. Spread on toast and garnish with minced red onion and speck.
CROSTINI AL TONNO *Tuna Crostini*	Drain Italian tuna and puree with a few capers until smooth. Spread the tuna on toast and garnish with whole capers.
CROSTINI ALLA ZUCCA *Squash Crostini*	Roast winter squash until tender, then puree until smooth with a pinch of salt; garnish with shavings of aged sheep's cheese.
BRUSCHETTA ALL'AGLIO *Garlic Bruschetta*	The original garlic bread: Rub the surface of the bread with a cut garlic clove. Drizzle with copious amounts of your best extra-virgin olive oil and season with salt.
BRUSCHETTA AL POMODORO *Tomato Bruschetta*	Chop the freshest tomatoes you can find and toss them with salt and a scattering of torn basil leaves. Rub the surface of the bread with a cut garlic clove and spoon the tomatoes and their juices on top.
BRUSCHETTA SICILIANA *Sicilian-Style Bruschetta*	Rub the surface of the bread with a cut garlic clove. Brush with extra-virgin olive oil. Combine ricotta with any or all of the following: minced fresh oregano, crushed red pepper flakes, minced red onion, and minced black olives. Spread the ricotta mixture in a thin layer on the bread.

You won't find an empty bread basket in Italy. Bread, like pasta and pizza, is synonymous with the tastes of the Mediterranean. No Italian meal is complete without it.

How to
"FARE LA SCARPETTA"

WE ITALIANS DON'T SPREAD BUTTER ON OUR BREAD. Instead, we use bread to nudge food onto our forks and especially to clean our plates at the end of a tasty meal. The small piece of bread used to clean your plate is called a *scarpetta*, which literally means "little shoe."

1. Pull the heel from the bread basket or filch it from a friend's plate.

2. Place the heel, cut side down, onto your plate at the edge of a pool of sauce.

3. Holding onto the butt end, drag the heel through the sauce, sopping up as much as possible. Pop it into your mouth.

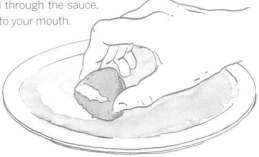

MULINO MARINO

In the modern world, we tend to forget that flour is a plant food. After all, it's widely available in sacks and cartons on supermarket shelves. But flour is ground from plants—most commonly wheat—and like all plant foods it loses flavor and character as it passes its peak. Flour can "go bad," albeit not as quickly or as notably as, say, an apple. Mulino Marino grinds traditional, organically farmed grains, which have not been hybridized or genetically modified, into flour using three natural stone mills in the town of Cossano Belbo, in Piemonte. Its flours are fresh-tasting and noticeably "wheaty," and they retain much of the nutritional power of the grain.

The flours are completely unrefined, and the millstones are still treated via a traditional hammering procedure. Because the natural stone surface doesn't overheat (unlike the surface of the steel rollers used in industrial mills), the germ and bran in these flours remain alive. This type of flour truly tastes of wheat and is both more nutritious and easier to digest than typical "industrially produced" flour.

Mulino Marino also has its own laboratory, used for quality testing and selection. In addition to wheat flour, the company produces rye, kamut, spelt, and other types of flours, all of which make a significant difference in the final taste of bread, cakes, and just about anything else made with flour.

PANE RUSTICO
COUNTRY-STYLE BREAD

1 loaf

---

3 cups bread flour

1 cup whole wheat flour

7 ounces (about 1 cup) starter (see page 121)

1 tablespoon fine sea salt

¼ teaspoon instant yeast

This is Eataly's house bread, made daily using our natural yeast, with a little boost of fresh yeast added. You can make it this way at home once you have a starter (see page 121). Or replace the starter with additional yeast if you prefer, or leave out the yeast and just rely on the starter. The results will be a little less predictable without the extra yeast, but they will be delicious. You may be surprised to discover that we mix the flour with the water and then set the bowl aside for several hours. You can cut this step a little short if you're in a hurry, but do let the flour and water rest together for at least 30 minutes before proceeding. This step is known as the autolyze, and it allows the water to hydrate the flour thoroughly and evenly. It makes the dough easier to knead and imparts a stronger wheat flavor to the finished loaf. Plus, it doesn't require any effort—just mix the two together until they're roughly combined and then wait. You'll see that as the mixture sits, it gets smoother. One last note: The whole wheat flour you use for this bread must be "hard" whole wheat flour. Bakers term flour "hard" or "soft" depending on the protein content. Whole wheat pastry flour is soft and will not develop enough gluten to make good bread. Most flour that is simply labeled as whole wheat is hard flour.

PLACE both flours in a large bowl. Stir in 1⅓ cups lukewarm water until the mixture is shaggy. (You can use a wooden spoon or your hand.) Cover the bowl with plastic wrap. Set aside to rest for at least 30 minutes and up to 4 hours.

ADD the starter to the bowl and knead with the flour and water to combine. Remove about ¼ cup dough (no need to measure—simply pinch off a piece) and transfer it to a clean jar with a tight-fitting lid to use for the next batch of bread.

SPRINKLE on the salt and the instant yeast. Transfer the dough to an unfloured work surface. Knead until the dough is smooth and compact, about 10 minutes, using a bench scraper if necessary. The dough will start out fairly sticky, but it will get easier to handle as you knead it. Do not add flour unless the dough is runny like a batter. When the dough is ready, you should be able to stretch a piece of dough so that a "windowpane" forms. If the dough simply snaps apart, keep kneading.

(continued)

Variations

PANE RUSTICO CON FICHI (FIG BREAD): *Fold about ½ cup roughly chopped dried figs into the dough after kneading and before proofing. Serve with soft cheeses.*

PANE RUSTICO CON UVETTA (RAISIN BREAD): *Fold about ½ cup black raisins into the dough after kneading and before proofing. Serve with jam or honey, or pair with salumi for a sweet/savory contrast.*

PANE RUSTICO CON NOCI (WALNUT BREAD): *Fold about ¾ cup shelled walnuts into the dough after kneading and before proofing. Serve with fall salads.*

PANE RUSTICO CON OLIVE (OLIVE BREAD): *Fold about ½ cup pitted black olives and 2 to 3 tablespoons of lightly ground dried herb mix (any or all of the following: rosemary, fennel seed, savory, thyme, basil, tarragon, lavendar, chervil, marjoram, and oregano) into the dough after kneading and before proofing. Serve with vegetable soups.*

PANE RUSTICO CON SCORZA DI ARANCIA CANDITA (BREAD WITH CANDIED ORANGE PEEL): *Fold about ½ cup diced candied orange peel into the dough after kneading and before proofing. Serve with ricotta and honey, gianduia (see page 250), or plain. Making your own candied orange peel is a snap: Remove peel with a paring knife or peeler, leaving the white pith behind. Cut peel into ½-inch strips. Make a sugar syrup of equal amounts water and sugar in a medium saucepan and place over medium heat. Cook, stirring occasionally, until the sugar has melted. Add the peel to the syrup, adjust the heat to a simmer, and simmer until the peel is very soft and translucent, about 45 minutes. Remove the strips of peel with a strainer and set on a rack to dry.*

PLACE the dough in a proofing basket (or a colander lined with a lightly floured flat-weave dishtowel) and set aside to ferment at room temperature. After 30 minutes, fold and turn the dough. (To fold and turn dough, very lightly flour the dough and the work surface, then gently turn the dough onto the work surface. Pull the right side of the dough—where the 3 would be on a clock—out to the right to stretch it, then fold that stretched portion of dough over the main body of the dough. Repeat where the 6, 9, and 12 would be on a clock, pulling away and then folding the stretched portion of dough over the dough. Turn the dough so that the smooth side is now on top and return it to the basket, using the bench scraper if needed.) After another 30 minutes, repeat folding. Then let the dough ferment untouched until puffy, about 1½ hours.

TURN the dough back onto the work surface with the smooth side down. Shape the dough. If at any time during shaping the dough resists, set it aside and come back to it 20 minutes later. Very gently tug the dough into a thick rectangle. (Try not to deflate the dough.) Fold the dough in thirds like a letter. Seal the seam with the flat part of your hand by rolling the dough toward you slightly and pressing the seam together against the work surface. Roll the dough under the palms of your hands to round the shape and taper the ends.

PLACE the shaped loaf on a parchment-lined baking sheet, cover loosely with plastic wrap, and place in the refrigerator. Ferment until the dough is very puffy and smooth looking and feels dry, about 8 hours. (Fermenting in the refrigerator slows the process and allows flavor to develop. If you are in a hurry, you can ferment the loaf at room temperature for a couple hours—though it will not have the same depth of flavor as bread given a longer rise.)

WHEN you are ready to bake the bread, if you are using a baking stone, place it on the middle rack of the oven. Preheat the oven to 500°F. Place a pan on the bottom rack of the oven for steam.

IF you have a peel and are using a baking stone, transfer the loaf (still on the parchment) to the peel. With a sharp knife or razor blade, make 3 or 4 diagonal slashes in the top of the loaf. Using the peel, slide the loaf onto the baking stone with the parchment. (If you don't have a baking stone, simply place the baking sheet in the oven.) Pour water into the pan on the bottom shelf, then quickly close the door. Bake until the bread is well risen, the crust is dark and crisp, and you hear a hollow sound when you knock on the bottom, about 50 minutes.

LET the bread cool completely on a rack before slicing.

How to
MAKE A STARTER

THE EASIEST WAY TO MAINTAIN A LIEVITO MADRE, or natural yeast starter, is to stash a bit of bread dough each time you bake bread, before you add the salt to the dough. Just sock it away in a clean glass jar, either at room temperature if you plan to bake bread within the next few days, or in the refrigerator if you think you'll need it further into the future.

Once you get into the rhythm of baking bread regularly, this system becomes second nature, but the starter for your first batch of dough has to come from somewhere. A starter is nothing more than flour and water fermented to create yeast and bacteria. (Please don't be put off by the word "bacteria"—these are beneficial substances like the bacteria in yogurt.) Rye flour is a natural source of some of the bacteria you want, so it's helpful to begin your starter with rye flour, but if all you have is wheat flour, that will work, too.

1. Stir together equal parts (about ½ cup each) flour (preferably rye flour) and water in a glass jar with a tight-fitting lid. At first your starter will look like nothing much. Screw the lid on tightly and set the starter aside for a couple of days at room temperature.

2. The flour will get dark (and a little smelly) and will begin to bubble. Throw out about half of the starter and wash the jar. Return the reserved starter to the jar and again stir in equal parts water and flour, about ¼ cup this time. Cover and set aside at room temperature.

3. Each time the dough darkens and bubbles, repeat step 2. The starter will bubble on an increasingly fast schedule. When it bubbles and almost doubles in size, looks frothy and smells tart (but not overly alcoholic and "beery") in 8 hours or less after you feed it, you're ready to go.

4. A starter will last almost indefinitely in the refrigerator. Bring it to room temperature and refresh as described above until it is again active and bubbly within 8 hours of being fed—this may take up to 1 week if it has been refrigerated for a long time.

PIZZA E FOCACCIA

Perhaps Italy's most famous food after pasta is the globally beloved flatbread known as pizza. Pizza hails from the Campania region, and while these days you can find flatbreads labeled "pizza" almost anywhere in the world, pizza eaten at the source is especially delicious. Italian pizza is always a single-serving round pie that bakes in a very hot wood-burning oven for a short time—about 3 minutes—until its crust is soft and blistering. It is served piping hot. In order to safeguard the pizza tradition, in 2009 Italy petitioned the European Union for the *Specialità Tradizionale Garantita* denomination for Neapolitan pizza, which was granted.

The Italian Way with
CLASSIC PIZZAS

While you've probably seen pizza topped with everything from pineapple to corn, there are certain classic pizzas that every Neapolitan-style pizzeria must serve.

NAME	MEANING	TOPPING
MARGHERITA	named for the queen of Italy in honor of her 1889 visit to Naples	tomato sauce, buffalo or fior di latte mozzarella, basil
MARINARA	sailor-style	tomato sauce, oregano, garlic
NAPOLETANA	Neapolitan	tomato sauce, mozzarella, anchovy fillets, capers
QUATTRO STAGIONI	four seasons	tomato sauce and mozzarella with four toppings in separate quadrants, typically olives, artichokes, mushrooms, and prosciutto
CAPRICCIOSA	based upon the whims of the chef	different in every pizzeria, but pretty much anything goes

The Italian Way with
SANDWICHES ON FOCACCIA

Focaccia is delicious on its own, and thicker focaccia can be sliced in half horizontally and filled to make a number of delicious sandwiches. Below are some of the most popular combinations at Eataly. Don't forget to drizzle a little olive oil on the filling.

IL BOSCAIOLO	sautéed mixed mushrooms, Taleggio, and arugula
IL CALABRESE	spicy soppressata and sliced provolone cheese
IL CASARO	sliced mozzarella, sliced heirloom tomatoes, sea salt, and basil oil
IL MAIALINO	roasted pork loin, shaved fennel, capers, and bagna cauda
IL PORCHETTARO	thick-sliced porchetta (see page 210) and giardiniera
L'ALPINO	prosciutto cotto, sliced fontina, and fig mostarda

PIZZA MARGHERITA
PIZZA MARGHERITA

Makes 6 individual pizzas   *Campania*

3½ cups 00 flour or unbleached
all-purpose flour

3½ cups bread flour

½ ounce (about 1 tablespoon)
starter (see page 121)

1 tablespoon plus 1 teaspoon fine
sea salt, plus more to taste

½ teaspoon instant yeast

1½ cups crushed tomatoes

1 clove garlic, minced

¼ cup extra-virgin olive oil,
plus more for drizzling

1 pound mozzarella, thinly sliced

18 fresh basil leaves

This recipe makes enough dough for six individual pizzas, and you could halve it if you like, but pizza dough freezes nicely and is great to have on hand. Instructions for freezing unused dough are included on page 125. In any case, unless you have an unusually large oven and baking stone, you will be able to bake only one pizza at a time. If you are lucky enough to have a wood-burning oven, this is the time to use it. Otherwise, just turn your oven as high as it will go and be sure to preheat it thoroughly with the baking stone in place. One of the biggest challenges of opening our Eataly stores around the world is that there is no one-to-one correspondence when it comes to flour. In Italy, we rate flour as 00, 0, and so forth, but that is a description of how finely ground the flour is, not the protein content. If you cannot purchase 00 flour, unbleached all-purpose flour is a fine substitute.

IN a large bowl, combine the flours with 2 cups lukewarm water. Mix by hand to combine into a shaggy dough, cover the bowl with plastic wrap, and set aside at room temperature for 1 hour.

ADD the starter (dissolved in a little water if it is very stiff) to the bowl and stir to combine. Remove about ¼ cup dough (no need to measure—simply pinch off a piece) and transfer it to a clean jar with a tight-fitting lid to use for the next batch of bread.

SPRINKLE on the salt and yeast. Turn the dough out onto a lightly floured work surface and knead until thoroughly combined and soft, about 15 minutes.

TRANSFER the dough to a clean bowl (no need to oil it), cover the bowl with plastic wrap, and set aside at room temperature to ferment for 1 hour.

TURN the dough out onto a lightly floured work surface and use a bench scraper to cut it into 6 equal pieces. (If you want to be exact, use a scale to weigh them. Each piece should be 10 to 12 ounces.)

LIGHTLY flour a tray or baking sheet and set aside. Place 1 piece of dough in front of you on the work surface, smooth side up. Cup the dough with your hands and gently turn it while pressing the edges of the dough underneath so that it forms a round ball with a smooth top stretched tightly. Transfer the rounded dough to the prepared tray or pan and repeat with the remaining dough.

COVER the tray or pan with plastic wrap and refrigerate the dough until it is very puffy, at least 8 hours and up to 24 hours. (If you don't plan to make 6 pizzas, you can freeze risen balls of pizza dough. Simply slip them into small zippered food-storage bags and freeze; bring them back to room temperature before using and proceed as described below.)

ABOUT 1½ hours before you want to make pizza, remove the dough from the refrigerator and let it sit, covered, until it comes back to room temperature.

PLACE a baking stone on the lowest rack of the oven. Remove the other racks. Preheat the oven as high as it will go, at least 500°F.

IN a small bowl, stir together the crushed tomatoes, garlic, and olive oil and season to taste with salt.

PLACE 1 ball of dough on a lightly floured work surface. Stretch the pizza dough (see page 127) into a disk about 10 inches in diameter. The dough should be quite thin (but take care not to tear it) with a slightly thicker perimeter. If it resists, set it aside for a few minutes to relax.

TRANSFER the disk of dough to a piece of parchment paper, then move paper and dough to a peel (or an inverted baking sheet or cookie sheet if you don't have a peel). Spread about ¼ cup tomato sauce on the dough, leaving an uncovered border. Top with a few slices of mozzarella.

SLIDE the pizza, still on the paper, onto the baking stone. While the pizza is baking, stretch the next ball of dough. Bake until the crust is blistering and golden and the cheese has melted, 4 to 7 minutes, depending on how high the oven temperature goes. Remove the pizza (with the peel if you have one) and transfer to a plate. Top with three basil leaves and brush a little additional oil on the uncovered crust. Repeat with remaining dough, tomato sauce, cheese, and basil.

How to
EAT PIZZA

WE'LL JUST COME OUT WITH IT: You've been eating pizza all wrong. It's not your fault.

1. Use a knife and fork to cut a triangular slice of pizza.

2. Use the knife and fork to cut off the point end of that slice and transfer it to your mouth. Continue to work your way up toward the crust, cutting off bite-size pieces with your knife and fork.

3. When the pizza has cooled and only a small portion of your slice is left, it is acceptable to pick it up and eat it. There is no need to fold the pizza slice. A folded pizza is known as a calzone, and even that should be eaten with a knife and fork.

4. Repeat with remaining pizza.

How to
STRETCH PIZZA DOUGH

YOU KNOW THOSE IMAGES OF DISKS OF PIZZA DOUGH BEING TOSSED IN THE AIR? There's a reason for this practice. Pizza dough should never be rolled with a rolling pin, but should be gently stretched into a circle. Assuming you don't have the confidence to whirl your dough over your head, you can do this on a floured wooden work surface.

1. Place one proofed ball of dough on the work surface. Flatten the top with the palm of one hand.

2. Cup your hands and position them inside the perimeter of the dough. (The section of the dough that remains beyond your hands will remain thicker and form the crust.)

3. Gently pull your hands outward and away from each other, flattening them as you go, while turning the dough.

4. Repeat until you have a thin, even circle of dough with a thicker edge.

FOCACCIA GENOVESE
FOCACCIA

Makes one 12-by-17-inch focaccia   *Liguria*

1¾ cups unbleached all-purpose flour

1¾ cups bread flour

1 ounce (about 2 tablespoons) starter (see page 121)

1 tablespoon fine sea salt

½ teaspoon instant yeast

2 tablespoons plus 1 teaspoon extra-virgin olive oil, plus more for oiling bowl and pan

1 teaspoon coarse sea salt

1 tablespoon minced fresh rosemary leaves

Variations

FOCACCIA ALLA CIPOLLA (ONION FOCACCIA): *Thinly slice or shred red onions, toss with olive oil, salt, and rosemary, and spread on top of the focaccia in place of the olive oil and water mixture. Bake as for Focaccia Genovese.*

FOCACCIA ALLE ZUCCHINE (ZUCCHINI FOCACCIA): *Thinly slice 1 large zucchini and 1 large yellow summer squash and toss with a few tablespoons extra-virgin olive oil, salt and freshly ground black pepper, and grated grana. Omit olive oil and water mixture and bake focaccia for about 8 minutes. Spread about ½ cup ricotta on top of the focaccia, sprinkle on the sliced zucchini mixture, and return to the oven until the focaccia is golden and the squash slices are lightly browned, about 8 additional minutes. Tear fresh basil leaves over focaccia.*

Fresh focaccia is a joy. Just before baking, you lavish a mixture of water and olive oil on top of the dimpled dough. As the focaccia bakes, the water evaporates and the little dimples fill with salt and olive oil as the crust turns crisp and brown. We use a combination of starter and yeast for our focaccia at Eataly. You can leave out the starter if you like and increase the amount of yeast to 1 teaspoon.

IN a bowl, combine the flours with 1⅓ cups lukewarm water and stir to combine. Add the starter (dissolved in a little more water if it is very stiff) and stir to combine. Remove about ¼ cup dough (no need to measure—simply pinch off a piece) and transfer it to a clean jar with a tight-fitting lid to use for the next batch of bread.

SPRINKLE on the fine sea salt and yeast. Drizzle on 1 tablespoon plus 1 teaspoon of the olive oil. To knead by hand, turn the dough out onto a lightly floured work surface and knead until thoroughly combined and soft. To knead in a food processor, use the dough blade and process until the dough cleans the sides of the bowl, about 2 minutes. Process for an additional 45 seconds.

LIGHTLY oil a bowl, turn the dough into the bowl, cover with plastic wrap, and set aside at room temperature until doubled in size, about 1½ hours.

GENEROUSLY oil a 12-by-17-inch baking sheet. Turn the dough out onto the baking sheet. With your fingertips, begin to stretch the dough (see page 132) to fill the pan. It will most likely spring back and resist. Do not tear the dough. If the dough does resist, cover loosely with plastic wrap and set the pan aside for up to 1 hour. Stretch the dough so that it fills the pan. Again, if it stretches somewhat but then springs back into the middle, set the dough aside and wait. By the third try, the dough should relax enough that you can stretch it to fill the pan.

WHEN the dough fills the pan, set it aside to rest at room temperature for 30 minutes. If you are using a baking stone, place it on the lowest rack of the oven. Remove the other racks. Preheat the oven to 425°F.

IN a small bowl, stir the remaining 1 tablespoon olive oil with 1 tablespoon water. Pour the mixture all over the focaccia. Press with your fingers to make dimples about 1 inch apart across the entire surface of the focaccia. Sprinkle on the coarse salt and the rosemary leaves.

BAKE, turning front to back about halfway through, on the bottom rack (on the stone if using) until the top of the focaccia is golden and the bottom is a little darker and crisp, about 15 minutes. Serve hot or at room temperature.

focaccia de recco

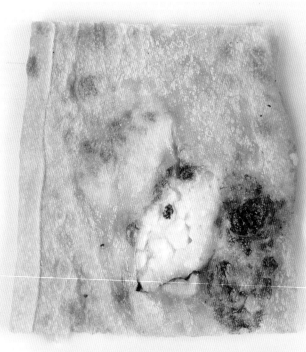

focaccia with sausage, onion, and peppers

focaccia with parmacotto and mozzarella

focaccia with tomato and mozzarella

focaccia with zucchini and squash

focaccia with tomato and oregano

focaccia Genovese

focaccia with onions

How to
FORM FOCACCIA

FOCACCIA COMES BY ITS DIMPLED SURFACE HONESTLY—as you're pressing the dough into the pan, you create those little indentations that are perfect for capturing little pools of oil and salt.

1. Place the focaccia dough on an oiled pan.

2. Press lightly with your fingertips while pushing outward on the dough.

3. If the dough resists, let it sit for at least 10 minutes or up to 1 hour. When you come back to it, the gluten will have relaxed and the dough will easily stretch to fit the pan.

PIADINA
FLATBREADS

Makes 12 flatbreads   *Emilia–Romagna*

4 cups unbleached all-purpose flour

1 tablespoon fine sea salt

1 teaspoon baking soda

½ cup whole milk

⅓ cup extra-virgin olive oil or melted leaf lard (see Note)

The rustic flatbreads known as *piadine* are one of the signature dishes of the Romagna area, where they are often folded to enclose simple fillings such as garlic spinach (see page 168) or soft, spreadable cheese like stracchino and slices of prosciutto or salami. We like to serve them as part of a casual meal with friends, letting everyone create his or her own combinations.

PLACE the flour, salt, and baking soda in the work bowl of a food processor fitted with the dough blade. Pulse a few times to combine.

IN a measuring cup with a spout, whisk together the milk and olive oil or lard. With the food processor turned on, add the liquids in a thin stream through the feed tube.

FILL the measuring cup with 1 cup water. Again with the food processor turned on, add the water in a thin stream through the tube. Stop when the dough forms a ball that cleans the side of the work bowl and sits on top of the blade. (You may not need all of the water, or you may need a little more than 1 cup.) The dough should be soft and moist.

ON an unfloured work surface, cut the dough into 12 equal pieces. Set 11 pieces aside and cover them with an overturned bowl to keep them from drying out. Roll 1 piece of the dough into a disk about 8 inches in diameter and ⅛ inch thick. Set it aside and repeat with the remaining pieces of dough. Do not stack the rolled disks. If a piece of dough is very difficult to roll and the edges keep springing back in, set it aside for a few minutes and go back to it.

NOTE: *Piadine are traditionally made with* strutto, *or lard, but more and more often today they are made with olive oil. Piadine made with olive oil are just as tasty as those made with lard, but they tend to turn crispy once they cool off. Their flavor is good, but a proper piadina is pliable and can be folded without breaking, while after cooling, an olive oil piadina resembles a cracker. Piadine should be served warm right after they are made, but if you find yourself with leftover olive oil piadine and want to return them to a softer state, try reheating them gently in a steamer basket over boiling water.*

WHEN all the pieces of dough have been rolled out, heat a 10-inch cast-iron skillet or griddle over medium heat until hot enough that a drop of water sizzles. Place 1 disk on the skillet or griddle and cook for 10 seconds. Flip and cook for an additional 10 seconds. Both sides should now be dry looking. Use a fork to pierce the flatbread and rotate it slightly (about one-eighth of the way around). Cook until black spots dot the underside, then turn and do the same for the other side, about 2 minutes per side. If black spots are developing too quickly, or large areas are scorching, turn down the heat; if the surface of the bread remains pale and does not develop spots, turn up the heat. Repeat with the remaining disks of dough. (You may need to continue to regulate the heat.) Stack the flatbreads as they cook. Serve warm.

PANE SECCO

Bread is ubiquitous in Italy, where it is stored in a bread box and sliced for lunch and dinner (and often dipped in milky coffee for a quick breakfast). Italians have a way with leftovers in general, but leftover bread—especially bread that has gone hard and stale—is a prized commodity in Italy. With a little ingenuity, it is turned into breadcrumbs, used in bread salads and bread puddings (both savory and sweet), or used as a thickener for soups and sauces. Bread such as our Pane Rustico (page 119), made with a natural starter, has a longer life than bread made with industrial yeast, and it makes better leftover bread, too. When stale it gets very hard (much too hard to bite without breaking a tooth), but it doesn't develop mold and its flavor doesn't turn.

We like to keep a plastic zipper bag in the freezer and toss in any leftover ends of bread—the heel or a bit that was cut for a meal but went uneaten. Breadcrumbs, too, can be frozen for several months. For flavored breadcrumbs, in a food processor fitted with the metal blade, grate stale bread with rosemary and/or sage, black pepper, and a pinch of nutmeg (optional) to the desired consistency (for unflavored breadcrumbs, omit seasonings). Drizzle in a little olive oil, then gently toast the breadcrumbs in a pan until just golden before using to stuff a whole fish, top baked cardoons (page 176) or other vegetables, use as an extender in meatballs or meat loaf, or toss with pasta.

Bread is the most important food *in the world. In Italia, when we say someone is a good person, we say "È buono come il pane!" (He's good like bread!)*

coarse breadcrumbs

crostini

fine breadcrumbs

bread cubes

The Italian Way with
LEFTOVER BREAD

SFORMATO DI PANE *Savory Bread Pudding*	Soak slices of stale bread in milk until soft. Remove the bread from the milk (don't squeeze dry) and arrange some of the slices to cover the bottom of an oiled or buttered baking dish. (A glass dish is useful for judging doneness.) Top the slices of bread with some browned onion, grated fontina cheese, and grated Parmigiano Reggiano or Grana Padano. Season with salt and pepper. Top with another layer of soaked bread slices and continue, alternating layers, until you've used up all the bread. Top with a generous amount of grated cheese and bake in a preheated 400°F oven until the top is browned and there is no liquid in the bottom of the pan, about 30 minutes to 1 hour—it will depend on the amount of bread, the amount of milk, the size of the pan, and a host of other factors. Allow to sit for 10 minutes before serving.
PANCOTTO *Bread Soup*	In a soup pot, brown a couple of peeled garlic cloves in extra-virgin olive oil, add water, a Parmigiano Reggiano or Grana Padano rind, salt, and pepper and simmer for about 10 minutes. Add stale bread in large chunks and cook, stirring frequently, until the bread has fallen apart. Remove the rind. Lightly beat about 1 egg per person and whisk the eggs into the liquid off the heat. Whisk in a generous amount of chopped flat-leaf parsley and some butter.
CANEDERLI *Trentino Bread Dumplings*	Cut stale bread into a small (about ¼-inch) dice and toss with beaten egg and milk to cover. Set aside to rest for a couple hours, then add minced speck, minced parsley, grated nutmeg, salt, and pepper. Add enough flour to make a moist mixture that clumps when you squeeze a piece in the palm of your hand. With damp hands, roll pieces of dough into balls 3 to 4 inches in diameter (just as you would do to make meatballs). Cook in boiling water or boiling broth until they float to the top, and serve with grated cheese or in the broth used to cook the dumplings.
PINZA OR MACAFAME *Stale Bread Fruitcake*	Although halfway between a cake and a bread, this dish from the Veneto isn't served as a dessert and it isn't terribly sweet. Soak stale bread in milk until soft, then crumble the bread. Add a small amount of cornmeal and stir to combine. Stir in sugar, pine nuts, raisins, minced dried figs, ground fennel seeds, a splash of grappa, a teaspoon of vanilla extract, and a peeled, cored, and diced apple. Stir in enough lightly beaten eggs to make the mixture moist, but not a true batter. Transfer the mixture to a cake pan (the mixture should be at least 2 inches thick—choose pan size accordingly) and bake in a preheated 350°F oven until the top springs back when pressed with a finger, about 1 hour. Cool completely before serving.
TURTA DE MICHELAC *Brianza Chocolate Bread Cake*	Soak stale bread in milk overnight to soften. Combine crumbled bread with cocoa powder, sugar, crumbled amaretti, vanilla extract, grated lemon zest, raisins, melted butter, and a pinch of salt. The batter should be runny. If it is too dry, add a small amount of milk. If it is too liquid, add a small amount of additional crumbled amaretti. It also should be a dark brown; if it is too pale, add a little more cocoa powder. Transfer to a buttered cake pan. Traditionally, additional pine nuts are arranged in a floral design on top of the cake. Bake in a preheated 350°F oven until a tester inserted in the center comes out clean, about 30 minutes. Refrigerate and serve cold.

PASSATELLI IN BRODO
BREADCRUMB NOODLES IN BROTH

Serves 6 as a first course   *Emilia–Romagna*

1½ quarts capon broth (see page 72) or beef broth

⅔ cup grated Grana Padano or Parmigiano Reggiano, plus more for serving

1½ cups fine plain (unflavored) breadcrumbs (see page 134)

Grated zest of 1 lemon

½ teaspoon grated nutmeg

2 large eggs, lightly beaten

In Italy, you can purchase a special type of food mill for creating breadcrumb noodles, or *passatelli*, but a potato ricer with large holes works fine. If you like thicker noodles, you can also roll them out by hand. (First shape them into ropes about ¼ inch thick, then cut them into noodles.) The hand-rolled noodles will cook in about 5 minutes. This is traditionally served in capon broth or beef broth, but it's delicious in chicken broth, too.

BRING the broth to a boil in a large pot.

IN a bowl, combine the cheese, breadcrumbs, lemon zest, and nutmeg. Make a well in the center of the mixture and add the eggs. Mix by hand until thoroughly combined. The dough should be damp but firm. You may need to incorporate additional breadcrumbs or a few drops of water.

PLACE about half the dough in a potato ricer fitted with the attachment with the largest holes. Squeeze the dough so that noodles are extruded. Cut the noodles off in 3-inch lengths, letting them drop directly into the boiling broth. Repeat with the remaining dough.

GENTLY stir the passatelli and cook until they float to the surface, about 2 minutes. Ladle broth and noodles into individual serving bowls. Serve additional grated cheese on the side.

PANZANELLA
BREAD SALAD

Serves 4 as a first course or side dish   *Toscana*

1 red onion, halved and thinly sliced

About 8 ounces stale Pane Rustico (see page 119) or other country-style bread

5 ripe tomatoes, cored

1 tablespoon red wine vinegar

3 tablespoons extra-virgin olive oil

Fine sea salt to taste

Freshly ground black pepper to taste

1 cucumber

¼ cup pitted black and green olives

12 fresh basil leaves

Don't be put off by the instructions to soak bread in water. If you are using good-quality bread, it won't disintegrate but will turn moist and spongy. This is a very flexible recipe. You can adjust the proportions to your liking, and you can add all kinds of other vegetables to this salad, or capers, or even some canned tuna if you want to make it a little heartier. The only constants are perfectly ripe tomatoes (use a mix of variously colored heirloom varieties for best flavor and color) and leftover bread that is given new life. Indeed, panzanella is one of the great joys of summer. Not only is it served cool, but it benefits from being made in advance, allowing ample time for the rehydrated bread to really soak up the tomato juices.

SOAK the onion slices in water while you prepare the salad. This helps to lessen the bite of raw onion.

PLACE the bread in a mixing bowl, add water to cover, and set aside until soft. (The time it takes will depend on how stale the bread is and how large the pieces are—probably about 15 minutes for bread that is 3 days old.)

MEANWHILE, chop the tomatoes and place them in a large salad bowl. In a small bowl, whisk together the vinegar and olive oil, season with salt and pepper, and pour about half over the tomatoes. Toss to combine and set aside.

PEEL, seed, and chop the cucumber and add it to the bowl with the tomatoes. Add the olives, then tear the basil leaves into the bowl. Drain the onion and add it to the bowl. Toss to combine.

WHEN the bread is soft, remove it from the water with your hands and squeeze out as much water as possible. Break the bread into chunks and place in a medium bowl. Pour the remaining vinaigrette over the bread and toss to combine. Add the bread to the vegetables and toss. Taste and adjust seasoning (add more olive oil if you like, too), then set the salad aside to rest for at least 1 hour and up to 3 hours before serving, tossing occasionally. Serve at cool room temperature.

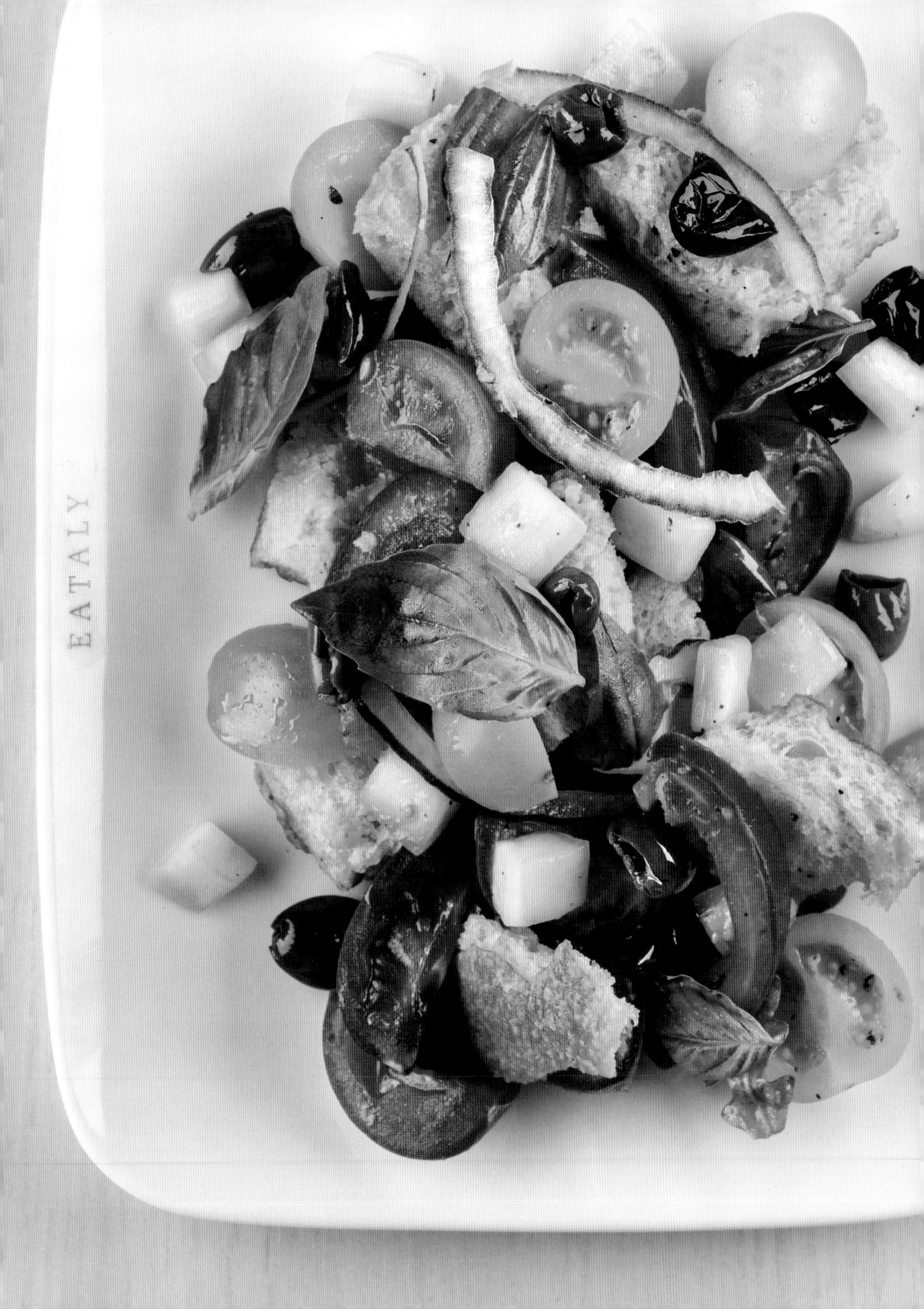
EATALY

PAPPA COL POMODORO
TOMATO-BREAD SOUP

Serves 4 as a first course   *Toscana*

2 tablespoons extra-virgin olive oil, plus more for finishing

1 large onion, thinly sliced

Fine sea salt to taste

3 cloves garlic, thinly sliced

1 teaspoon crushed red pepper flakes

2 pounds fresh tomatoes, peeled, seeded, and roughly chopped (see Note)

Leaves of 2 sprigs fresh basil

2 cups roughly diced day-old Pane Rustico (see page 119) or other country-style bread

Freshly ground black pepper to taste

This soup highlights the brilliant, garden-fresh tomatoes available in summer, but you can make it "off-season" by replacing the fresh tomatoes with 4 cups of canned whole peeled tomatoes. The bread will crumble somewhat in the soup and thicken it—if you prefer a smoother soup, puree it after adding the bread. Leftovers are delicious at room temperature. In the 1960s, Rita Pavone had a popular hit with her song "Viva la Pappa col Pomodoro."

HEAT 2 tablespoons olive oil in a large pot over medium-high heat. Add the sliced onion, season with salt, and sauté for a few minutes until the onions turn translucent. Add the garlic slices and red pepper flakes. Sauté until fragrant, another 1 to 2 minutes.

ADD the tomatoes and basil. Stir to combine. Bring the soup to a boil, then reduce the heat to a simmer and continue simmering until slightly thickened, about 30 minutes.

PUREE the soup in the pot with an immersion blender. Add the bread and return the soup to a simmer, stirring occasionally. Taste and season with additional salt, if necessary, and pepper. Taste the bread to be sure it is soft. If not, let the soup sit for 5 to 10 minutes.

TO serve, ladle the soup into individual soup bowls and drizzle generously with additional olive oil.

NOTE: *To peel fresh tomatoes, bring a pot of water to a boil and prepare a large bowl of ice water. Cut a small X in the base of each tomato with a paring knife. Drop the tomatoes into the boiling water and let them boil for about 30 seconds, then remove with a slotted spoon to the ice water. (Work in batches if necessary.) When the tomatoes are cool enough to handle, the peel should lift off easily.*

POLPETTINE DI PUNTA DI PETTO DI MANZO
BRISKET MEATBALLS

Serves 6 to 8 as a main course

½ cup fine breadcrumbs
(see page 134)

½ cup whole milk

2 pounds ground brisket

½ cup grated Parmigiano Reggiano

½ cup grated pecorino Romano

1 tablespoon minced garlic

1½ teaspoons fine sea salt

¼ teaspoon freshly
ground black pepper

¼ cup chopped fresh flat-
leaf parsley leaves

1 large egg

1 egg yolk

We like to roast these meatballs, but you can also brown them in a skillet in a small amount of olive oil (you won't need much). These can be served alone, as they are exceptionally moist, but you can also serve these meatballs in the tomato sauce on page 30.

PREHEAT the oven to 375°F.

PLACE the breadcrumbs and milk in a large bowl and soak for 5 minutes. To the bowl with the milk mixture, add the brisket, both cheeses, garlic, salt, pepper, and parsley. Lightly beat the egg and the yolk and add them as well. Stir in ¼ cup water. Mix by hand until thoroughly combined.

WITH your hands, shape the ground-meat mixture into meatballs about 1½ inches in diameter. Place them in a baking dish that will hold them in a single layer.

ROAST the meatballs, turning them once, until they are nicely browned, 20 to 30 minutes. With tongs, remove the meatballs to a platter, letting some of the fat drain off of them back into the pan. Serve hot.

CEREALI

Pasta may be Italy's most famous *primo,* or first course, but rice is equally crucial to Italian cuisine, especially in the northern parts of the country. During the Renaissance, the swamps of Lombardia were turned into rice paddies, and ever since, rice has played a key role in Milanese cuisine, especially in the city's famous risotto with saffron. Rice is also eaten very frequently in the Veneto region, where it appears in *risi e bisi* (a very soupy risotto with peas) and many soups. But rice isn't the only grain game in town. Whole grains such as wheat berries and barley are used frequently in Italy, and farro—a kind of wheat eaten by the Etruscans—is cooked whole and also ground into flour. Corn is eaten in Italy largely in the form of polenta; *polenta taragna* is buckwheat polenta. (Technically, buckwheat is not a grain, but it is handled as if it were.) Buckwheat flour is also used to make delicious pizzoccheri noodles, enjoyed in Valtellina, usually in a casserole with potatoes, cabbage, and copious amounts of Alpine cheese. Fregola, though technically a type of pasta, resembles a grain in size and shape and is often cooked in similar ways as grains.

The Italian Way with RICE

Risotto is always made with short-grain Italian rice specifically labeled for risotto. This rice is never rinsed—the starch it gives off is critical to creating a creamy risotto. These are the four most common types of Italian rice:

ARBORIO *named after a town in the region of Piemonte in northwest Italy*	Arborio's short, plump grains contain more starch than most other rice varieties, which makes it ideal for risotto. It is also well suited for dishes where the rice must retain its shape.
CARNAROLI *a short-grain, plump Italian white rice grown in Piemonte and Lombardia*	It has a larger grain than the other Italian white rice varieties, but still cooks into a creamy consistency with a firm body. Carnaroli rice is usually more expensive than other Italian rice varieties, but it is more forgiving when cooked as it absorbs more liquid and seems to reach the creamy al dente texture more easily.
VIALONE NANO *a semi-fino rice that is most popular in the Veneto region*	It is classified as such not because of its quality or cooking characteristics, but because of its length-to-width ratio. It is shorter and fatter and even lower on the stickiness scale than Carnaroli. These factors lend it a great capacity for absorption and expansion when cooking and it yields a creamier risotto that flows on the plate. Vialone Nano suits many of the seafood risottos that are traditional in the Veneto region.
ORIGINARIO *has a round grain, which is very suitable for soups*	The round, small, pearly grain fully absorbs the flavors of the seasonings. Once also used to make risotto, this rice is more suitable for the preparation of rice desserts.

durum wheat semolina

fregola

arborio

SIGNS OF QUALITY

Risotto can be made only with short-grain Italian rice grown specifically for that purpose. No other type of rice will release enough starch to make a proper risotto.

vialone nano

polenta

carnaroli

farro

brown carnaroli rice

venere black rice

VERDURE ALLA PIASTRA CON FARRO
GRILLED VEGETABLES WITH FARRO

Serves 8 as a first course or 4 as a light main course   *Toscana*

3 cloves garlic

¾ cup extra-virgin olive oil

½ cup farro

Fine sea salt to taste

1 small head radicchio,
cut into ribbons

¼ cup roughly chopped chicory

2 tablespoons red wine vinegar

2 tablespoons sparkling water

¼ teaspoon dried basil

¼ teaspoon dried oregano

½ bunch broccoli rabe, chopped

1 zucchini

1 large red onion

4 to 6 baby turnips

1 red bell pepper

8 ounces brussels sprouts, halved

¼ cup chopped scallions

¼ cup toasted pine nuts

A *piastra* is a flat-topped grill or griddle that gives vegetables a lovely char. A well-seasoned cast-iron skillet makes a fine substitute, but this salad can also be prepared in a regular skillet. You can prepare the farro and the vegetables a day or two ahead, making this is a terrific choice for a buffet. The farro adds a hearty touch to this salad, but the vegetables are really the stars.

PLACE the garlic in a small saucepan and pour in ¼ cup olive oil. (The pan should be small enough that the oil covers the garlic—if not, add a little more oil). Place over very low heat and poach gently until the garlic is meltingly soft, about 1 hour. In a mini food processor or with a fork, blend the garlic with the oil into a thick paste.

MEANWHILE, place the farro in a medium dry saucepan over medium heat. Cook, shaking the pan occasionally, until the farro begins to emit a toasty aroma, about 5 minutes. Add 3 cups water, season with salt, bring to a boil, reduce the heat to a simmer, and cook until the farro is al dente, about 30 minutes. Drain the farro and transfer it to a bowl; set aside.

WHEN the farro is cool, toss the radicchio and chicory with the farro. In a small bowl, whisk together the vinegar, sparkling water, ¼ cup olive oil, and the dried basil and oregano. Season with salt. Toss with the farro mixture and set aside.

BRING a pot of salted water to a boil and blanch the broccoli rabe until tender. Shock in cold water, drain, and set aside.

CUT the zucchini, onion, and turnips into thick slices. Core and seed the bell pepper and cut it into thick slices. Place the zucchini, onion, turnips, pepper, broccoli rabe, and brussels sprouts in a bowl. Drizzle on the remaining ¼ cup olive oil, season with salt and pepper, and toss to coat the vegetables thoroughly.

HEAT a cast-iron griddle or skillet over high heat until a drop of water sizzles on it. Cook the vegetables, turning them once, until slightly soft and nicely browned around the edges, about 3 minutes per side. Work in batches to keep from crowding the pan—remember that you are searing or grilling the vegetables, not sautéing them.

REMOVE the cooked vegetables from the heat and toss them with the pureed garlic.

TO serve, place a portion of the farro mixture on the center of each plate and arrange the grilled vegetables around and over it. Scatter the pine nuts on top. Serve at room temperature.

POLENTA ALLA GRIGLIA
CON RAGÙ DI FUNGHI
GRILLED POLENTA WITH MUSHROOM RAGÙ

Serves 4 as a first course   *Friuli—Venezia Giulia, Lombardia, Piemonte, Veneto,*

1 cup polenta, any grind

Fine sea salt to taste

½ ounce dried porcini (about ½ cup loosely packed)

2½ pounds mixed mushrooms

¼ cup extra-virgin olive oil, plus more for brushing on the polenta

4 tablespoons (½ stick) unsalted butter

6 medium shallots, minced

1 cup minced yellow onion

About 3 cups vegetable broth

Leaves of 3 sprigs fresh thyme, minced

Leaves of 1 sprig fresh rosemary, minced

1 sprig fresh sage with 4 big leaves, minced

⅓ cup tomato paste

1 cup dry Marsala wine

Freshly ground black pepper to taste

Minced parsley for finishing

This recipe gives instructions for grilling rectangles or triangles of the cooled polenta, but if you prefer, you can skip this step and serve the hot polenta straight out of the pan. Simply spoon it into pasta bowls and serve the sauce on top. If you'd rather make grilled polenta, you need to make the polenta in advance and allow it to cool completely before cutting it into slices. You can also make the sauce in advance—it will keep for a week in the refrigerator and for several months in the freezer. Polenta matches well with all kinds of hearty sauces and roasted meats.

COOK the polenta with the salt (see page 148). Pour the polenta onto a wooden board or a jelly-roll pan to form a rectangle about ¾ inch high. Smooth the top with a spatula and allow to cool completely.

SOAK the porcini in warm water until soft, about 20 minutes. Squeeze out the soaked porcini, and slice them into pieces about ¼ inch wide. Strain the soaking water through cheesecloth or a coffee filter into a bowl, and keep it in a warm spot.

CLEAN, trim, and slice the fresh mushrooms just under ¼ inch wide.

PLACE the olive oil and butter in a large skillet over medium heat. When the butter has melted, add the shallots and onions. Season lightly with salt and stir to combine. Slowly raise the heat until the onions are sizzling and cook, stirring frequently, until the onions are soft and shiny but not browned, about 6 minutes.

MEANWHILE, bring the broth to a boil in a small saucepan. Reduce the heat to a simmer and keep it at a simmer.

ADD the dried and fresh mushrooms to the skillet with the onions and toss to combine. Sprinkle with a small amount of additional salt, add the thyme, rosemary, and sage, toss briefly, raise the heat a bit, and cover the skillet. Cook, covered, shaking the skillet now and then, until the mushrooms give up their liquid, about 3 minutes.

UNCOVER the skillet and continue to cook over medium-high heat, stirring frequently, as the mushrooms shrink and the liquid evaporates, about 5 additional minutes.

(continued)

WHEN the liquid has evaporated and the mushrooms begin to brown, clear a spot in the pan, drop in the tomato paste, and cook, stirring just the tomato paste, for 1 minute, then stir the paste together with the mushrooms.

WHEN the vegetable mixture is sizzling and browning again, and just starting to stick, add the Marsala, pouring it all around the skillet. Stir constantly as the wine thickens and evaporates.

WHEN the mushrooms again start sticking to the bottom of the pan, pour in the warm mushroom water and about 2 cups hot broth. Bring to an active boil, stirring up any caramelized bits on the bottom of the pan. Lower the heat to keep the sauce bubbling gently all over the surface and cover the skillet. Cook for about 20 minutes, occasionally stirring and adding small amounts of broth to keep the mushrooms nearly covered with liquid; you may not need all the broth. Adjust the heat to keep the sauce at a steady simmer, but not boiling rapidly.

UNCOVER the skillet and cook, maintaining the simmer and adding broth (if you run out of broth, use water) until the mushrooms are thoroughly tender and the sauce is thick but still pourable, about 20 minutes. Taste and add salt, if needed, and pepper to taste.

WHEN you are ready to serve the dish, cut the polenta into rectangles or triangles, brush them lightly with olive oil, and place on a hot outdoor grill or grill pan, turning once with tongs, until they are crisp and seared with grill marks, 4 to 5 minutes per side.

PLACE the grilled polenta on individual serving plates, top with the warm ragù, sprinkle on minced parsley, and serve immediately.

The Italian Way with POLENTA

Traditionally, polenta is prepared in a *paiolo*, a special copper kettle. It is stirred constantly for an hour or more. Then it is poured out onto a wooden board. We love those traditions and rituals, but we were tired of nursing our sore arms after we'd finished cooking polenta, so we experimented a little and came up with a new method. You can still do it the old-fashioned way if you'd rather—but we've been eating polenta since we were kids and can't tell the difference.

Bring 4 cups of water for every 1 cup polenta to a boil in a Dutch oven or other heavy pot. Salt the water and reduce the heat to a simmer. While stirring constantly, drizzle in the polenta extremely slowly, letting it run between your fingers in a thin stream, as if you could add a single grain at a time. If any lumps form, smash them against the side of the pot. When all the polenta has been added and it is completely smooth and integrated—there is no longer liquid on top of the pot—reduce the heat to very low and allow the polenta to cook uncovered. A thick skin will form on top of the polenta. Cook until the polenta is very thick (it will resemble bubbling lava) and no longer tastes raw, about 45 minutes for fine-ground polenta, 1 hour for medium-grind polenta, and 1 hour 20 minutes for coarse-ground polenta. You can check under the skin occasionally to test for doneness, but don't disturb it too often—the polenta is steaming underneath. If you prefer the old-fashioned way, simply continue stirring constantly after the polenta is completely smooth and there is no longer liquid on top of the pot.

The Italian Way with RISOTTO

To cook risotto, bring the broth to a boil in a small pot, then reduce the heat and keep at a simmer. In a sauté pan over low heat, sauté minced yellow onion in a small amount of olive oil until just golden, about 5 minutes. Add the rice to the pan and toast it, stirring continuously with a wooden spoon, for about 3 minutes. Season with salt. (It is important to salt risotto early so that the salt penetrates the grain; otherwise you'll end up with unsalted rice in seasoned liquid.)

As soon as the rice begins to stick to the bottom of the pan, add about ½ cup white wine and cook, stirring constantly, until the liquid has evaporated. At this point, add about ½ cup of the warm broth. Continue to add the broth in small amounts, stirring continuously between additions. As the rice cooks, decrease the amount of broth in each addition. Always wait until the previous addition has been absorbed completely before adding more broth. To check, draw the spoon across the bottom of the pan. If liquid immediately runs in to fill the "canal," there is still too much liquid; if the bottom remains relatively dry, add more broth.

When the rice is cooked al dente, add one last splash of broth, a few tablespoons of butter and grated Parmigiano Reggiano or Grana Padano, stir in to melt, then cover and set aside for a few minutes. Serve with additional grated cheese on the side. The best thing about risotto is that it can serve as a blank canvas for almost any addition you can imagine. The following are just a few ideas:

RISOTTO COI FUNGHI *Mushroom Risotto*	Before toasting the rice, sauté sliced button mushrooms with the onion until soft.
RISOTTO CON ZAFFERANO E FIORI DI ZUCCA *Risotto with Saffron and Zucchini Blossoms*	Toast a pinch of saffron threads in a small pan over low heat. Crumble the toasted saffron and combine it with a small amount of warm water. When the rice is almost cooked, add the saffron liquid along with the final addition of broth. Stir in strips of zucchini blossom after the rice is cooked.
RISOTTO PRIMAVERA *Risotto with Spring Vegetables*	Use a couple of spring onions in place of the yellow onion and with it sauté chopped asparagus, peas, and green garlic (fresh garlic available in spring that resembles scallions and is then "cured" to create the more familiar bulbs). Garnish the finished risotto with chopped fresh parsley.
RISOTTO AI GAMBERI CON DRAGONCELLO *Shrimp and Tarragon Risotto*	In the skillet where you will cook the risotto, sauté shrimp of any size until opaque (about 1 minute) and set aside. Use chopped scallion in place of the yellow onion. Use a broth made with shrimp shells, if possible, or chicken broth. After adding the wine and before beginning to add the broth, add a squeeze of fresh lemon juice, and when the rice is almost cooked, grate in a little lemon zest. Omit the cheese. Stir chopped tarragon leaves and the sautéed shrimp into the finished risotto before setting aside to rest for a few minutes before serving.

SUPPLÌ AL TELEFONO
ROMAN RICE CROQUETTES

Makes 20 croquettes   *Lazio*

1 quart beef broth

2 tablespoons extra-virgin olive oil

1 yellow onion, minced

Fine sea salt to taste

Freshly ground black
pepper to taste

2 cups rice for risotto
(see page 142)

1 cup grated Parmigiano
Reggiano or Grana Padano

2 large eggs

1½ cups fine untoasted (plain)
breadcrumbs (see page 134)

8 ounces mozzarella, diced

Vegetable oil for frying

The supplì of Lazio are quite similar to the arancini of Sicilia, but don't mention that to the residents of either of those two regions or you'll get quite an earful. The *al telefono*, or "telephone-style" part of the name comes from the long, stretchy strings of mozzarella that form when you pull apart one of these croquettes—they're meant to resemble telephone wire. Supplì were originally a simple snack made with leftover cooked rice (and you can certainly make them with leftover risotto), but these days they're often served as an appetizer before a casual meal. You can prepare the rice a day or two in advance and refrigerate it, but supplì do need to be fried shortly before they are served.

BRING the broth to a boil in a small pot. Reduce the heat to a simmer, and leave at a gentle simmer. Line a baking sheet with parchment paper and set aside.

IN a large skillet over medium heat, heat the olive oil. Sauté the onion until soft and golden, about 6 minutes. Season to taste with salt and pepper.

ADD the rice, stir to combine thoroughly, and reduce the heat to a simmer. Cook, stirring constantly, adding the broth in small amounts, as for risotto (see page 149). Cook until the rice no longer has a brittle core but is still al dente, about 15 to 20 minutes, although cooking time will vary. This rice should be less soft and have much less remaining liquid than risotto. You may not use all of the broth.

REMOVE the skillet from the heat and stir in the grated cheese. Spread the cooked rice on the prepared baking sheet and allow to cool until you can handle it comfortably.

ONCE the rice has cooled, divide it into 20 equal portions, each about the size of an egg. In a shallow bowl, beat the eggs. Place the breadcrumbs in another shallow bowl.

WITH damp hands, roll 1 portion of rice between your palms to form a ball. Dig into the center of the ball with your thumb, insert 2 or 3 cubes of mozzarella into the hole, then close the ball again between your palms, tapering it to make it slightly oval. No mozzarella should be visible. Set aside and repeat with the remaining rice and mozzarella. Wet your hands occasionally to keep the rice from sticking.

ONE at a time, dredge each croquette in the beaten eggs and then the breadcrumbs and set aside.

IN a cast-iron skillet over medium heat, warm 1 to 2 inches vegetable oil until hot but not smoking—you want the oil to be hot enough to melt the cheese in the center of the croquettes without burning the rice. Working in batches to avoid crowding the pan if necessary, add the croquettes to the skillet and fry for about 5 minutes total, moving them around with a slotted spoon or strainer to brown all sides.

AS the croquettes are browned, remove them with a slotted spoon or strainer to drain briefly on paper towels. Serve warm.

FRUTTA E VERDURA

Bottom line: Mom was right.
Vegetables are good for you.
When you buy them fresh,
they are full of flavor.

FRUTTA

In Italy, fruit is by far the most common dessert. Every household keeps a fruit bowl filled with a few different selections that is placed on the table at the end of lunch and dinner. Each person at the table selects a piece of ripe fruit, peels it (in Italy most fruit is peeled, though with the increase in organic farming that's become less necessary), cuts it into quarters, if the fruit is large, and eats it. Fruit is also incorporated into savory dishes—it matches particularly well with game—and it is often used to make simple home-style desserts, too.

The Italian Way with
FRUIT DESSERTS

FRUTTI DI BOSCO *Macerated Berries*	Sprinkle whole blackberries, blueberries, raspberries, or sliced hulled strawberries (or a combination of two or more) with sugar. Toss gently and allow to macerate at room temperature or in the refrigerator for at least 2 hours before serving.
MACEDONIA *Fruit Salad*	Cut apples, pears, kiwis, melons, pineapples, bananas, and any other ripe fruit into ½-inch pieces. Place in a large bowl. Sprinkle with sugar and a generous amount of lemon juice and toss to combine. Taste and adjust sugar and lemon juice.
MELE COTTE *Baked Apples*	Preheat the oven to 375°F. Core apples but leave them whole. Place the apples in a baking dish so that they are touching. Sprinkle with sugar and ground cinnamon. Pour in water at the side of the dish until it comes 2 inches up the side. Bake until the apples are so soft they collapse.
PERE SCIROPPTE *Poached Pears*	In a small saucepan combine water and sugar (or honey) and simmer until the sugar is dissolved. Quarter, peel, and core pears and add them to the syrup along with a vanilla bean. Simmer until the pears are tender. Store in the syrup.
PESCHE RIPIENE *Stuffed Peaches*	Halve and pit (don't peel) peaches and scoop out a little of their flesh. In a food processor fitted with the metal blade, grind amaretti cookies with the peach pulp. If dry, moisten with a little water or wine. Stuff the peaches with the amaretti mixture. If the peaches aren't perfectly ripe, bake them briefly in a preheated 350°F oven to soften.

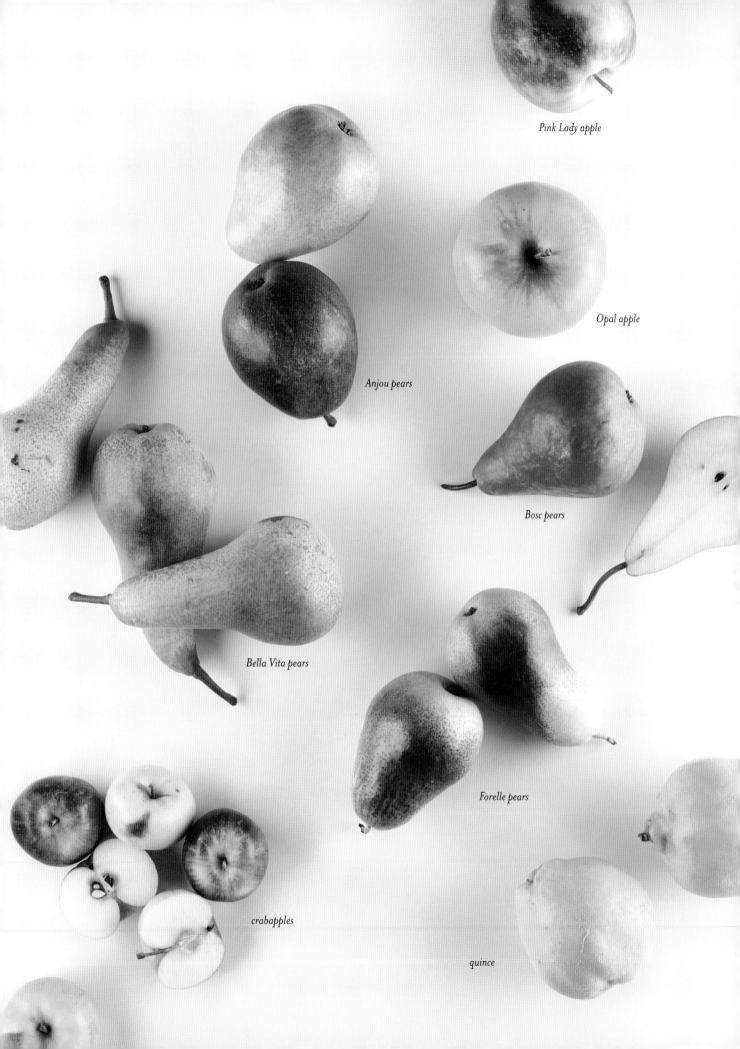

Pink Lady apple

Opal apple

Anjou pears

Bosc pears

Bella Vita pears

Forelle pears

crabapples

quince

INSALATA DI FINOCCHIO E AGRUMI
FENNEL AND CITRUS SALAD

Serves 4 as an appetizer or side dish   *Sicilia*

2 medium bulbs fennel, trimmed, fronds reserved

1 blood orange

1 grapefruit

Juice of ½ lemon

¼ cup extra-virgin olive oil

Fine sea salt to taste

Freshly ground white pepper to taste

¼ cup pine nuts

Pale green fennel is a highly versatile vegetable. When eaten raw, it tastes like anise; when cooked, it turns soft and sweet. Look for round fennel bulbs for salad—the longer, narrower bulbs are better for cooking. A mandoline is handy for making paper-thin slices. Fennel doesn't marry well with vinegar, but it is wonderful with citrus. If you can't find a blood orange—the deep red oranges grown in Sicily—feel free to substitute a navel orange.

SLICE the fennel as thinly as possible, using a mandoline if you have one, and place in a salad bowl.

SET a strainer over a mixing bowl. Peel and section the orange and grapefruit over the strainer, collecting any juice in the bowl. Discard any pith, white membrane, and seeds that collect in the strainer.

ADD the grapefruit and orange sections to the salad bowl with the fennel. Combine the lemon juice with the reserved orange and grapefruit juices. Whisk in the olive oil and season with salt and white pepper. Pour the juice and oil mixture over the fennel and fruit and toss to combine.

IN a skillet over low heat, toast the pine nuts just until fragrant and golden, about 3 minutes. Scatter the toasted nuts over the salad. Garnish with a few chopped fronds from the fennel and serve immediately.

pink striated lemon

etrog citron

mandarin orange kumquats

fukushu kumquats

blood oranges

satsuma mandarin oranges

Cara Cara oranges

kumquats

sweet lime

Meyer lemons

heirloom navel orange

RISOTTO PERE E MONTASIO
PEAR AND MONTASIO RISOTTO

Serves 6 as a first course   *Veneto*

2 quarts chicken or vegetable broth

4 tablespoons (½ stick) unsalted butter

2 medium shallots, diced

2½ cups rice for risotto, preferably Vialone Nano (see page 142)

Fine sea salt to taste

2 Bosc pears, peeled, cored, and diced

½ cup white wine

Freshly ground black pepper to taste

⅔ cup grated aged Montasio cheese

Pears and cheese are frequently served side by side in Italy because their flavors complement each other so well. (There's even an old Italian proverb, "Never let the farmer know how good cheese and pears taste together," presumably because he'd eat them all if he ever found out.) Montasio, a cow's milk cheese with a nutty undertone from the Veneto region, is particularly well-suited to pears. Bosc pears stand up well to cooking. In this recipe, we add some of the pear to the pan at the start, so it becomes meltingly soft as the rice cooks, and the rest closer to the end of the cooking time, so it retains a little crunch. If you prefer all the pears cooked or all crisp, adjust the recipe accordingly. For more on cooking risotto, see page 149.

BRING the broth to a boil in a small pot, then reduce the heat and leave at a simmer.

IN a large sauté pan over low heat, melt 2 tablespoons butter. Add the shallots and cook, stirring frequently with a wooden spoon, until soft, about 5 minutes. Do not allow the shallots to brown.

ADD the rice to the pan and season with salt, then toast, stirring, until the rice becomes translucent. Stir in about half the pears. Add the wine and cook, stirring, until it is mostly absorbed. When you draw a wooden spoon across the diameter of the pan, very little liquid should run into the space.

ADD about 1 cup broth. Simmer, stirring frequently, until the broth is almost absorbed by the rice. Continue adding broth ½ cup at a time, stirring constantly and allowing each addition to evaporate almost completely before adding more; use the spoon test above, but don't let the pan get so dry that the rice sticks. When the rice begins to release some of its starch and the mixture is creamy, about 30 minutes total, stir in the remaining pears. Continue cooking until the rice is tender but still slightly firm to the bite. (You may not need all of the broth.) Adjust salt and season with pepper.

REMOVE the pan from the heat and stir in the remaining 2 tablespoons butter and the grated cheese. Set aside to rest, covered, for 2 minutes. Serve piping hot.

VERDURE

Dark leafy greens—broccoli rabe, chard, savoy cabbage, Tuscan kale—are an integral part of Italian cooking. Spinach arrived in Italy from Persia "only" about one thousand years ago, but Italians have an even longer tradition of foraging for leafy greens and, to this day, enjoy dandelion, purslane, and all manner of wild greens. These are often available only locally and identified by names in dialect. Generally, we use the stalks as well as the leaves. If the stalks are harder and more fibrous than the leaves, as with Swiss chard, we separate the two and cook the stalks a little longer, then add the leaves to the pan later. Bitter greens with thick leaves, such as broccoli rabe and dandelion, are best blanched before sautéing to temper their strong taste. Cook in boiling salted water for 4 to 5 minutes, then transfer to a colander, run cold water over them, and squeeze them dry.

SIGNS OF QUALITY

Look for fruits and vegetables at the proper degree of ripeness, without soft spots or excessive blemishes. Conversely, fruits and vegetables with a perfectly smooth and shiny skin have often been treated with wax or sprays and are best avoided.

Out-of-season fruits and vegetables are rarely satisfying—they have been harvested too early and have traveled too far. Whenever possible, choose fruit that is in season in your area and grown locally.

Most fruit can be stored at room temperature and will benefit from not being refrigerated, assuming you will consume it within a few days of purchase. Most vegetables are best stored in your refrigerator's crisper, with the exception of mushrooms, which should be kept on the refrigerator shelves, and tomatoes, which should never be chilled.

Vegetables will make you smile. How can you not fall in love with something that tastes good and makes you look good?

puntarelle

Tuscan kale

chicory

dandelion greens

red leaf lettuce

arugula

escarole

RIBOLLITA
TUSCAN VEGETABLE SOUP

Serves 8 as a main dish   *Toscana*

1 bunch Tuscan kale

1 head savoy cabbage

1 bunch Swiss chard

2 russet potatoes

3 large carrots

2 zucchini

1 rib celery

2 leeks, white parts only

2 cloves garlic

2 cups cooked cannellini beans

3 tablespoons extra-virgin olive oil, plus more for finishing

½ teaspoon crushed red pepper flakes

2 cups canned whole peeled tomatoes

1 bay leaf

Leaves of 1 sprig thyme

Fine sea salt to taste

1 to 2 cups 2-inch cubes stale bread

Calling a soup made from scratch *ribollita* is a bit of a misnomer—the word means "reboiled" and indicates a dish of leftover soup thickened with stale bread. Ribollita is meant to be very dense—traditionalists say it should be eaten with a fork, not a spoon. The ingredient list is long, but like most soups, this one is in no way difficult to execute.

CUT the kale leaves, cabbage, and chard into 2-inch ribbons. Peel and dice the potatoes and carrots. Dice the zucchini and celery. Slice the leeks and garlic. Puree about half the cannellini beans and set aside.

PLACE the olive oil, leeks, and garlic in a large soup pot over low heat. Cook, stirring frequently, until the leeks and garlic are soft but not browned, about 5 minutes. Add the carrots and celery and cook, stirring frequently, until the vegetables have softened but not browned, about 8 minutes. Add the potatoes and zucchini and cook, stirring frequently, until the vegetables have softened but not browned, about 8 minutes. Add the kale, cabbage, and chard leaves and cook, stirring frequently, until the greens are very soft, about 8 minutes. Stir in the red pepper flakes.

ADD the tomatoes and their juice, squeezing the tomatoes between your fingers to break them up (see page 31). Add 2 quarts water, the bay leaf and thyme, and all of the beans. Season to taste with salt.

BRING to a boil and then reduce the heat to a simmer and cook until the vegetables are very tender, about 30 minutes. Remove and discard the bay leaf.

ADD the bread cubes to the soup and simmer until the bread is breaking apart and the soup is very thick, about 10 minutes more. Let the soup rest off the heat for several minutes, then ladle into bowls. Drizzle a generous amount of extra-virgin olive oil over each portion before serving.

red endive

tardivo radicchio

Castelfranco radicchio

endive

Chioggia radicchio

trevisano radicchio

PUNTARELLE IN SALSA
PUNTARELLE SALAD

Serves 4 as a side dish   *Lazio*

1 head Italian puntarelle

2 anchovy fillets, rinsed

1 large clove garlic

1 teaspoon crushed
red pepper flakes

1 egg yolk

¼ cup fresh lemon juice

1 cup extra-virgin olive oil

Fine sea salt to taste

Freshly ground black
pepper to taste

Puntarelle is a variety of chicory with long, spear-shaped leaves that have a bracing taste and crunchy texture. This classic Roman salad offers a refreshing contrast to the city's meaty cuisine. Don't skip the soaking, which not only leaches out some of the chicory's natural bitterness, but also makes the leaves curl up in characteristic fashion. Be aware that the dressing contains a raw egg yolk, which might be a health issue for some.

PREPARE a large bowl of ice water. Remove and discard the dark green outer leaves from the puntarelle. Separate the shoots from the root and cut lengthwise into ⅛-inch strips. Place the strips in the bowl of ice water and soak for at least 2 hours.

JUST before you serve the salad, prepare the dressing: In a blender or a food processor fitted with the metal blade, combine the anchovy fillets, garlic, red pepper flakes, egg yolk, and about three-quarters of the lemon juice. Puree until the garlic and anchovies are finely minced.

WITH the blender or food processor running, add the olive oil in a thin stream. Season with salt and pepper, but taste first, as the anchovies may be sufficiently salty. If the dressing is too thick, thin by whisking in some or all of the remaining lemon juice.

REMOVE the strips of puntarelle from the ice water and dry thoroughly with paper towels. Dress the puntarelle with the anchovy mixture (you may not need all of it), toss, and serve immediately.

The Italian Way with
SPINACH

Rinse spinach in several changes of cold water until no sand remains at the bottom of the bowl when you lift it out. Cook the spinach in the water that clings to the leaves until wilted (this will take only a minute or two). Keep in mind that the volume of fresh spinach will be greatly reduced once cooked. Squeeze steamed spinach dry and chop, then use in any of the following recipe ideas (or in a frittata, page 191, or spinach pasta, page 55):

SPINACI ALL'AGRO *Lemon Spinach*	Dress spinach with a small amount of olive oil and a generous amount of fresh lemon juice. Season with salt and pepper and serve at room temperature.
SPINACI ALL'AGLIO *Garlic Spinach*	Brown 2 to 4 crushed garlic cloves in a generous amount of olive oil, then add the spinach and toss over medium-high heat until warmed through. Season with salt and pepper and serve warm.
SPINACI CON UVETTA E PINOLI *Spinach with Raisins and Pine Nuts*	Rehydrate golden or black raisins in a small amount of warm water, then drain; toast pine nuts. Sauté the spinach in butter, then add the raisins and pine nuts. Sauté for a few minutes and serve hot.
FRITTELLE AGLI SPINACI *Spinach Pancakes*	Mince the spinach finely, transfer to a mixing bowl, and stir in an egg, a minced shallot, grated grana cheese (see page 104), and a tablespoon or two of flour. (Use a light hand with the flour—you don't want the mixture to be too stiff.) Brush a cast-iron skillet or griddle with olive oil and place over medium heat; once hot, drop spoonfuls of the batter on the surface. Flatten slightly with the back of the spoon. Cook until nicely browned, flipping once, about 5 minutes total. (If the pancakes are browning before their centers are cooked, turn down the heat.)
CRESPELLE AGLI SPINACI *Spinach Crepes*	Mince spinach and combine with ricotta and minced prosciutto cotto. Season with salt and pepper and set aside. To make the crespelle, whisk together 1 cup milk and 2 eggs. Gradually add ¾ cup flour, whisking constantly until the batter is very thin with no lumps. (An immersion blender works well; strain to remove lumps if necessary.) Whisk in a little salt. Set the batter aside to rest (up to 8 hours) if you have the time. When you're ready to make the crespelle, lightly grease a nonstick pan, crepe pan, or cast-iron skillet and place over medium heat. Once hot, add a small amount of batter, about 2 tablespoons for an 8-inch pan, and swirl the pan to coat the surface very thinly with the batter. Cook until the crepe is brown around the edges, flip, and cook the other side. Repeat with remaining batter. Fill each of the crespelle with some of the spinach mixture and roll each up into a cylinder. Tuck the rolled crepes side by side in a baking dish (seam side down), and then, just before serving, bake or broil briefly to heat through. Sprinkle with a little grated grana cheese (see page 104) before baking or broiling if desired.

CICORIE ALLA GRIGLIA
GRILLED CHICORY WITH PINE NUTS, CURRANTS, AND PARMIGIANO

Serves 4 as an appetizer or side dish

1 head escarole

2 heads white endive

1 head Chioggia radicchio

¼ cup pine nuts

¼ cup extra-virgin olive oil, plus more if needed

Fine sea salt to taste

Freshly ground black pepper to taste

¼ cup currants

4-ounce piece Parmigiano Reggiano, preferably aged for 36 months

¼ cup aged balsamic vinegar

The members of the chicory family—which includes escarole, endive, and radicchio—have a pleasantly bitter edge that can be tamed just enough by the heat of the grill. This composed salad makes a terrific light lunch.

QUARTER the escarole. Cut the endive in half the long way. Quarter the radicchio. Toast the pine nuts in a skillet until fragrant and light brown, about 3 minutes, then set aside.

PREPARE an outdoor grill or heat a grill pan over high heat. In a large bowl, toss the escarole, endive, and radicchio with the olive oil. The greens should be coated generously in oil—if not, add a little more. Season with salt and pepper. Place the greens on the preheated grill, cut sides down, and cook, without moving, until charred and slightly wilted, about 5 minutes. Turn over and cook the uncut sides just to soften, about 3 minutes.

TRANSFER the greens directly from the grill to individual serving plates. Sprinkle 1 tablespoon toasted pine nuts and 1 tablespoon currants over each. Shave the Parmigiano Reggiano over the salads using a vegetable peeler. Drizzle with balsamic vinegar and serve.

ORTAGGI

It is the rare lunch in Italy that does not include a salad composed of greens or other garden vegetables of some kind. Italians also rely heavily on the triumvirate of minced carrots, onion, and celery to create soffritto, the sautéed mirepoix mixture that forms the base of most sauces and soups. Finally, tomatoes are, of course, the signature vegetable of Italy, though in reality they are neither a vegetable (tomatoes are properly classified as fruit) nor native to the land. Tomatoes originated in the Americas and were brought back to Italy in the sixteenth century along with many other food products, including coffee, chocolate, eggplants, and potatoes. Tomatoes can be preserved beautifully (learn more about canned and jarred tomato products in the pantry chapter on page 28), but a fresh, ripe, juicy tomato knows no equal. Italians enjoy them only in season, aware that those available in the off-season are pallid imitations. Other popular garden vegetables include artichokes, cauliflower, and broccoli, especially the cone-shaped light green Romanesco variety, which originated in Italy and has a mild flavor. Long, squat-bottomed Italian eggplants are another favorite, as are red bell peppers and spicy chili peppers, especially in the south.

The Italian Way with SALADS

INSALATA DI CAROTE *Carrot Salad*	Grate peeled or scraped carrots on the large holes of a four-sided box grater. Toss with a dressing of extra-virgin olive oil and fresh lemon juice. Garnish with chopped fresh parsley if desired.
INSALATA VERDE *Green Salad*	Nothing easier. Tear a variety of tender lettuces into bite-size pieces. Dress with a classic vinaigrette (see page 26). For insalata mista (mixed salad), top lettuce with grated carrots, chopped peeled and seeded cucumber, and quartered tomatoes before tossing with the vinaigrette.
INSALATA DI RUCOLA *Arugula Salad*	Combine arugula leaves (torn if large) with a handful of toasted walnuts and peeled, cored, and quartered pears. Toss with olive oil and salt and top with a few shavings of aged cheese.
INSALATA DI CARCIOFI *Artichoke Salad*	Tender baby artichokes can be eaten raw. Trim as on page 178, slice very thinly (a mandoline works best), and toss with a dressing of extra-virgin olive oil, fresh lemon juice, and minced fresh parsley and/or mint leaves. Allow to sit for 15 to 30 minutes in the refrigerator before serving.

See also Pomodoro e Mozzarella (page 100), Insalata di Finocchio e Agrumi (page 157), and Insalata Tricolore (page 26).

romanesco cauliflower

fennel

hot peppers

eggplant

porcini mushrooms

broccoli rabe

artichokes

acorn squash

cranberry (borlotti) beans

PINZIMONIO

SHAVED VEGETABLE SALAD WITH CITRONETTE

Serves 4 to 6 as an appetizer   *Toscana*

¼ cup fresh lemon juice

1 tablespoon fresh thyme leaves, minced

Pinch ground cayenne pepper

¾ cup extra-virgin olive oil

2 tablespoons acacia honey

Fine sea salt to taste

Freshly ground black pepper to taste

6 cups thinly sliced seasonal vegetables (see suggestions below)

Although the concept of eating raw vegetables in dip feels very modern, pinzimonio actually dates back to the Renaissance. At banquets, grand centerpieces featured cut-up vegetables that were eaten at the start or the end of the meal. The flavor and texture of the vegetables are front and center here—whichever vegetables you use, make sure they have great snap and crunch. At Eataly, we like to serve the dish as a salad, tossing the vegetables with the olive oil mixture. This ensures that they are thoroughly coated. If you have a mandoline, use it now, as the vegetables need to be cut very thinly.

COMBINE the lemon juice, thyme, and cayenne pepper in a bowl. Add the olive oil in a thin stream while whisking constantly. Whisk in the honey and continue whisking until the honey is completely dissolved. Season generously with salt and a small amount of pepper.

TOSS vegetables with the olive oil mixture and distribute among the salad plates.

SEASONAL VEGETABLES for PINZIMONIO

SPRING	SUMMER	FALL	WINTER
ASPARAGUS	CARROTS	BRUSSELS SPROUTS	CELERY ROOT
BEETS	CELERY	CAULIFLOWER	PURPLE CABBAGE
RADISHES	CHERRY TOMATOES	CELERY ROOT	WINTER SQUASH
	CUCUMBERS	FENNEL	
	GREEN BEANS	SUNCHOKES	
	PEPPERS		
	SUMMER SQUASH		

CARDI GRATINATI
BAKED CARDOONS

Serves 6 as a side dish   *Piemonte*

4 tablespoons (½ stick) butter, plus more for buttering dish

½ lemon

8 large cardoons

Fine sea salt to taste

2 cups whole milk

3 tablespoons all-purpose flour

Pinch grated nutmeg

¼ cup grated Parmigiano Reggiano or Grana Padano

¼ cup fine untoasted (plain) breadcrumbs (see page 134)

Cardoons are quite popular in the Mediterranean, where they have been consumed since the days of the ancient Romans, and they deserve a wider audience. These thistle plants are related to artichokes, and they taste very similar to artichoke stems, though they look more like celery. Many other vegetables—including endive, fennel, and radicchio—can be prepared using the following method, which yields a pleasant combination of creaminess and crunch.

PREHEAT the oven to 350°F. Butter a baking dish and set it aside. Prepare a large bowl of ice water. Juice the lemon into the bowl and add the lemon half to the water.

REMOVE and discard any leaves from the cardoons. Use a paring knife or vegetable peeler to remove any fibrous strings. (They should pull off easily.) Cut the cardoons in half lengthwise, then into ½-inch pieces. Add the cardoons to the bowl with the ice water to prevent them from turning brown.

BRING a large pot of water to a boil, season with salt, and cook the cardoons until they are tender enough to pierce with a fork but not mushy, about 4 minutes. Drain the cardoons and set them aside to cool.

PLACE the milk in a small saucepan and heat very gently over low heat. Do not allow it to boil.

IN a small sauté pan, melt the 4 tablespoons butter over low heat. Gradually sprinkle in the flour, whisking constantly, and continue whisking for 2 minutes. Do not allow the flour to brown. Still whisking constantly, add the warm milk to the flour mixture in a thin stream. If the sauce begins to clump, stop adding milk and whisk until smooth, then resume. Season with a touch of salt and the nutmeg.

TOSS the cardoons with the sauce and transfer to the prepared baking dish. Smooth the cardoons into an even layer. Combine the cheese with the breadcrumbs and sprinkle on top of the cardoons. Bake until the top is browned, about 15 minutes. Allow to rest for 15 minutes before serving.

How to
TRIM AN ARTICHOKE

1. Fill a large bowl with water and the juice of 1 lemon.

2. Remove any leaves from the artichoke stem, and then cut the stem, leaving an inch or two. Pull off and discard any hard, dark-colored leaves.

3. When you have revealed the light green portion of the artichoke, peel any tough skin off the outside of the stem.

4. Cut off the top of the artichoke's leaves.

5. If leaving the artichoke whole, place it upside down on the counter and press down firmly to open it up. Use a small paring knife to cut out and discard the hairy choke. If slicing the artichoke, cut it in half the long way, then into quarters, and simply cut out the choke with a paring knife (as if coring an apple or pear).

6. Drop the artichoke into the lemon water and repeat with the remaining artichokes.

Cut off the top of the artichoke's leaves

Place upside down and press firmly

Drop into lemon water

*Eat in season: When you do, the vegetables
will be more flavorful and cost less.*

SCAFATA
SPRING VEGETABLE STEW

Serves 4 as a main course   *Umbria*

4 to 6 leaves tender Swiss chard

6 to 8 stalks asparagus, preferably wild

4 baby artichokes

½ cup white wine

¼ cup extra-virgin olive oil

½ cup shelled fresh fava beans (see Note)

½ cup shelled fresh peas

2 spring onions, quartered

Fine sea salt to taste

Freshly ground black pepper to taste

¼ cup loosely packed fresh basil leaves

This restorative dish is served in early spring, when the first green shoots begin to sprout. As with so many Italian recipes, the key to scafata isn't a tricky technique or pricey equipment. The secret is to find the freshest spring vegetables possible—from asparagus to baby artichokes to fresh fava beans—and prepare them simply, so that their delicious flavor shines. Serve this stew with lots of crusty bread.

SEPARATE the Swiss chard stalks from the dark green part of the leaves. Roughly chop the stalks and leaves, keeping them separate. Trim the asparagus and cut into ½-inch pieces. Trim and quarter the artichokes (see page 178).

COMBINE the wine and olive oil in a medium pot and place over medium heat. Add the chard stalks, asparagus, artichokes, fava beans, peas, and onions. Simmer until the vegetables are tender, about 15 minutes. If the wine boils off and the pot begins to look dry, add small amounts of water (guard against sputtering). The finished dish should not be soupy, but it should be moist.

WHEN all the vegetables are tender, stir in the chard leaves and cook for 5 minutes more, until the greens are wilted. Season to taste with salt and pepper. Let the stew cool slightly, about 15 minutes, then tear and add the basil leaves, stir to combine, and serve.

NOTE: *Preparing fresh fava beans takes some effort because you have to remove not just an outer pod, but an inner skin as well. (If you're lucky enough to come across extremely young and tender beans, the inner skin will not be fully formed yet, but unless you're growing your own fava beans, these are hard to find.) In Italy, we often avoid this task by serving a rustic appetizer of sheep's cheese paired with fava beans still in their pods and letting people peel the beans themselves. But sometimes you'll want to peel the beans for a prettier presentation. Remove the beans from the pod, then remove the skin around each bean.*

PASTA CON RAGÙ DI ZUCCA E SCAMORZA

PASTA WITH SQUASH AND SCAMORZA

Serves 6 as a first course   *Abruzzo, Campania, Molise, Puglia*

2 tablespoons extra-virgin olive oil

4 cloves garlic, smashed

2 yellow summer squash, cut into ½-inch cubes

2 zucchini, cut into ½-inch cubes

Fine sea salt to taste

Freshly ground black pepper to taste

1 pint grape tomatoes, halved

Coarse sea salt for pasta cooking water

1 pound short dried pasta, such as Vesuvio or penne

8 ounces scamorza cheese, cut into ½-inch cubes

¼ cup fresh mint leaves

1 cup grated pecorino Romano

Green zucchini and yellow summer squash make a lovely contrast in this summer dish, which is perfect for a relaxed al fresco dinner with friends. For a memorable evening, pair this first course with a well-chilled white wine, such as a Falanghina, and follow it with a light seafood main course—the whole grilled fish on page 228 would be ideal.

BRING a large pot of water to a boil for cooking the pasta.

PLACE the olive oil and the garlic cloves in a large sauté pan. Set over medium heat. Cook the garlic in the olive oil, stirring frequently, until the garlic is soft (but do not allow it to brown). Remove and discard the garlic.

INCREASE the heat to medium-high and add the summer squash and zucchini cubes. Season lightly with salt and pepper. Cook them, stirring occasionally, until they have released any liquid and begin to brown slightly, about 6 minutes. Add the grape tomato halves and continue to cook until they, too, have released their liquid.

MEANWHILE, when the water in the large pot boils, add salt (see page 20), and then add the pasta. Cook, stirring frequently, until the pasta is al dente (see page 74). Drain the pasta and add it to the sauté pan to coat with the sauce. Toss vigorously over medium heat until combined, about 2 minutes.

REMOVE the pan from the heat and toss in the cubes of scamorza. Mix well, and then tear and sprinkle the mint leaves all around the pan. Sprinkle in the grated pecorino, stir to incorporate, and serve immediately.

How to
ROAST RED PEPPERS

ROASTING A BELL PEPPER SOFTENS ITS FLAVOR AND BRINGS OUT ITS SWEETNESS, and makes it a little easier to digest. This method works with red, yellow, and orange peppers. (We don't eat unripe green peppers in Italy.) Roasted peppers can be cut into strips and placed in a lidded glass jar with olive oil to cover and refrigerated for up to one week. You can also seed peppers, cut them into triangles, toss them with a little olive oil, salt, and herbs of your choosing, and roast them in a 450°F oven, shaking them occasionally, until soft, about 20 minutes.

1. Preheat the broiler (or an outdoor grill).

2. Arrange whole peppers on a foil-lined baking sheet for broiling.

3. Broil or grill (place the peppers directly on the grate), turning occasionally with tongs, until the skin is charred and black in spots and the peppers are collapsing, 15 to 20 minutes.

4. When the peppers are cool enough to handle, slice in half the long way and pull out the stems and seeds, which should come away in one piece. Use a paper towel to wipe out any stray seeds.

5. Peel off most of the charred skin, leaving little flecks behind to impart smoky flavor.

"RADICI" E TUBERI

Roots, or tubers, aren't the sexiest members of the vegetable family. They're usually brown or beige, and they—quite literally—develop out of sight. But there is little that is more comforting than a roasted potato that's crunchy on the outside and creamy on the inside, or as crisp and refreshing as a raw radish dipped in sea salt. Though not technically a root vegetable as it grows above ground, winter squash is included here, too.

The Italian Way with
COOKED POTATOES

SUBRÌCH *Piemontese Potato Fritters*	Peel potatoes and put them through a potato ricer, then combine the riced potatoes with beaten egg, grated Parmigiano Reggiano, salt, and pepper. Form the mixture into small balls or patties, dredge them lightly in flour, and fry in olive oil until golden and crisp.
INSALATA DI PATATE *Potato Salad*	Combine diced peeled and cooked potatoes, chopped cooked green beans, a few rinsed capers, and a thinly sliced red onion. Dress with a classic vinaigrette (page 26), toss, and serve at room temperature.
PURÈ DI PATATE *Mashed Potatoes*	Peel potatoes and put them through a potato ricer. In a pot, combine the riced potatoes with butter or extra-virgin olive oil (or a combination of the two), grated Parmigiano Reggiano, and enough milk to create a creamy consistency. Place over low heat and whisk constantly until heated through. Serve warm.
FRITTATA DI PATATE *Potato Frittata*	Peel and dice potatoes. Heat a generous amount of olive oil in a (preferably cast-iron) skillet over medium heat. Spread the diced potatoes in a layer and cook without stirring until they are browned underneath. Turn and cook until browned on the other sides, then remove with a slotted spoon or spatula and set aside. Cook a sliced yellow onion in the same oil, then remove and set aside with the potatoes. In a mixing bowl, whisk eggs (2 per person is a good rule of thumb), season with salt and pepper, and stir in the potatoes and onion. Pour the egg and potato mixture into the skillet. Cook, pushing in the edges of the eggs as they cook and tilting the pan to let the raw eggs run to the outside. When the bottom of the frittata is brown, run the pan under the broiler for a few minutes to set the top. Serve warm or at room temperature. (See page 191 for more on the cooking technique for a frittata.)
PATATE CON LO SGOMBRO *Potatoes with Mackerel*	Preheat the oven to 450°F. Peel and thinly slice potatoes. Toss the potatoes with a little olive oil, salt, pepper, minced fresh parsley, and minced garlic and spread in a baking dish. Top with mackerel fillets, skin side down. Brush a little additional oil on the mackerel and season with salt and pepper. Bake until the fish is cooked through and the potatoes around the edge of the pan are browned, 15 to 20 minutes.

INSALATA DI SEDANO RAPA E MELE
CELERY ROOT AND APPLE SALAD

Serves 4 as a side dish   *Valle d'Aosta*

1 large celery root (about 8 ounces)

1 tablespoon white wine vinegar

2 large eggs

Juice of ½ lemon

Fine sea salt to taste

About 2 cups extra-virgin olive oil

½ cup walnuts

2 Golden Delicious apples

Knobby celery root—popular in the northern regions of Italy—has an astringent flavor only faintly reminiscent of celery and can be eaten either raw or cooked. Because it stores well, it can be enjoyed during the long winters when fresh vegetables may be in short supply. Here it pairs beautifully with sweet apples and slightly bitter walnuts. It is always cooked with either vinegar or lemon juice to prevent discoloration. Be aware that the dressing contains raw eggs, which might be a health issue for some.

PEEL the celery root. Cut it in half, and if it has a woody core, cut it away and discard it. Cut the remaining celery root into matchsticks.

BRING a pot of water to a boil and add the vinegar. Blanch the celery root until tender, about 10 minutes, then drain and let stand at room temperature for 1 hour.

MEANWHILE, whisk the eggs and lemon juice with a pinch of salt until thoroughly combined. Whisking constantly, slowly drizzle in the olive oil, drop by drop, to make a mayonnaise. You may not need all the oil. Stop when the mayonnaise is creamy but not runny. Taste and adjust salt. (You can also do this with an immersion blender or in a food processor.)

LIGHTLY toast the walnuts in a dry skillet until fragrant, about 5 minutes, then chop them roughly.

PEEL, core, and quarter the apples, then thinly slice and transfer to a large salad bowl. Add the celery root and the mayonnaise and toss until thoroughly combined. Sprinkle with the toasted walnuts and serve at room temperature.

BRUSCHETTA CON ZUCCA E "VINAIGRETTE" DI TARTUFO NERO
BRUSCHETTA WITH BUTTERNUT SQUASH AND BLACK TRUFFLE VINAIGRETTE

Makes 12 bruschette   *Piemonte*

---

1 butternut squash (about 2½ pounds), peeled, seeded, and diced

Fine sea salt to taste

Freshly ground black pepper to taste

6 tablespoons extra-virgin olive oil

2 medium shallots, minced

2 tablespoons chopped fresh black truffle or truffle paste

2 tablespoons apple cider vinegar

12 (½-inch-thick) slices Pane Rustico (see page 119) or other country-style bread

These pretty *bruschette* (the plural of *bruschetta*) are a lovely way to start a meal, and they can even make a light vegetarian dinner on their own. You can prepare the squash a couple days ahead of time (bring it back to room temperature before using), but grill the bread right before serving for best results.

PREHEAT the oven to 375°F.

IN a large mixing bowl, season the squash with salt and pepper and toss with 2 tablespoons olive oil. Spread in a single layer on a baking sheet and roast until lightly golden and tender, about 30 minutes. Set the squash aside to cool.

WHEN cool, puree the squash in a food processor fitted with the metal blade until smooth. Set aside.

COMBINE the minced shallots, truffle, and vinegar in a bowl. Season with salt and pepper. Whisking constantly, add the remaining 4 tablespoons olive oil in a thin stream. Taste and adjust salt.

HEAT a cast-iron grill pan over medium-high heat or use an outdoor grill. Grill the bread until golden brown, about 4 minutes per side.

SPREAD about 2 tablespoons squash puree over each piece of toast. Drizzle each bruschetta with about 1 tablespoon truffle vinaigrette. Serve warm.

NOTE: *Truffles are intensely perfumed fungus that grow underground on tree roots. They vary in size and there are two types—white truffles from the Piemonte region and black truffles from the Marche and Umbria—but they all share one thing: They are extremely pricey. There are, however, plenty of ways to enjoy truffles without shelling out the money to purchase a fresh one (though we do carry those in season). Truffles can be purchased in cans and jars, and truffle puree is sold in tubes. However, you will never find truffle oil on the shelves in Eataly—it is a chemically enhanced product that both overpowers dishes and stints on true truffle flavor.*

GATTÒ DI PATATE
POTATO CAKE

Serves 6 as a light main dish   *Campania, Sicilia*

2½ pounds Yukon gold or russet potatoes, peeled

6 sun-dried tomatoes

3 large eggs, lightly beaten

½ cup whole milk

½ cup grated aged pecorino cheese

¾ cup diced mozzarella

2 tablespoons chopped fresh parsley

2 tablespoons chopped fresh basil

Butter for greasing ramekins

½ cup fine breadcrumbs (see page 134)

1 tablespoon extra-virgin olive oil

Fine sea salt to taste

The word *gattò* is the Italian spelling of the French word for cake, or *gâteau*. French-inspired dishes like this one hail from the Sicilia and Campania regions, which developed a rich tradition of French cooking during the eighteenth century, when they were ruled by the French House of Bourbon. These days this gattò is usually served as a rather humble one-dish meal, albeit one that never fails to please. We like to make it a little more special by baking it in individual ramekins, so that each diner gets a small cake. Pair with one of the simple salads on page 172 for contrast. In this recipe, we rehydrate dry sun-dried tomatoes, but if you prefer you can use the type that come jarred in oil. Simply drain them—no need to rehydrate—and drizzle a little of the tomato oil on the finished dish. At Eataly we serve this vegetarian version with a heavily dressed chicory salad that balances the richness.

PREHEAT the oven to 350°F.

BRING a large pot of water to a boil and boil the potatoes. Once the potatoes are tender enough to be pierced easily with a fork or the tip of a paring knife, 15 to 40 minutes depending on their size, remove them with a slotted spoon, peel them when they are cool enough to handle, and crush them in a large mixing bowl leaving some chunks.

MEANWHILE, place the sun-dried tomatoes in a heatproof bowl. Add enough boiling water to just cover the tomatoes. Set aside to rehydrate until the tomatoes are flexible, about 10 minutes.

DRAIN the rehydrated tomatoes and cut them into a ¼-inch dice. Combine the tomatoes, eggs, milk, pecorino, mozzarella, parsley, and basil, then fold the egg mixture into the crushed potatoes by hand until thoroughly combined.

BUTTER 6 individual ramekins, then coat the bottom and sides of each with about 1 tablespoon breadcrumbs, shaking out any excess. Fill the ramekins with the potato mixture, smoothing the tops. Combine the remaining 2 tablespoons, plus excess, breadcrumbs with the olive oil and season with a pinch of salt. Sprinkle the breadcrumb mixture on top of the cakes and place the ramekins on a baking sheet.

BAKE the ramekins until the tops are golden brown and crisp, about 20 minutes. Remove from the oven and allow to cool for about 20 minutes, then either run an offset spatula around the perimeter of each dish, unmold, and serve, or simply serve the cakes in the ramekins.

ZUCCA CON LENTICCHIE NERE

ACORN SQUASH WITH BLACK LENTILS

Serves 4 as an appetizer or side dish

1 acorn squash (about 1¾ pounds)

3 tablespoons extra-virgin olive oil

Fine sea salt to taste

Freshly ground black pepper to taste

12 cipolline onions, unpeeled

1 sprig fresh sage

2 sprigs fresh thyme

½ teaspoon whole black peppercorns

1 carrot

1 rib celery

1 medium shallot

1 cup black beluga lentils

Aged balsamic vinegar for finishing

Diminutive black lentils—known as beluga lentils because of their resemblance to caviar—add a touch of class to any dish. If you've got only brown lentils on hand, though, feel free to substitute them. They'll take a little longer to cook—closer to 30 minutes.

PREHEAT the oven to 350°F.

PEEL the outermost part of the ribs of the squash, but leave stripes of skin on the indented parts to create a striped effect. Halve lengthwise, scoop out the strings and seeds and discard them, then cut the squash into crescents.

LINE a baking sheet with parchment paper. Toss the squash with 2 tablespoons olive oil and season to taste with salt and pepper. Spread the squash in a single layer on the baking sheet and roast until the skin is crispy and the flesh is soft, about 35 minutes.

MEANWHILE, place the cipolline onions in a baking dish or on another parchment-lined baking sheet and roast until tender, about 8 minutes. Let the roasted onions cool until they can be handled comfortably, then snip off the ends with kitchen shears. Leave the onions whole, or cut in half lengthwise.

PLACE the sage, thyme, and peppercorns in a cheesecloth sachet. Mince the carrot, celery, and shallot, and place in a saucepan with the remaining 1 tablespoon olive oil. Cook over low heat until the vegetables are softened but not browned, about 5 minutes. Add the lentils and cook, stirring occasionally, for 2 minutes. Add 1½ cups water and the herb sachet and bring to a boil. Reduce the heat to a simmer, and cook until the lentils are soft but still hold their shape and most of the liquid has been absorbed, about 15 minutes. Remove and discard the sachet. Season the lentils with salt and set aside to cool.

TO serve, arrange a bed of lentils on each serving plate. Top with a few slices of squash and a few onions. Drizzle with aged balsamic vinegar and serve at room temperature.

ERBE AROMATICHE

Pungent basil, zesty flat-leaf parsley, earthy oregano—fresh herbs are the secret weapon of the Italian kitchen. They add a zap of flavor to almost any dish. As a rule of thumb, add "hard-textured" herbs, such as rosemary, at the start of cooking a dish and incorporate "soft-textured" herbs, such as mint, at the end.

The Italian Way with
HERB-ESSENTIAL DISHES

Italians use herbs frequently and copiously, but these are dishes where herbs really take center stage.

PESTO ALLA GENOVESE *Genoese Pesto*	See page 108 for Liguria's famous uncooked basil sauce.
PATATE AL ROSMARINO *Roasted Potatoes with Rosemary*	The mandatory accompaniment to any Sunday lunch. Peel potatoes and cut them into 2-inch chunks. Toss with salt, pepper, lots of fresh rosemary needles, and olive oil. Spread on a baking sheet or baking pan in a single layer and roast at 350ºF until crisp.
RAVIOLI DI BORRAGINE E RICOTTA *Borage and Ricotta Ravioli*	Borage is an herb that grows so prolifically it is used as a green. Replace the spinach in the filling for the pansotti (page 70) with borage, or use a mixture of borage and spinach.
PASTA CON LE SARDE *Pasta with Sardines*	Sardines are essential in this dish from Sicilia, but fennel is equally important. In Sicilia, wild fennel is used, but you can make do with the feathery tops of a cultivated fennel bulb. (Either reserve the bulb for another use or chop it and add it with the onion below.) Cook chopped fresh sardines in a skillet with a little onion and a chopped anchovy fillet. Add pine nuts and toast right in the pan, then add currants, chopped thin stalks of fennel, chopped feathery fennel leaves, and a pinch of saffron dissolved in a small amount of water. Cook bucatini until al dente, toss the pasta with the other ingredients in the pan, and top with toasted breadcrumbs.
MELANZANA ALLA MENTA *Mint Eggplant*	In Calabria and Sicilia, chili peppers and mint often appear together. Slice an eggplant in half the long way, brush the cut side with olive oil, cut slits in the eggplant, insert whole cloves of garlic into the slits, and roast in a preheated 400ºF oven until browned and soft, 15 to 30 minutes. Cut the cooked eggplant into cubes and toss with sliced fresh chili pepper and plenty of torn fresh mint leaves. Drizzle on a little white wine vinegar and serve.

The Italian Way with FRITTATE

Learn how to make a frittata and you will never go hungry. Almost any savory ingredient will make a good frittata, and even a plain frittata made with just eggs, salt, and pepper can serve as a plain-yet-satisfying supper in a pinch.

Use an oven-safe skillet if you plan to finish the frittata under the broiler (a cast-iron pan is best). In a large bowl, beat 2 eggs per person (4 eggs minimum) with a pinch of salt and freshly ground black pepper. Heat extra-virgin olive oil in the skillet over medium-low heat. Pour in the eggs. Every few seconds, tilt the pan and push the more solid eggs from the edge into the center so that the still-uncooked egg fills in the space. When the bottom of the frittata is firm but the top is still soft, cook undisturbed for 2 to 3 minutes until the bottom is browned and the top has a narrow margin of cooked egg around the perimeter. Either slide the frittata onto a plate, turn the skillet upside down over the plate, and flip the plate and skillet together to return the frittata to the pan (use oven mitts for this maneuver!) and cook for 2 to 3 minutes to brown the bottom—or run the pan under a broiler for 1 to 2 minutes, watching closely, to brown the top.

FRITTATA ALLE ERBE *Herb Frittata*	Mince a generous amount of fresh parsley, chives, oregano, chervil, marjoram, or a combination of two or more. Stir into the beaten eggs before pouring them into the skillet.
FRITTATA DI VERDURE *Frittata with Greens*	Squeeze cooked greens (spinach, chard, escarole, and kale are all good candidates) until dry, mince them, and stir them into the beaten eggs before pouring them into the skillet.
FRITTATA AI FUNGHI *Mushroom Frittata*	Sauté sliced mushrooms in the skillet, then pour the beaten eggs over them and continue.

CARCIOFI ALLA ROMANA
ROMAN-STYLE ARTICHOKES

Serves 4 as a side dish   *Lazio*

---

3 cloves garlic

¼ cup loosely packed fresh parsley leaves, chopped

¼ cup loosely packed fresh mint leaves, chopped

¼ cup extra-virgin olive oil

8 Romanesco artichokes, trimmed and left whole (see page 178)

Fine sea salt to taste

Freshly ground black pepper to taste

¼ cup white wine

Italians are crazy about artichokes. This is the classic Roman preparation, and it is best made with Romanesco artichokes, which don't have spiky leaf tips and are round and large, with purple outer leaves. You may want to wear gloves when working with artichokes, as they can stain your hands brown. The artichokes themselves will quickly turn brown once cut—for that reason, always keep a large bowl of water with lemon juice at hand so that you can drop the artichokes into it immediately once they are trimmed. Roman-style artichokes are always cooked stems up in the pot, so choose a pot tall enough to contain the stems, but narrow enough that the artichokes are pressed up against one another—they shouldn't be floating in the liquid. You can easily double or triple this recipe.

MINCE together the garlic, parsley, and mint. Mix in a small bowl with 1 tablespoon olive oil. Stuff the trimmed artichokes with the garlic mixture.

PLACE the remaining 3 tablespoons olive oil in the bottom of a tall, narrow pot. Arrange the artichokes side by side and stems up in the pot. Season with salt and pepper. Cook, uncovered, over medium heat for 5 minutes.

POUR in the wine and enough water to come about 2 inches up the side of the pot. Cover the pot with a tight-fitting lid wrapped in a flat-weave dishtowel. (Use caution—be sure the ends of the dishtowel don't hang down near the flame.) Place a heavy nonflammable item, such as a meat pounder, on top of the lid to hold it in place. Place over medium heat and simmer (turn down the flame if the liquid begins to boil) until the artichokes are extremely tender and easily pierced with a fork, about 45 minutes. Check occasionally, and if the pot seems very dry, add water in small amounts, but keep in mind that your ultimate goal is to have very little liquid.

WHEN the artichokes are tender, remove the lid, turn the heat up to high, and boil until most of the liquid has evaporated and just the oil remains in the pot. (You may be able to skip this step if there is very little liquid in the pot.) Remove the artichokes with a slotted spoon and set aside to cool, reserving the cooking liquid.

WHEN the artichokes are cool, drizzle the oil from the pot over them. Serve warm or at room temperature.

CARNE

All of the meat we offer is processed following
the "NEVER EVER" guidelines:
No antibiotics EVER!
No added hormones EVER!
No growth-promoting drugs EVER!

MANZO, VITELLO E AGNELLO

In Italy, as in most parts of the world where beef is eaten, a rich and mineral-flavored steak is a symbol of luxury. For many years, Italy was not a wealthy country, and beef was a special treat reserved for Sundays and holidays. Even then, it often served a dual purpose—first as the flavoring for a sauce that would be served over pasta, and then as a main course on its own. These days, most Italians can afford to eat beef more frequently, but it is still treated with reverence and every part of the animal is used. Adjusting cooking technique to the specific cut is key: When braised, tougher cuts with more connective tissue grow fork-tender. A tasty steak, preferably from one of the cattle breeds native to Piemonte or Toscana, can be grilled with little more than a sprinkling of sea salt and a drizzle of olive oil. Lamb is eaten only in spring in Italy (when lambs about four months old are slaughtered) and is traditionally served as the centerpiece of an Easter meal. And Italians have long worked wonders with veal, especially in the form of scaloppine (often called *fettine,* or small slices), which are slices about ¼ inch thick cut against the grain from the top round.

The Italian Way with
REGIONAL BEEF, LAMB, and VEAL DISHES

REGION	SPECIALTY
VALLE D'AOSTA	Cotoletta alla Valdostana: a veal cutlet dredged in egg and breadcrumbs, panfried, and topped with thin slices of prosciutto and cheese.
PIEMONTE	Bollito misto: a variety of cuts of beef cooked together in a big pot and served with red and green sauces.
LOMBARDIA	Ossobuco: a slowly braised veal shank topped with refreshing gremolata sauce (also the name of the special cut of shank used to make this dish).
TOSCANA	Bistecca alla Fiorentina: a grilled T-bone steak, traditionally from the local Chianina breed of cattle.
LAZIO	Abbacchio: very young lamb, usually roasted.

Piemontese tagliata

chops

Piemontese porterhouse

Piemontese fillet

SIGNS OF QUALITY

A real old-fashioned butcher cuts meat to order rather than selling it prepackaged.

Select the proper cut for the technique you plan on using: Tougher meats are suitable for long braises, while more tender cuts can be seared or grilled.

Raw beef and lamb should be bright red in color; veal should be a rosy pink.

lamb chops

lamb sausage

osso buco

veal cutlets

The Italian Way with
VEAL CUTLETS

Instructions for all: Heat a generous amount of olive oil in a skillet. When the oil is hot, dredge veal cutlets in lightly seasoned unbleached all-purpose flour and brown the cutlets in the oil, about 2 minutes per side. Remove from the pan and keep warm. Deglaze the pan with your choice of the ingredients below, and return the cutlets to the pan just long enough to warm them through in the sauce. Serve immediately.

MARSALA WINE AND A SMALL AMOUNT OF BUTTER

FRESH LEMON JUICE, CAPERS, AND MINCED PARSLEY

CANNED WHOLE PEELED TOMATOES, CHOPPED, AND THEIR JUICES; after returning the veal to the pan, top it with thin slices of mozzarella, if you like, and allow the cheese to melt on top of the cutlets

MINCED GARLIC, CHOPPED ANCHOVY FILLETS, AND WHITE WINE

HEAVY CREAM AND MINCED FRESH THYME

We source our meat from clean, sustainable farms and ranches where the animals graze daily in open pastures and are humanely handled. The health of both the animals and the land on which they are raised has a direct impact on the quality and flavor of the meat once it reaches your table and your mouth.

CARNE CRUDA
BEEF TARTAR

Serves 4 as an appetizer   *Piemonte*

---

12 ounces Razza Piemontese top round beef (see Note)

¼ cup mellow extra-virgin olive oil, preferably from Liguria

Flaky sea salt to taste

This simple dish illustrates the Eataly philosophy: If you purchase stellar ingredients and prepare them in a way that lets them shine, you will always create something special. Using a meat grinder is the easiest way to prepare the beef tartar. (A food processor fitted with the metal blade will turn the beef to mush.) Most of the manufacturers of stand mixers sell handy attachments that can be used to transform their mixers into meat grinders. If you don't have a meat grinder, you can have the butcher grind the meat for you, but have it ground as close as possible to the time that you will be serving the dish to avoid oxidization. You want the finished dish to retain its ruby-red color. Alternately, chop the meat very finely with a sharp knife. (Be sure not to leave any chunks, as they will be unpleasantly chewy.) This is a classic Piemontese dish, but there is very little olive oil produced in Piemonte, so we like to opt for an oil from Liguria, a neighboring region. One other detail: Chill the bowl you will be using in advance to keep the meat cool. Savor carne cruda with bread or crackers as an appetizer. In Piemonte, it is eaten at all hours as a snack, appetizer, or meal—even at breakfast!

CUT the beef into 1-inch cubes. Grind the beef in a meat grinder or stand mixer fitted with a meat grinder attachment.

PLACE the ground meat in a chilled bowl. Pour the olive oil evenly over the meat. Sprinkle on salt to taste. With a large spoon, gently fold together the ingredients until combined. Do not mash the meat or stir vigorously.

DIVIDE the mixture among 4 plates and serve immediately.

NOTE: *Using the best ingredients available is especially crucial when making a recipe such as this one with only three ingredients, and when served raw, beef must be absolutely fresh. The meat should be bright red and very lean—cut away any fat or sinew before grinding it. Be sure that it is very cold before you begin handling it.*

CARPACCIO
THINLY SLICED RAW BEEF

Serves 4 as an appetizer   *Piemonte*

12 ounces Razza Piemontese tenderloin beef, trimmed and sliced paper-thin (see Note)

1 tablespoon extra-virgin olive oil

1 teaspoon fresh lemon juice

Fine sea salt to taste

Freshly ground black pepper to taste

½ cup loosely packed arugula

Like the Carne Cruda on the opposite page, this preparation requires the freshest possible ingredients, so purchase the thinly sliced beef only a few hours before you plan to serve it. For a luxurious appetizer, pair the two raw beef dishes and serve them together.

ARRANGE the beef slices in a single layer on 4 chilled appetizer plates.

IN a small bowl, whisk together the olive oil and lemon juice and season to taste with salt and pepper. Dress the arugula with the olive oil mixture and arrange a few pieces of arugula on each serving of carpaccio. Serve immediately.

NOTE: *A proper carpaccio is sliced paper-thin—only a meat slicer will do the job, and the meat must be frozen in advance. Your best bet is to order the sliced beef from your butcher. If you can't find a butcher who will slice it for you, you can wrap the beef tightly in plastic wrap, freeze it for at least 1 hour, cut the frozen beef by hand as thinly as possible, and then place the slices between sheets of plastic wrap and pound them even thinner. However, this technique will diminish the quality of the meat and should be employed only in case of emergency.*

RAZZA PIEMONTESE

This is a breed of cattle native to the Piemonte region. Due to a genetic particularity, the resulting meat has a lower percentage of fat and less connective tissue than meat from other breeds, making it delicious in general and ideal for these recipes. But that's not all Piemontese beef has going for it: It is lower in saturated fat and higher in polyunsaturated fat (the good fat). It's the avocado of beef! It also has more omega-3 fatty acids and more protein than standard beef. We chose certified Piemontese beef as part of our commitment to environmental stewardship and sustainability, humane animal-handling practices, farm-to-fork traceability, and, of course, taste and quality.

COSTATA DI MANZO AI PORCINI CON ACETO BALSAMICO

BEEF SHORT RIBS WITH PORCINI RUB AND BALSAMIC VINEGAR

Serves 4 as a main course   *Emilia-Romagna*

½ cup dried porcini mushrooms (about ½ ounce), ground

¼ cup light or dark brown sugar

2 tablespoons fine sea salt

2 tablespoons crushed red pepper flakes

2 tablespoons freshly ground black pepper

2 pounds boneless short ribs

Aged balsamic vinegar to taste

These unusual short ribs are rubbed with a spicy ground mushroom mixture, then grilled until juicy. A drizzle of aged balsamic vinegar provides a sweet-tart finish. Grind the dried porcini mushrooms in a blender. Serve the steak with potatoes tossed with olive oil and sprinkled with rosemary and sage, then roasted until golden brown and crisp.

IN a small mixing bowl, combine the ground mushrooms, sugar, salt, red pepper flakes, and black pepper. Mix thoroughly.

PREHEAT a gas or charcoal grill or broiler on high. Pat the meat dry and rub it with the porcini mixture, coating well on all sides. Grill or broil the meat for about 2 minutes on each side, or until an instant-read thermometer registers an internal temperature of 115°F for medium-rare.

ALLOW the meat to rest for a few minutes before carving to avoid losing the juices on the cutting board. Carve the meat on a bias into ½-inch slices, drizzle with aged balsamic vinegar, and serve immediately.

The Italian Way with
MUSHROOM PRODUCTS AND TRUFFLES

DRIED PORCINI MUSHROOMS	These particularly meaty mushrooms grow in pine forests. Reconstitute dried mushrooms in water until pliable and then use the soaking liquid (spooned out of the bowl and leaving any grit at the bottom) in risotto or soup, or grind the dried mushrooms into a powder.
SLICED PORCINI MUSHROOMS IN OIL	Drain slices of these meaty preserved mushrooms and serve as part of an antipasto platter.
TRUFFLE BUTTER	A dab of black or white truffle butter can be brushed onto hot grilled meats.
TRUFFLE FLOUR	Use truffle flour in place of a small amount of all-purpose flour when making pasta.
TRUFFLE PUREE	Stir a little of this potent mixture (either the white or the black version) into mashed potatoes or spread on toasted bread for crostini.
TRUFFLE SALT	Sprinkle a little of this flavored salt on a plain or herb frittata.

AGNELLO ALLA SCOTTADITO
SEARED LAMB CHOPS

Serves 6 as a main course   *Lazio*

¼ cup fine sea salt

2 tablespoons sugar

1 tablespoon freshly
ground black pepper

1 teaspoon grated lemon zest

1 tablespoon fresh mint
leaves, chopped

1 tablespoon fresh rosemary
leaves, chopped

12 lamb chops (about 3 pounds;
see Note)

3 tablespoons extra-virgin olive oil

Scottadito means "finger burning," but we think picking up these tender lamb chops while they're piping hot is worth the risk of blisters. At Eataly, we use an olive oil from Lazio in this recipe.

IN a bowl, combine the salt, sugar, pepper, lemon zest, mint, and rosemary. Cover the chops with the rub and let them stand at room temperature for up to 2 hours or refrigerate, covered, for up to 1 day.

WHEN you are ready to cook the chops, heat a heavy griddle or large cast-iron skillet over medium heat and brush lightly with olive oil. Drizzle the remaining olive oil onto the chops.

PLACE as many chops as you can fit on the griddle without crowding it. Cook, turning once, until the chops are well browned outside and rosy pink in the center, about 3 minutes per side. (For more well-done chops, cook 1 to 2 minutes longer.) Repeat with the remaining chops, if any. Serve piping hot.

NOTE: *For this dish, rib chops cut from a rack of lamb are best because of the length of the bone. If you prefer the cleaner, less rustic look of frenched chops, ask the butcher to french them for you, or do it yourself: Cut the meat and fat away from the bone starting at the point where the "eye" of meat meets the bone. Scrape the bone clean with the back side of a knife. There should be a 1½- to 3-inch bone protruding. Save any meat and fat scraps and use them to make a quick stock.*

How to EAT SCOTTADITO

THE NAME SAYS IT ALL: *scottadito* literally means "finger burner." Pick up a chop by pinching the bone between your index finger and thumb, then gnaw away.

ANIMELLE DI VITELLO DORATE
PANFRIED VEAL SWEETBREADS

Serves 4 to 6 as an appetizer   *Lazio*

1 pound veal sweetbreads

1 tablespoon coriander seeds

1 cup white wine vinegar

1 carrot, minced

1 rib celery, minced

1 small yellow onion, minced

1 small bulb fennel, minced

Fine sea salt to taste

6 tablespoons extra-virgin olive oil

1 cup unbleached all-purpose flour

In ancient Rome, offal—organ meats—was considered a great delicacy. At one time slaughterhouse workers were even paid in offal in lieu of cash. In Italy today, and particularly in Rome and the Lazio region, tripe, kidneys, spleen, liver, and both lamb and veal sweetbreads are still enjoyed with gusto. The Romans even have an expression for these tasty bits: the *quinto quarto*, or "fifth quarter." In Italy, we like the earthy flavor of sweetbreads front and center, but if you prefer a milder flavor, soak the cleaned sweetbreads in cold water for a couple of hours before cooking.

PEEL off the membrane from the sweetbreads and discard. (It may be helpful to do this under cold running water.)

TOAST the coriander seeds in a dry skillet until fragrant, about 5 minutes.

IN a pot, combine the coriander seeds, vinegar, carrot, celery, onion, and fennel with 1 cup water and salt to taste. Bring the liquid to a very gentle simmer. Add the sweetbreads and poach over low heat until they are tender but not falling apart, about 6 minutes.

REMOVE the sweetbreads with a slotted spoon and set aside to cool. Check for any remaining bits of membrane and remove them.

CUT the sweetbreads into bite-size pieces. Dry them well with paper towels. Heat the olive oil in a sauté pan over medium-high heat. Dredge the sweetbreads in the flour and, working in batches if necessary to keep from crowding the pan, fry the sweetbreads until golden brown on all sides, 3 to 4 minutes. Sprinkle on a little additional salt and serve hot.

MAIALE

Nowhere is the "nose-to-tail" philosophy of cooking and eating that Italy exemplifies more obvious than in its consumption of pork. A whole pig roasted on a spit is not an uncommon sight in many parts of the country, and good use is made of pig ears, tails, trotters, and innards. *Strutto*, or lard, is also used for cooking, lending extra savory flavor to traditional dishes. At Eataly, we sell heritage breed pork. This pork is derived from the original breed of pig, which predates modern crossbreeding. Raised on pasture-based, sustainable farms, heritage breed pigs produce highly flavorful quality pork because of their better living conditions.

The Italian Way with
FRESH PORK SAUSAGES

Different types of fresh pork sausages are made in a number of regions (see page 84, for more about dried pork sausages and other cured pork products). Central Italy in particular has a way with pork, and the town of Norcia in Umbria is justly famous for the skill of its pork butchers, which is why specialty pork butcher shops are often known as *norcinerie* in the region and elsewhere.

COTECHINO	From Modena in Emilia-Romagna, this robust sausage is made with pork, fatback, and pork rind and contains nutmeg and cloves; zampone is a pig's trotter stuffed with the same filling used in cotechino.
LUGANEGA	This mild pork sausage made with pork shoulder and grated Parmigiano Reggiano is coiled rather than portioned into links.
PROBUSTO	Trentino–Alto Adige in northeastern Italy is home to a variety of German-style sausages known collectively as wurst. Probusto is a type of wurst that can be either boiled or panfried.
SALSICCIA NORCINA	The Umbrian town of Norcia is famous for its pork and boar products (both fresh and dried), including sausage. Two of the area's other signature products, lentils and mushrooms, make wonderfully earthy partners for the local sausage.

hot Italian sausage

pancetta

chops

sweet Italian sausage

loin

ARISTA IN PORCHETTA
BONELESS PORK ROAST

Serves 4 to 6 as a main course   *Lazio, Marche, Umbria*

¼ cup sugar

1½ cups fine sea salt, plus more for seasoning belly

About 1 gallon water

4 pounds boneless pork loin, sinew and fat trimmed

4 pounds boneless pork belly with skin

Freshly ground black pepper to taste

¾ cup fennel seeds

¾ cup black peppercorns

2 tablespoons minced garlic

Porchetta is traditionally a seasoned whole suckling pig that is slowly roasted until the meat is tender and the skin is crisp, but these days it is frequently made with just the loin and belly of a larger pig. Porchetta hails from central Italy, where at outdoor events, carts often sell succulent sandwiches made of thick slices of porchetta on crusty rolls. You will need a large container to brine the pork. Be sure to make room for it by clearing some shelves in your refrigerator before you start the process. The pork loin is brined for 24 hours and the pork belly is seasoned and then refrigerated for 8 hours. A convenient way to handle this is to begin brining the loin the morning of the day before you wish to cook the porchetta, and then season the pork belly that evening and refrigerate it overnight. In a pinch, you can brine the loin overnight only, but the longer soaking time increases flavor and tenderness.

PLACE the sugar and ½ cup salt in a container large enough to hold the pork loin in the brine. Bring a large pot of water (about 1 gallon) to a boil and pour into the container. Whisk until the salt and sugar are dissolved. Add a generous amount of ice to cool the water—you want enough liquid to fully submerge the loin. Place the loin in the cold brine (add water to cover if needed) and refrigerate for 24 hours.

IN a spice grinder, grind the fennel seeds and black peppercorns. Combine with the remaining 1 cup salt. Reserve about half of this spice mixture in a small bowl and set aside.

SEASON the pork belly with the other half of the spice mixture; discard any that isn't used. Cover the pork belly and refrigerate for at least 8 hours.

WHEN you are ready to roast the porchetta, preheat the oven to 350°F. Combine the reserved spice mixture with the minced garlic and stir to combine.

Heritage breed pork is the original breed, what our ancestors were eating before crossbreeding.

REMOVE the loin from the brine and pat dry. (Discard the brine.) Completely coat the loin and the pork belly with the garlic spice mixture. Use some of the reserved rub, if needed, to cover all of the meat's surface area. Wrap the belly around the pork loin so that the loin is completely covered. Truss the meat with twine, tying knots about 1 inch apart. (The easiest way to do this is to start in the middle of the porchetta and work your way to the ends.) Place the porchetta on a rack set in a roasting pan. Place in the preheated oven and cook until the middle of the pork loin reaches an internal temperature of 138°F and the skin is crispy, which will likely take at least 1 hour 15 minutes but may take up to 2 hours. Allow the porchetta to rest before slicing.

SALSICCIA FRESCA
EATALY'S HOUSEMADE SAUSAGE

Makes 10 to 15 4-inch sausages

2½ pounds boneless pork shoulder, trimmed and cut into 1-inch cubes

¾ pound fatback, frozen and cut into ½-inch cubes

3 teaspoons freshly ground black pepper

2½ teaspoons fine sea salt

2½ teaspoons sugar

1 tablespoon fennel seeds

¼ teaspoon ground nutmeg

10 to 15 feet of hog casings, soaked and rinsed (see box)

This is the recipe for the housemade sausages at Eataly in New York. There are numerous different types of fresh sausage made in Italy from all different kinds of meat. For example, in the Langhe area of Piemonte you will find salsiccia di Bra, made with a combination of veal and pork and a long list of spices, including coriander and cloves. Making your own sausages at home is a bit of a project, but the results are rewarding. You will need some basic equipment: a meat grinder with a medium-coarse blade and a sausage stuffer (you can purchase both tools as an attachment for a stand mixer if you have one). A dedicated wooden rack for drying the sausages is handy. You'll also need casings, which you can purchase from a butcher shop. Grinding, mixing, and stuffing tend to heat up the sausage mixture, so start with very cold meat just out of the refrigerator, freeze the fat, and use a chilled (metal works well) bowl for mixing. (If it's a warm day and you're especially concerned about temperature, you can set the bowl in a larger bowl filled with ice.) Refrigerate the meat grinder before using as well.

GRIND the pork shoulder on a medium-coarse blade. Then grind the fatback on the same blade.

PLACE the ground meat and fat in a large (preferably chilled metal) bowl. Sprinkle on the pepper, salt, sugar, fennel seeds, and nutmeg. Add 1 cup cold water (without water, the stuffing will be more like hamburger, which will result in a dry and crumbly sausage) and toss by hand until the spices are evenly distributed. Do not knead the mixture as you would for meat loaf or meatballs.

HOG CASINGS are packed in salt to preserve them. Soak them overnight, changing the water once or twice, then rinse them thoroughly. Rinse the inside of the casings by holding the open end under the faucet, filling the casing with water, pinching the end closed, and sloshing the water around a little. As you are doing this, check for holes. Empty the water completely. Place the soaked and rinsed casings in a clean bowl of water while you are preparing the meat mixture. Hog casings are long—you may need only one casing for this amount of sausage.

PANFRY a small amount of the mixture until browned; taste and adjust seasoning if desired.

PLACE a casing over the end of the stuffing tube, leaving about 6 inches hanging off at the end. Place the sausage mixture in the sausage stuffer and tightly fill the casing, coiling the sausage as it fills. When the casing is tightly filled, tie off the end with a double knot. Use a toothpick to poke holes in the casing 1 to 2 inches apart. If you see any air bubbles, poke holes in them to deflate them. Hold the end of the sausage in one hand and, with the other hand, pinch the sausage about 4 inches down the length. Spin the pinched area to make a link. Continue pinching and spinning, every 4 inches, down the length of the sausage. Tie off the other end of the casing. Check again for air bubbles and poke any you find with the toothpick.

HANG the sausages, preferably on a rack, in a cool, dry place (or in the refrigerator if your kitchen is warm) to dry for 1 to 2 hours, then store in the refrigerator. Unlike preserved meat, these need to be eaten in a day or two. Freeze for longer storage.

ANIMALI DA CORTILE

Chicken and other poultry are popular in Italy for the same reason they are popular everywhere—they are a handy, relatively inexpensive canvas for all kinds of flavors. Rabbit, widely available in Italy, is included in that group as well. Indeed, rabbit is the chicken of Italy—a lean meat that can serve as the foil to any number of flavors and tastes equally terrific roasted simply, perhaps with some herbs and potatoes accompanying it in the roasting pan. If you like the skin of your chicken extra-crispy, refrigerate the bird, uncovered, skin side up, the night before you plan to cook it—this allows the greatest amount of moisture to evaporate.

The Italian Way with
CHICKEN INVOLTINI

Instructions for all: Pound boneless, skinless chicken breasts (or veal scaloppine) until thin (just under ¼ inch) and cut in half. Spread a small amount of your filling of choice (see below) on top of each half. Roll jelly-roll style and seal with kitchen twine or toothpicks. In a skillet large enough to hold the involtini in a single layer, brown them on all sides. Add white wine and cook until the liquid has evaporated. Add enough stock to come about halfway up the sides of the involtini, cover, and cook until the chicken is cooked through. If desired, deglaze the pan to make a sauce. Remove twine or toothpicks before serving.

CHOPPED SAUTÉED SPINACH AND RICOTTA

SAUTÉED CHOPPED MUSHROOMS AND MINCED PARSLEY

CARAMELIZED ONIONS AND GORGONZOLA CHEESE

BREADCRUMBS AND MINCED PANCETTA

MINCED OLIVES AND CAPERS

POLLO ALLA DIAVOLA
PEPPERY CORNISH HEN

Serves 2 as a main course

¼ cup freshly ground black pepper

1 to 2 cups extra-virgin olive oil for marinating

2 lemons, thinly sliced into rounds

1 Cornish hen, breast separated from thigh

6 grape tomatoes

¼ cup loosely packed arugula

A Cornish hen or poussin is a special type of chicken that is the perfect size for two people. Of course, you can easily double this dish, but you will probably need two sauté pans. This method gives you plenty of crispy skin—always the best part of a chicken. For food-safety reasons, the olive oil can't be reused after the chicken marinates in it, so you may want to opt for a less expensive bottle. The large amount of pepper in this dish makes it extra-spicy; you can use a little less if you're afraid it will be overwhelming.

IN a small bowl, combine the black pepper and 1 cup olive oil. Arrange half of the lemon slices in a layer in the bottom of an 8-by-8-inch baking pan. Top the lemon slices with the pieces of chicken and cover with a second layer of the remaining lemon slices. Pour over the olive oil mixture. If the oil doesn't cover the chicken, add a little more. Marinate in the refrigerator for at least 4 hours and up to 48 hours.

PREHEAT the oven to 350°F.

SET a rack over a jelly-roll pan or platter. Remove the chicken from the olive oil marinade and place on the rack, letting the oil drip off of the chicken.

PLACE a large ovenproof sauté pan over medium-high heat and heat until very hot. Add the chicken, skin side down, and cook until the skin is brown and crispy. Turn the chicken, toss the grape tomatoes into the pan, and transfer to the oven. Bake until the chicken is cooked through and the juices run clear, 4 to 5 minutes. Cut the chicken into 6 pieces and transfer to a serving platter with tomatoes. Scatter arugula on top. Serve hot.

QUAGLIE IN SALSA DI PANE
QUAIL IN BREADCRUMB SAUCE

Serves 2 as a main course *Emilia-Romagna, Piemonte, Toscana, Umbria*

1 cup seedless red grapes

1 sprig fresh rosemary

3 tablespoons unsalted butter

Fine sea salt to taste

Freshly ground black
pepper to taste

About 2 tablespoons olive oil

4 quail (about 4 ounces
each), semi-deboned

1 cup red wine

About 2 tablespoons finely ground
breadcrumbs (see page 134)

Roasting grapes intensifies their flavor so that they nicely balance the gamier taste of quail. Be sure to use a light hand when adding the breadcrumbs to the sauce—you want a pourable sauce and not a crumbly topping.

PREHEAT the oven to 400°F.

LINE a baking sheet with parchment paper. Place the grapes and sprig of rosemary on the pan. Dot with 2 tablespoons butter and season with salt and freshly ground pepper. Cook the grapes in the preheated oven until they have burst open and released their juices, about 10 minutes. Remove from the oven and immediately drain off the liquid into a bowl, reserving both liquid and grapes. Leave the oven on.

HEAT a large ovenproof sauté pan over medium-high heat. Add enough olive oil to the pan to coat the bottom. Add the remaining 1 tablespoon butter. Season the quail on both sides with salt and pepper. Add the quail to the pan, breast side up. Sear until the skin is golden brown and crispy. Flip the quail, and then transfer the pan to the oven and roast until the quail is cooked to desired doneness, about 4 minutes.

REMOVE the pan from the oven. Remove the quail from the pan and set them on a rack to rest. Place the pan on the stove and deglaze with the wine (reduce the liquid over medium heat, stirring to combine the wine with the cooking juices and scraping any browned bits from the bottom of the pan). When the wine has reduced slightly, add the reserved grape liquid. Taste and season with salt. If the sauce is very sticky or thick, thin with a small amount of water. Stir in the breadcrumbs gradually to thicken the sauce slightly, but leave it thin enough to pour. (You may not need all the breadcrumbs.) Spoon the grapes and sauce on 2 serving plates and place 2 quail on each plate. Serve immediately.

PAPPARDELLE AL SUGO DI CONIGLIO
PAPPARDELLE WITH RABBIT SAUCE

Serves 6 as a first course   *Emilia–Romagna*

1 rabbit (about 2 pounds), cut up

Fine sea salt to taste

¼ cup extra-virgin olive oil

2 carrots

2 leeks

½ cup chicken stock

¼ cup tomato puree

Fresh pappardelle made with approximately 6 cups unbleached all-purpose flour and 6 large eggs (see page 54)

Coarse sea salt for pasta cooking water

1 tablespoon unsalted butter

¼ cup grated Parmigiano Reggiano

This preparation brings the somewhat subtle taste of rabbit to the fore. If you are lucky enough to have access to duck fat, use a combination of half olive oil and half duck fat to cook the rabbit for even more flavor. Rabbit is relatively lean, so it should be cooked for a long time at a low temperature, as it is here.

PREHEAT the oven to 200°F.

SEASON the rabbit generously with salt and place in a roasting pan large enough to fit the pieces in a single layer. Heat the olive oil until warm and pour it over the rabbit. Roast until tender and browned, about 2 hours.

MEANWHILE, dice the carrots and the white part of the leeks. Bring a small pot of water to a boil, add the vegetables, and cook until the carrots are soft, about 8 minutes. Drain and reserve.

BRING a large pot of water to a boil for cooking the pasta.

WHEN the rabbit is cooked (an instant-read thermometer registers an internal temperature of 160°F) and cool enough to handle, remove the meat from the bone. (You can pull it off with your fingers—you want it to be in pieces.) Discard the bones and save for use in a stock.

PLACE a large skillet over medium heat. Add the cooked carrots, leeks, chicken stock, and tomato puree, and stir to combine. Season with salt and simmer over low heat while preparing the pasta.

MEANWHILE, when the water in the large pot boils, add salt (see page 20), and then add the pappardelle. Cook, stirring frequently with a long-handled fork, until the pappardelle rise to the top and are cooked al dente (see page 55).

ADD the rabbit meat to the simmering sauce and cook until heated through. When the pasta is cooked, drop the butter into the pan with the sauce and stir it in. Drain the pasta in a colander. Transfer the pasta to the pan with the sauce. Toss vigorously over medium heat until combined, about 2 minutes. Remove from heat and stir in the cheese. Serve immediately.

PATÉ DI FEGATINI DI POLLO
CHICKEN LIVER PÂTÉ

Makes about 2 cups pâté   *Toscana*

1 pound chicken livers, cleaned and patted dry

About ¼ cup extra-virgin olive oil

1 large red onion, halved and thinly sliced

Fine sea salt to taste

2 cups Vin Santo

Freshly ground black pepper to taste

To serve this pâté as crostini, a classic Tuscan antipasto, thinly slice a Rustic loaf or other bread with a dense crumb and lightly toast the slices. Spread pâté on each slice and serve. You can also arrange this on a platter with crackers. At Eataly, we use a drum-shaped sieve with a flat bottom called a tamis to strain the pâté, but a fine-mesh sieve of any kind will work. It does need to be strained, though, or it will be unappealingly grainy. Vin Santo is a sweet dessert wine that provides contrast to the gaminess of the livers, but white wine will work here as well.

LINE a plate with paper towels and put the livers on the towels to dry. Blot the tops of the livers with a clean paper towel.

LIGHTLY coat the bottom of a medium saucepan with olive oil and place over medium heat. Add the onion, season with salt, and cook until the onion is soft and browned.

WHEN the onion is soft, add the wine. Cook over medium-high heat until the liquid is reduced by half. Set aside to cool slightly.

MEANWHILE, in a large sauté pan over high heat, add enough olive oil to coat the bottom of the pan. When the oil is shimmering, add the livers in a single layer and season generously with salt and pepper. When the livers are seared on one side, turn them and cook briefly on the other side until just pink in the center, about 2 minutes total.

TRANSFER the chicken livers to the work bowl of a food processor fitted with the metal blade. Add about half of the wine and onion mixture. Process until very smooth, 2 to 3 minutes. Scrape down the sides of the work bowl as necessary. Taste and season with salt and/or more of the wine and onion mixture. Continue to process, taste, and adjust seasoning until you are pleased with the balance. Process one last time until very smooth.

TO strain the pâté, scoop it into a fine-mesh sieve set over a bowl and push the pâté through the sieve with a flexible bench scraper or spatula.

NOTE: *Store the pâté in a tall container with a narrow opening in order to reduce the surface area exposed to air. Press a piece of plastic wrap against the exposed surface before closing the container with a tight–fitting lid and refrigerating. Pâté can also be frozen for longer storage. When ready to serve, thaw the frozen pâté and process it in a food processor fitted with the metal blade until creamy.*

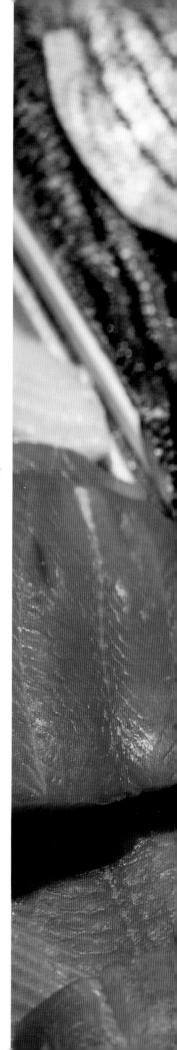

PESCE

*One of the greatest sources of joy is what
happens around a dinner table.*

PESCE INTERO E FILETTI

Italians have always eaten a diet heavy in fish. The long, narrow peninsula of Italy is flanked by the Adriatic and Mediterranean seas. It has more than 4,700 miles of coastline and includes two islands (Sardegna and Sicilia), making fish readily available. Fish steaks, whole fish, and fillets are often grilled or roasted for simple second courses.

The Italian Way with FISH FILLETS

These recipes will work with any number of types of fish. Fillets commonly served in Italy include hake, sole, sea bass (branzino), sea bream (orata), and turbot. Always run your hands over fillets to check for any stray bones and, if serving with the skin, check for any scales that have remained attached. Bonus: Fillets cook quickly.

PESCE ALL'ACQUA PAZZA *Fish in "Crazy Water"*	In a large skillet, cook peeled and crushed garlic over medium heat until browned, then remove and discard. Add minced onion and cook until transparent. Add a single layer of cherry tomatoes and season with salt and pepper. Cook until about half of the tomatoes have burst their skins. Add a mixture of equal parts white wine and water and bring to a simmer. Arrange fillets (preferably with skin) on top of the tomatoes and simmer, covered, until the fillets are opaque, about 6 minutes. When the fish is cooked, baste the top of the fillets with a little liquid from the pan, then remove the fish to a serving platter. Cook spaghetti until quite al dente, drain, and then add to the pan. Toss vigorously with the tomato sauce over medium heat until the pasta is cooked.
PESCE ALL'ADRIATICA *Adriatic-Style Fish*	Toss some breadcrumbs with enough olive oil to moisten them; the mixture should look like wet sand. Add minced fresh parsley and season with salt and pepper. Place fillets on a parchment- or foil-lined baking sheet and spread the breadcrumb mixture on top of the fish. Place the pan in a preheated broiler (not too close to the heat source or you'll burn the breadcrumbs) and broil until the fillets are opaque and the breadcrumbs are browned, about 7 minutes.
PESCE AL LIMONE *Fish with Lemon Sauce*	Lightly dredge skinless fillets in flour. Film a pan with olive oil and brown the fish over medium heat until opaque, turning once, about 5 minutes. Remove the fillets and keep warm. Pour a mixture of white wine, lemon juice, and capers into the pan and cook, scraping up any browned bits, until the liquid has reduced to a silky sauce, 1 to 2 minutes. Pour the sauce over the fish and serve.
PESCE IN CARTOCCIO *Fish in Parchment*	Tear off a large piece of parchment paper and set one skinned fillet in the center. Top with thin slices of lemon, thin strips of scallion, and a few stalks of asparagus. Drizzle with a little olive oil. Fold up the parchment and crimp the edges together. Repeat. Place the parchment packages on a baking sheet and bake at 350°F for 15 minutes. Open the packets at the table, but watch for escaping steam.
PESCE IN SAOR *Fish in Sweet-and-Sour Sauce*	Dredge skinless fillets lightly in flour and brown in a generous amount of oil; set aside. Strain the oil and return a few tablespoons of it to the skillet. Cook a generous amount of sliced yellow onion in the same skillet until soft, but not brown. Add 1 cup white wine vinegar and cook for a few additional minutes. Add pine nuts and raisins (soaked to rehydrate a little if they are hard) to the sauce. Layer the onion sauce with the cooked fish, cover, and refrigerate, preferably overnight. Bring to room temperature before serving, or serve slightly chilled. This is also sometimes made with whole sardines.

SIGNS OF QUALITY

Look for fish cleaned and cut in-house to ensure that you receive the most pristine product.

Fish is as regional as fruits and vegetables—always look for fish caught in your area.

Good fish smells like the ocean, not "fishy," and has smooth, firm flesh.

ACCIUGHE MARINATE ALLA LIGURE
LIGURIAN MARINATED ANCHOVIES

Serves 8 as an appetizer   *Liguria*

2½ pounds small to medium fresh anchovies, cleaned and scaled

Fine sea salt to taste

Juice of 4 lemons

2 tablespoons extra-virgin olive oil

4 to 5 fresh basil leaves

Liguria offers some of Italy's freshest-tasting fare, including many light fish dishes like this one. The acid in the lemon juice "cooks" the fish as it sits. Serve these anchovies on the bone or fillet them before serving—they are a key component to a mixed seafood antipasto. We find it convenient to make this in a glass storage container with a tight-fitting lid.

REMOVE the heads from the anchovies. Rinse the fish and transfer to a nonreactive flat-bottomed container. Season with salt to taste.

POUR the lemon juice over the anchovies. Cover and refrigerate until the fish is opaque, 5 to 6 hours. Store in the refrigerator for up to 5 days, though the anchovies will become more acidic as they sit in the lemon juice.

TO SERVE, remove the anchovies from the lemon juice and transfer to a serving dish. Drizzle on the olive oil. Tear the basil leaves and scatter over the fish.

SGOMBRI AL FINOCCHIO
MACKEREL WITH FENNEL

Serves 4 as a main course   *Marche*

Fine sea salt to taste

2 mackerel (about 2 pounds each),
cleaned and scaled (see below)

10 pearl onions

4 carrots

1 rib celery

1 medium bulb fennel,
including tops

Leaves of 1 sprig flat-leaf parsley

1 clove garlic

1 strip orange zest

3 tablespoons extra-virgin olive oil

Freshly ground black
pepper to taste

1 tablespoon tomato paste

Juice of ½ lemon

Mackerel, along with tuna, is part of a family known as *pesce azzurro*, or blue fish, in Italian—not to be confused with bluefish, pesce azzurro are simply fish rich in oil. That said, if you can't locate mackerel in your area, Atlantic bluefish (which isn't available in Italy) makes a fine substitute. Traditionally, this dish is prepared with whole mackerel that are then filleted, but if you prefer, you can use mackerel fillets and poach them in an inch or so of water rather than boiling them.

BRING a pot of salted water to a boil. Add the mackerel, turn the heat down to a simmer, and cook the mackerel until the flesh near the bone is opaque, 7 to 10 minutes. Remove with a skimmer and set aside to cool. When the mackerel are cool, fillet them (see page 228 for instructions). Set on a platter in a single layer and reserve.

CHOP the onions, carrots, celery, fennel bulb, and fennel fronds. Mince the parsley, garlic, and orange zest.

HEAT the olive oil in a medium saucepan over medium-low heat. Add the onions, carrots, celery, fennel, parsley, garlic, and zest. Cook, stirring frequently, until soft, about 10 minutes. Season with salt and pepper.

STIR the tomato paste with 1 tablespoon water and whisk smooth. Add the tomato paste mixture to the pan and cook until thickened, about 5 minutes more.

TAKE the sauce off the heat and whisk in the lemon juice. Pour the sauce over the mackerel fillets. Serve at room temperature.

How to
CLEAN AND SCALE A FISH

AT EATALY, WE ALWAYS CLEAN AND SCALE your fish for you, but to do it yourself:

1. Make a long slit along its belly, from the throat almost to the tail (use a knife with a narrow, sharp blade).

2. Reach in with your hand and pull out the guts. Discard the guts and rinse out the cavity.

3. Snip off the gills and fins with kitchen shears.

4. Use the flat side of a butter knife to scale a fish—hold the blade at a 45-degree angle near the tail and push up toward the head. Scales will fly around, so if you have a deep sink, set the fish in the sink to do this. Run your fingertips up the body of the fish to check for any stray scales.

PESCE ALLA GRIGLIA
WHOLE GRILLED FISH

Serves 4 as a main course   *Campania, Liguria, Sicilia, Toscana*

2 lemons

¼ cup extra-virgin olive oil

**2 sprigs fresh rosemary
or marjoram**

**2 whole fish, about 2 pounds each,
cleaned and scaled (see page 227)**

Fine sea salt to taste

**Freshly ground black
pepper to taste**

This recipe is simple and beautifully highlights the tender flesh of fresh fish. If you have a grill basket, use it for this recipe—the skin of the fish tends to stick to the grill and tear.

JUICE 1 lemon. Combine the lemon juice and the olive oil in a large nonreactive bowl.

PLACE 1 sprig of herbs in the cavity of each fish. Slice the remaining lemon and stuff the slices into the cavity of each fish. Place the fish in the bowl with the olive oil mixture and turn to coat. Season with salt and pepper. Set the fish aside while you prepare an outdoor grill. (If you don't have a grill, preheat a cast-iron grill pan or broiler, or preheat the oven to 450°F and roast the fish, about 10 minutes per inch of thickness.)

WHEN the grill is very hot, grill the fish, turning once (use a basket if you have one), until the flesh is opaque near the bone, about 8 minutes per inch of thickness.

ALLOW the fish to rest on a serving platter for a minute or two, then fillet (see below) and serve.

How to
FILLET A COOKED FISH

1. Set the fish on a work surface or platter on its side, and, with a sharp knife, cut along the top of the fish, just to the side of the ridge where its fin was located.

2. Make another cut from the left side of the first cut to the bottom of the fish (where the fish's neck would be if it had one).

3. Slide the knife blade flat along the bones of the fish, under the flesh, from the first cut down to the belly, gently working the flesh free of the bone. You should then be able to lift up the tail and the fish skeleton should release easily from the remaining fillet.

4. Cut off the head.

5. When working with a large fish, you may want to cut each fillet into 2 or more portions.

TONNO ALLA GRIGLIA CON PEPERONATA
GRILLED TUNA WITH PEPERONATA

Serves 4 as a main course   *Sicilia*

2 red bell peppers

2 yellow bell peppers

2 orange bell peppers

1 fresh red chili pepper

¼ cup plus 1 tablespoon extra-virgin olive oil, plus more for reheating the peperonata, if necessary

1 garlic clove, crushed

1 large yellow onion, diced

1 large bulb fennel, diced

2 bay leaves

Leaves of 1 sprig fresh rosemary, roughly chopped

Fine sea salt to taste

Freshly ground black pepper to taste

2 tuna steaks (about 1½ pounds total)

Peperonata is a classic southern Italian preparation that pairs beautifully with simple fish preparations. We serve it at Eataly with grilled fresh tuna steaks, or with marinated anchovies or sardines like the Ligurian Marinated Anchovies on page 226. You will notice that while this uses red, yellow, and orange bell peppers, green peppers are absent from this and any other Italian dish—we consider them unripe and indigestible.

CORE and seed the bell peppers and cut them into 2-inch-long matchsticks. Seed the chili pepper and cut it into thin matchsticks (thinner than the bell peppers).

OVER medium-high heat, heat ¼ cup olive oil in a sauté pan. Add the garlic and cook for about 2 minutes to soften. Add the onion and cook, stirring frequently, until translucent, about 7 minutes. Add the fennel, all the bell peppers, the chili pepper, bay leaves, and rosemary, and season with salt and black pepper to taste.

COOK until the vegetables are very soft and limp, with no crunch left in them, about 20 minutes. Store the peperonata at room temperature until ready to use, or refrigerate in a sealed container for up to 3 days.

WHEN you are ready to cook the tuna, preheat an outdoor grill (or cast-iron grill pan) until very hot.

BRUSH the tuna with the remaining 1 tablespoon olive oil and season with salt and black pepper. Grill, turning once, until the outside is seared but the inside is still red, about 5 minutes total per inch of thickness.

IF the peperonata was stored in the refrigerator, reheat it in a saucepan (with a little olive oil if needed to keep it from sticking).

CUT the tuna steaks into 4 portions. Serve hot with the peperonata on top.

229

BRANZINO AL SALE
BRANZINO IN SALT CRUST

Serves 4 as a main course

---

1 lemon

2 egg whites

6 cups fine sea salt

3 sprigs fresh marjoram

1 whole branzino (about 1½ pounds), cleaned and scaled (see page 227)

2 tablespoons extra-virgin olive oil

You can make this recipe with almost any whole fish. Branzino or sea bass is a popular choice, as is striped bass. When purchasing the fish, figure about ¾ pound per person. The salt crust doesn't make the resulting fish especially saline in flavor, but it does keep it extremely moist. Crack open the crust at the table if you want to make an impression. You can really use any herbs in the cavity of the fish that you like, and you can also flavor the salt mixture with ground spices. (See the salt rubs on page 20 for a few classic pairings.) The same technique also can be used for roasting a whole chicken or a beef roast or tenderloin.

PREHEAT the oven to 450°F.

SLICE the lemon into eighths and set aside.

IN a large bowl, whisk the egg whites with ¼ cup water. Add the salt and toss until the salt is thoroughly moistened. The mixture should have the consistency of wet sand. If it feels dry, add more water, about 2 tablespoons at a time, until the mixture is damp enough that when you squeeze a clump in your palm it remains in one piece.

SPREAD about one-quarter of the salt mixture in the bottom of a baking dish that is just slightly larger than the fish. (If you don't have a baking dish that is the right size, arrange the salt in a thin layer just slightly larger than the fish on a baking sheet.)

PLACE the lemon slices and marjoram in the fish cavity. Place the fish on its side on top of the salt bed. Pour the remaining three-quarters of the salt mixture all over the fish. Press with the palms of your hands to seal the crust around the fish.

BAKE for 25 minutes. Remove the fish and let it stand in the crust for 10 minutes, and then strike the top of the salt crust with the back of a wooden spoon to crack it. Remove the top crust (it should pull away in one piece). You can either fillet the fish in the baking dish or transfer it to a cutting board to fillet it. Either way, fillet the fish and divide into 4 servings. Gently brush off any salt clumps stuck to the skin and transfer the fish to individual serving plates. Drizzle with the olive oil and serve immediately.

SPIGOLA AL CAVOLO NERO
STRIPED BASS WITH TUSCAN KALE

Serves 4 as a main course   *Toscana*

1 pound Tuscan kale

2 tablespoons extra-virgin olive oil, plus more for finishing

1 onion, diced

1 clove garlic, minced

⅓ cup cooked chickpeas

Fine sea salt to taste

Freshly ground black pepper to taste

4 striped bass fillets (about 1½ pounds total), skin on

½ cup white wine or water

Bumpy-surfaced Tuscan kale, sometimes labeled "lacinato kale," cooks more quickly than curly kale. It is the main ingredient in Ribollita (page 164), but serves so many other purposes, as here, where it forms a savory bed for fish fillets. For extra-crispy skin, store the uncooked fillets, uncovered, skin side up, in the refrigerator for no more than 24 hours.

REMOVE any tough stems from the kale and either discard them or save them for another use. Cut the kale leaves into thin ribbons.

HEAT the oil in a large sauté pan over medium heat. Add the onion and cook, stirring frequently, until golden, about 3 minutes. Add the garlic, the chickpeas, and the kale. Season with salt and pepper. Cook, stirring frequently, until the kale is wilted, about 10 minutes. Meanwhile, season the fish lightly with salt and pepper.

REMOVE the kale from the pan and set aside. Place the fillets in the bottom of the pan, skin side down. Cook the fish undisturbed until the skin side is lightly browned, about 3 minutes.

REMOVE the fish from the pan and add the kale back to the pan, spreading it out so that it covers the bottom of the pan. Pour in the wine. Place the fish on top of the kale, skin side up. Cover and cook over low heat until the kale is very tender and the fish is cooked through, about 8 minutes more. (If the pan starts to dry out, add water in small amounts around the side of the pan; do not pour it over the fish or the skin will turn soft.)

FINISH with a drizzle of olive oil and serve hot.

PESCE SPADA ALLA SICILIANA
SWORDFISH SICILIAN-STYLE

Serves 4 as a main course   *Sicilia*

**4 slices swordfish (about
1 pound), about ⅔ inch thick**

Fine sea salt to taste

**¼ cup extra-virgin olive oil,
plus more for finishing**

¼ teaspoon dried oregano

¼ cup breadcrumbs (see page 134)

**Minced fresh oregano
leaves for garnish**

1 lemon, cut into eight wedges

Being an island, Sicilia offers some of the best seafood in Italy; its swordfish and tuna steaks are especially notable. Swordfish is also delicious sautéed.

SET a rack over a baking sheet or platter.

SEASON the swordfish with salt. Place the olive oil in a shallow bowl and place the swordfish steaks in the oil. Sprinkle on the oregano. Turn the swordfish in the bowl to coat both sides, then remove the swordfish to the rack and let any excess oil drain away.

PREHEAT an outdoor grill or cast-iron grill pan until very hot.

DREDGE the swordfish in the breadcrumbs and transfer to the grill. Cook, turning once, until just short of opaque in the center and browned on both sides, about 10 minutes.

SEASON to taste with salt, then drizzle with olive oil, sprinkle on fresh oregano leaves, and serve with lemon wedges.

*Fish cooked "Italian style" is extremely delicate with
no added fats and very few condiments.*

FRUTTI DI MARE

Seafood other than fish that is eaten in Italy can be divided into three categories: mollusks in shells, which include clams and mussels; cephalopods, which include cuttlefish, calamari, and octopus; and crustaceans, such as lobster, crab, and shrimp. Generally, the seafood in these categories is handled in a similar manner. Mollusks in shells are at their best when steamed open in a little white wine. Cephalopods should either be sautéed very quickly—squid can be ready in under a minute—or stewed at length. Anything in between will yield less-than-tender results. Crustaceans are delicious steamed or grilled, and often the meat is incorporated into pasta sauces.

Use less salt for tastier and healthier fish.

mussels

tiger shrimp

cockles

clams

oysters

razor clams

The Italian Way with CALAMARI

Squid are so closely identified with Italy that they are often labeled with their Italian name, calamari, even in English-speaking countries. Calamari are almost always sold cleaned, which means their ink sacs and cartilage have been removed. Calamari ink, also sold in small envelopes, can be used to color and flavor egg pasta (see page 55) and risotto, turning them a striking shiny black. Calamari are also irresistible when fried—simply follow the recipe for Fritto Misto di Pesce on page 245, substituting two additional pounds calamari for the shrimp and smelts. Baby octopus and cuttlefish are very similar to calamari and can be used in their place.

CALAMARATA *Neapolitan Pasta with Calamari*	This traditional Neapolitan dish contains two types of "calamari": squid and rings of pasta that go by that name. Slice the calamari bodies into 2-inch rings. In a saucepan, cook garlic and crushed red pepper flakes in extra-virgin olive oil. Add the calamari rings, toss for 1 to 2 minutes, then add white wine. When most of the wine has evaporated, add a generous amount of quartered cherry tomatoes. Cook until the tomatoes have collapsed and the calamari are tender, about 30 minutes. Cook the calamari pasta in abundant salted water until al dente, then drain and add to the pan. Toss to combine.
CALAMARI RIPIENI *Stuffed Calamari*	Separate the tentacles from the bodies and chop them. Quickly sauté the tentacles in a small amount of olive oil, then mix with minced garlic, fine breadcrumbs, and capers. Stuff the breadcrumb mixture into the bodies of the calamari. Close them with toothpicks if necessary. Grill, sauté, or roast the stuffed calamari until opaque.
CALAMARI IN UMIDO *Stewed Calamari*	Slice calamari bodies into 1-inch rings. In a pot, sauté minced garlic in olive oil, then add the calamari, a handful of pitted black olives, fresh marjoram leaves, and tomato puree and simmer until the calamari are tender, 35 to 45 minutes. Stir in chopped spinach and cook until the spinach is wilted.
INSALATA DI CALAMARI *Calamari Salad*	This dish is wonderful as part of a mixed seafood antipasto. Separate the tentacles from the bodies. Slice the tentacles in half the long way. Cut the bodies into rings. Cook the calamari in boiling water just until opaque, 1 to 2 minutes. Drain and, while still warm, toss with some cooked white beans and sliced red onion. Whisk together lemon juice and extra-virgin olive oil and dress the salad. Refrigerate until chilled. Serve with an additional spritz of lemon juice and some minced flat-leaf parsley.
RISOTTO NERO *Squid Ink Risotto*	Prepare a basic risotto as described on page 149. Thin squid ink with water or fish stock and add it to the risotto when it is about halfway cooked. Stir sliced calamari bodies and tentacles in with the final addition of broth. Finish with a generous amount of olive oil and serve hot. For a delicious variation, you can include a variety of other seafood, such as shrimp, along with the calamari.
SPIEDINI DI CALAMARI *Calamari Skewers*	Separate the tentacles and bodies and slice the bodies into 2-inch rings. Thread the calamari onto bamboo skewers so that the point goes through both sides of the rings. Intersperse cherry tomatoes with the calamari if desired. Top each skewer with the tentacles. Roll the skewers in a mixture of breadcrumbs, minced parsley, and minced garlic moistened with olive oil, then grill or broil them until opaque.

INSALATA DI FREGOLA
CON CALAMARI E CECI
FREGOLA SALAD WITH CALAMARI AND CHICKPEAS

Serves 4 as a main course   *Sardegna*

1½ pounds calamari

Coarse sea salt for cooking water

8 ounces (½ package) fregola

¼ cup extra-virgin olive oil

1 cup cooked chickpeas

1 small red onion, minced

Juice of ½ lemon

1 clove garlic, minced

2 tablespoons minced flat-leaf parsley

2 tablespoons minced fresh oregano leaves

Fine sea salt to taste

Freshly ground black pepper to taste

Fregola is Sardegna's answer to couscous—a toasted semolina flour pasta formed into little balls. Its rough surface is perfect for soaking up liquid, and it is served in room-temperature salads and in soups. Sardegna, of course, is an island, so it's natural that its signature pasta is frequently paired with seafood, particularly clams, mussels, and calamari. Fregola is sometimes made with a little saffron—that type will work nicely in this recipe.

CUT the calamari tentacles in half the long way and slice the bodies into rings.

BRING a large pot of water to a boil. Salt the water with coarse sea salt as for pasta (see page 20), add the calamari, and cook just until opaque, about 30 seconds. Remove with a slotted spoon or skimmer.

ADD the fregola to the water and cook as for pasta, stirring frequently, until the fregola is al dente, about 10 minutes. Drain, toss with 1 tablespoon olive oil, and set aside to cool.

COMBINE the calamari, chickpeas, red onion, and cooked fregola in a large bowl. In a small bowl, whisk together the remaining 3 tablespoons olive oil, the lemon juice, garlic, parsley, and oregano. Season with a little fine sea salt and pepper and pour the vinaigrette over the salad. Toss to combine.

SERVE at room temperature.

INSALATA DI POLPO E PATATE
OCTOPUS AND POTATO SALAD

Serves 4 as a main course   *Sardegna*

1 octopus (about 1½ pounds)

1 tablespoon fine sea salt, plus more to taste

2 medium Yukon gold potatoes

¼ cup loosely packed flat-leaf parsley leaves

1 red onion

1 tablespoon minced celery

2 teaspoons white wine vinegar

2 tablespoons extra-virgin olive oil

Freshly ground black pepper to taste

¼ cup loosely packed celery leaves

This main-course salad highlights the texture and flavor of octopus, but you could make it with almost any seafood or a combination of various types. Seafood salads are made all over Italy, with slight regional variations. This is Sardegna's version. In Puglia, it would include thinly sliced carrots and celery in place of the olives and potatoes, and in Calabria, you'll find it dressed with lemon juice rather than wine vinegar.

PLACE the octopus in a large pot and add water just to cover. Sprinkle in the 1 tablespoon salt. Bring to a boil, then lower the heat and simmer until the octopus is tender, about 50 minutes. Drain and set aside to cool slightly but not completely.

MEANWHILE, place the potatoes in a separate pot and add water to cover. Bring to a boil, then lower the heat and simmer until the potatoes are easily pierced with a paring knife, about 30 minutes. Drain and set aside to cool slightly but not completely.

WHEN the potatoes are cool enough to handle, peel them and cut into ½-inch slices. Place in a large bowl.

SEPARATE the octopus head and tentacles. Chop the tentacles and place them in the bowl with the potato slices. Remove the internal sac from the head if it hasn't been removed already, then chop the head and add to the bowl.

ROUGHLY chop the parsley and add to the bowl. Halve and thinly slice the onion and add that to the bowl along with the celery. In a small bowl, whisk together the vinegar and olive oil and season with salt and pepper. Drizzle the dressing over the salad and toss to combine.

THE salad benefits from sitting at room temperature for an hour or so, or you can refrigerate it and bring it back to room temperature before serving. Garnish with celery leaves.

BRODETTO
ADRIATIC FISH SOUP

Serves 6 as a main course   *Emilia-Romagna, Marche*

¾ cup dried cannellini beans

1 cup clam broth or fish stock (see Note)

3 to 4 dried chili peppers

4 cloves garlic, crushed

1 tablespoon extra-virgin olive oil

Fine sea salt to taste

Freshly ground black pepper to taste

1½ pounds clams

1½ pounds mussels

2 pounds scallops

½ cup tightly packed flat-leaf parsley leaves

½ cup tightly packed fresh basil leaves

Brodetto is made up and down the Adriatic coast, and each cook has a slightly different recipe. The clams and mussels need to be cleaned extremely thoroughly for this recipe, because you won't have a chance to strain their cooking liquid. Soak them in salted water until they don't give up any sand, and debeard the mussels. Scrub mussel shells against each other to remove any exterior grit. If you have cooked cannellini or other beans, feel free to use them and skip the soaking and cooking step—you'll need about 1 cup cooked beans. Brodetto is a rustic dish—keep the mussels and clams in their shells and let diners do the work. Some variations of brodetto include larger shellfish, and others incorporate whole fish or fish fillets. We love the concentrated flavor of the sea in this version with mussels, clams, and scallops.

SOAK the beans overnight, then cook until tender following the instructions on page 34. Reserve the cooking liquid.

IN a large heavy-bottomed pot with a tight-fitting lid, combine the clam broth with the reserved bean cooking liquid, chilis, garlic, and olive oil. Season to taste with salt and pepper. Bring to a boil.

ADD the clams, cover the pot, and cook until the clams open, 4 to 6 minutes. Discard any shells that haven't opened and set the clams aside.

ADD the mussels to the pot and cook until they open, 3 to 4 minutes. Discard any unopened shells and set the mussels aside.

ADD the scallops and cook until opaque, about 2 minutes, then return the clams and mussels to the pot. Chop the parsley and basil and stir them into the soup along with the cooked beans.

ADJUST the seasoning and serve hot.

NOTE: *To make clam broth, cook several pounds of clams in 2 cups water until the clams open, then strain the resulting liquid and reserve. For fish stock, when working with whole fish, save the heads and bones, rinse thoroughly, and soak in cold water for 8 hours, then make a stock by gently boiling the heads and bones in water with a carrot, a rib of celery, a couple of bay leaves, and some whole peppercorns. Strain and freeze the resulting stock. In a pinch, you can use plain water here in place of the stock—your brodetto won't have the same depth of flavor, but it will be delicious just the same.*

How to
DIG INTO BRODETTO

BRODETTO CAN BE A CHALLENGE. Don't wear a white shirt to eat brodetto unless you are an expert!

1. Roll up your sleeves. Tuck a napkin into the neck of your shirt.

2. Don't be afraid to use your hands to crack large shellfish. Eat the heads. Suck all the flesh out of the shells.

3. Discard shells in a bowl at the center of the table.

4. Soak up any remaining broth with thick slices of bread.

FRITTO MISTO DI PESCE
FRIED SEAFOOD

Serves 6   *Campania, Emilia–Romagna, Lazio, Liguria, Marche, Veneto*

1 pound medium shrimp

1 pound squid

1½ cups instant flour

1 cup cornstarch

Pinch sugar

Pinch ground cayenne pepper

2 teaspoons fine sea salt,
plus more to taste

2 teaspoons freshly
ground black pepper

6 cups olive oil

2 cups canola oil

1 pound smelts or sardines,
cleaned and left whole

2 cups whole milk

2 sprigs flat-leaf parsley

1 lemon, cut into eight wedges

Frying tends to intimidate people, but one bite of crispy fried fish and shellfish and you'll agree that it's worth the effort. The biggest objection people have to frying is that it makes a mess. Be sure to work with a pot with high sides and a small diameter to limit splattering as much as possible. Of course, if you have an electric fryer, it will be very useful here. Instant flour is a finely ground low-protein flour. Smelts are so small that they are entirely edible—bones, heads, and all.

PEEL and devein the shrimp. Separate squid tentacles from bodies. Leave the tentacles whole and slice the bodies into rings.

IN a bowl, combine the flour, cornstarch, sugar, cayenne pepper, 2 teaspoons salt, and pepper. Line a baking sheet with paper towels.

PLACE the olive oil and canola oil in a Dutch oven or stockpot (there should be 8 inches of oil). Clip a candy thermometer to the pot and place over medium heat. Bring the oil to 275°F and keep it at that temperature as you fry the fish.

DIP the fish and shellfish in the milk, then dredge in the flour mixture. Shake off any excess and fry in the hot oil until golden brown and crispy, about 5 minutes. Work in batches if necessary to keep the temperature of the oil steady.

AS the fish is ready, transfer it to the prepared baking sheet with a slotted spoon and salt immediately. When all of the fish is done, add the parsley sprigs to the oil and fry until crisp. Remove them, place them on the prepared baking sheet, and sprinkle them with salt, then transfer the fish to a serving platter and pull the fried parsley leaves off of the sprigs and scatter them on top. Serve piping hot with lemon wedges.

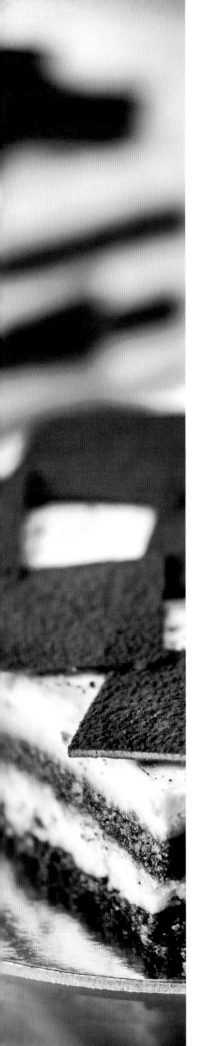

DOLCI

*Classic Italian pastries are
works of delicious art.*

CIOCCOLATO

The phrase *la dolce vita* may not have been referring to chocolate specifically, but chocolate is a big part of living a sweet life. We're not talking about consuming pounds of the stuff every day, but eating a small amount of high-quality chocolate can improve your mood. As far as we're concerned, chocolate is soul food, and life would be a lot less enjoyable without it.

The Italian Way with
PIEMONTESE CONFECTIONS

The region of Piemonte is famous for chocolate (as well as coffee and hazelnuts, which pair so well with chocolate) and for candies and confections in general. Chocolate production in Italy began in Piemonte in the sixteenth century, when the royal Savoy family popularized its consumption.

ALFIERINO	a praline with a portrait of Italian dramatist Vittorio Alfieri sculpted into it
BACI DI CHERASCO	bitter chocolate and hazelnut confections
BOTTONI DEL PRETE	colorful hard candies, often fruit-flavored
CIOCCOLATA DI SAVOIA	named for the royal family; a thick chocolate drink made with coffee, milk, and sugar
GIANDUIOTTO	chocolate-hazelnut confection shaped like an elongated pyramid that is extremely smooth in texture
MARRONS GLACÉS	candied chestnuts; despite the French name, these originated in Piemonte in the early fifteenth century
TORRONE DI NOCCIOLE	hazelnut nougat made with local honey
VIOLETTE CANDITE	candied violets—real flowers are dunked in hot syrup and then allowed to dry

white chocolate

chocolate with hazelnuts

cacao butter for cooking

chocolate with pistachios

gianduja candies

chocolate with candied fruit

triple cream gianduja candies

gianduiotti candies

milk chocolate

dark chocolate—covered pistachios

dark chocolate squares

cocoa powder

cuor di cacao candies

How to ENJOY CREME SPALMABILI

GIANDUIA IS SILKY CHOCOLATE WITH HAZELNUTS that is utterly irresistible—as addictive to us as any drug. It was invented in Piemonte in the 1860s, when cacao was rationed due to the Neapolitan wars. Hazelnuts grow widely in Piemonte, so they were used as a kind of extender for the scarce chocolate available. Strange but true: This ultimate match of flavors was born out of necessity. Today, gianduia is often served in the form of a creamy spread. It's the filling in Baci di Dama sandwich cookies (page 257), but we like it on almost anything.

1. Make a sandwich by spreading gianduia on a bun. This is a popular snack for Italian kids—sort of our version of peanut butter and jelly.

2. Fill a crêpe with gianduia, or spread a little gianduia on a piadina (page 133).

3. Insert spoon in jar. Place contents of spoon in mouth. Repeat. (We'd recommend using your finger, but that can get messy!)

hazelnut spread with milk

candied chestnut spread

chocolate and hazelnut spread

chocolate cream spread

dark chocolate spread

coffee spread

pistachio spread

SALAME DI CIOCCOLATO
CHOCOLATE "SALAMI"

Makes 1 salami, 10 to 12 servings

7 ounces dark chocolate

14 tablespoons (1¾ sticks) unsalted butter, softened

½ cup granulated sugar

2 large eggs

6 tablespoons rum

10 ounces crisp ladyfingers or other plain cookies

This dessert "salami" is very easy to make and always a crowd-pleaser—and it doesn't require turning on the oven. It is often served during the winter holidays. You can replace the rum with a different spirit if you like. Be aware that this dessert contains raw eggs, which may be a health issue for some.

PLACE a large sheet of waxed paper on a work surface.

MELT the chocolate in the top of a double boiler.

BEAT the butter with the sugar with a hand mixer until light and fluffy. Add the eggs and beat until incorporated. Add the melted chocolate and beat until incorporated. Add the rum and beat until incorporated. Crush the ladyfingers and fold them into the mixture.

POUR the chocolate mixture onto the prepared waxed paper and shape it into a cylinder, rolling the parchment paper around it and twisting the ends so that it resembles a large candy in a wrapper. Wrap the entire cylinder in aluminum foil and refrigerate until firm, at least 12 hours.

TO serve, unwrap the chocolate cylinder and use a serrated knife to cut thick slices.

BISCOTTI

Italians love cookies, and who could blame us? Over the major holidays, not only do we Italians enjoy lavish celebratory meals, but we also tend to visit friends and relatives on the days before and after at gatherings that are like an all-day open house. On those occasions, we like to have a plate of cookies (and maybe some nuts in the shells and some dried fruit) sitting out so that guests can help themselves.

The Italian Way with
TRADITIONAL COOKIES

AMARETTI *Little Bitter Ones*	Lombardia, Piemonte	bitter almond cookies
BRUTTI MA BUONI *Ugly But Good*	Piemonte	bumpy cookies made with hazelnuts and egg whites
CANESTRELLI *Little Baskets*	Liguria	daisy-shaped sugar cookies with a hole in the center and a hard-boiled egg yolk in the dough
CUCCIDATI *Little Bracelets*	Sicilia	pastry dough with a fig filling and colored sprinkles on top
CUDDURACI *Crowns*	Calabria	a lard dough is modeled into intricate shapes, often braided, and at Easter is wrapped around hard-boiled eggs
KRUMIRI *Crooked Ones*	Piemonte	bent, ridged, cylindrical cornmeal cookies whose shape was inspired by the handlebar mustache of King Victor Emanuel II
LINGUE DI GATTO *Cats' Tongues*	Piemonte	thin, crisp, oval vanilla cookies
MOSTACCIOLI *Wine Must Cookies*	Campania	spice cookies with wine must, honey, and dried fruit, often cut into diamond shapes and glazed
RICCIARELLI *Named for Ricciardetto della Gherardesca, said to have brought the idea back from the Crusades*	Toscana	dating to the fourteenth century; very light oval almond and orange peel cookies with sharply cracked surfaces that are sprinkled with confectioners' sugar
TORCETTI *Little Twists*	Piemonte	yeast-risen, not-too-sweet teardrop-shaped cookies coated in sugar

amaretti

cantucci

How to DIP CANTUCCI IN VIN SANTO

Tuscany's traditional twice-baked cookies like the cantucci on page 255 are dipped in Vin Santo, sweet dessert wine, to soften them.

1. Pour Vin Santo into a glass with a wide mouth (not a champagne glass) to a depth of two to three fingers.

2. Pick up a cookie. Holding one end of the cookie, immerse an inch or two of the other end in the glass. Hold for a count of five.

3. Eat softened portion of cookie. Repeat.

cappuccino

colazione

melighe

pine nuts

nougat

pistachios

dried fruit

dates

hazelnuts

almonds

raisins

prunes

red walnuts

CANTUCCI TOSCANI
TUSCAN ALMOND COOKIES

Makes about 60 cookies   *Toscana*

1¾ cups raw almonds

5 large eggs

1⅓ cups sugar

8 tablespoons (1 stick) unsalted butter, melted and cooled

4 cups pastry flour

1 teaspoon baking powder

These almond cookies are baked twice, which makes them extra crisp. They are traditionally served with Vin Santo, but they are also perfect for dunking in coffee or tea. They will keep for up to a week in a tin with a tight-fitting lid.

PREHEAT the oven or a toaster oven to 350°F.

TOAST the almonds in the preheated oven until fragrant and lightly golden, 8 to 10 minutes. Set aside to cool.

BEAT 4 eggs with the sugar. Pour in the butter and beat until combined. Add the flour and baking powder. Mix until well combined, then stir in the almonds. Refrigerate the dough until firm, about 1 hour.

WHEN you are ready to bake the cookies, preheat the oven to 350°F. Line 2 jelly-roll pans or cookie sheets with parchment paper and set aside.

TRANSFER the dough to a work surface and cut it into two equal portions. Shape each portion of dough into a log the length of the prepared pans. Whisk the remaining egg and brush it lightly onto the tops and sides of the logs, cleaning the brush of excess egg so that you don't drip it down the sides of the logs.

BAKE the logs of dough in the preheated oven for 20 minutes. Allow the logs to cool on the pans set on racks. (You can refrigerate them up to one day at this point if it's more convenient for you to continue at a later time.)

WHEN the logs are cool, use a sharp knife to cut them at an angle into slices about ½-inch thick. Place the cookies on the pans, cut sides down, and bake at 350°F, turning once, until golden, about 25 minutes.

PASTE DI MELIGA
CORNMEAL SHORTBREAD COOKIES

Makes about 50 cookies   *Piemonte*

½ vanilla bean

2 cups pastry flour, plus more for dusting

1 cup plus 3 tablespoons finely stone-ground cornmeal

½ teaspoon baking powder

14 tablespoons (1¾ sticks) unsalted butter

1 cup sugar

1 large egg

1 egg yolk

¼ teaspoon fine sea salt

Meliga is Piemontese dialect for "cornmeal," which gives these buttery cookies a pleasantly crisp and slightly gritty texture. This is one of two ways that you can make meliga cookies—the other is a softer dough that is piped onto cookie sheets with a pastry bag. Though these are very sophisticated cookies, they were born at a time when corn was a less expensive alternative to wheat. Serve these with the Zabaione al Moscato on page 284, eat them for breakfast as the Piemontesi often do, or emulate Italy's first prime minister, Camillo Benso, Count of Cavour, a Torino native who is said to have concluded every meal with a couple of meliga cookies dipped in mulled Barolo wine.

SCRAPE the seeds out of the vanilla bean and reserve seeds. Sift the pastry flour and cornmeal together with the baking powder into a small bowl.

PLACE the butter and sugar in the bowl of a stand mixer and mix with the paddle attachment until thoroughly combined.

ADD the egg, egg yolk, salt, and vanilla bean seeds. Mix to combine, then, with the mixer running, add the flour mixture, shaking it in gradually. Form the dough into a ball, wrap in plastic wrap, and refrigerate until firm, about 2 hours.

REFRIGERATE the dough until firm, about 2 hours.

PREHEAT the oven to 325°F. Line 2 baking sheets or jelly-roll pans with parchment paper and set aside.

TRANSFER the dough to a floured work surface and roll it out to about ⅓ inch thick. Cut out round cookies with a 3-inch round cookie cutter (or another shape if you prefer). Transfer the cut cookies to the prepared pans. Reroll any scraps and repeat. (Don't reroll scraps more than once.)

BAKE the cookies in the preheated oven, switching the pans top to bottom and back to front about halfway through, until dry and crisp and golden on the bottom, 10 to 15 minutes.

SLIDE the paper from the pans onto racks to cool. When the cookies are completely cooled, transfer them to a container with a tight-fitting lid.

BACI DI DAMA
"LADY'S KISSES" HAZELNUT COOKIES

Makes 50 sandwich cookies   *Piemonte*

18 tablespoons (2 sticks plus 2 tablespoons) unsalted butter, softened

1 cup sugar

2 cups unbleached all-purpose flour

2 cups plus 2 tablespoons hazelnut flour

¼ cup gianduia spread (see page 250)

No one is sure why these petite sandwich cookies are called lady's kisses. One theory is that from the side these resemble two lips pressed together tightly, and a true lady doesn't open her mouth while kissing. Another suggests that these are like a lady's kisses because they're delicate and irresistible—just one leaves you wanting more.

IN a stand mixer fitted with the paddle attachment, beat the butter and sugar. Add the flours about ½ cup at a time, beating to incorporate between additions. Refrigerate the dough until it is very firm, at least 8 hours.

PREHEAT the oven to 275°F. Line 2 baking sheets or jelly-roll pans with parchment paper and set aside.

ROLL the chilled dough into ropes about ½ inch in diameter. Cut the ropes into ½-inch pieces. Roll each piece between the palms of your hands to shape it into a round sphere and transfer to the prepared baking pans with at least 1 inch between them on all sides.

BAKE the cookies in the preheated oven, switching the pans top to bottom and back to front about halfway through, until lightly golden, about 10 minutes. The spheres will flatten on the bottom.

LET the cookies cool completely on the pans on racks.

WHEN the cookies are cool, make a sandwich cookie by spreading about ¼ teaspoon of the gianduia spread on the flat side of one cookie and gently pressing the flat side of another cookie against it. Repeat with the remaining gianduia and cookies.

DOLCI AL CUCCHIAIO

Spoon sweets—puddings, mousses, and the like—are very popular in Italy, and they are very commonly made at home. These sweet, mild treats could be prepared in a home kitchen back in the days when an oven was still a rarity.

The Italian Way with GRANITA

Granita is a flavored ice, a little chunkier than a sorbet. You can make an endless variety of types of granita. For basic granita, make a sugar syrup of equal amounts water and sugar and heat, stirring frequently, until the sugar is dissolved. Stir in flavoring (see below) and pour into a metal pan. Place the pan in the freezer. After 30 minutes, use a fork to break up the crystals that have begun to form. Stir the granita and return the pan to the freezer. Repeat this step every 30 minutes until the granita is frozen all the way through, about 3 hours. To serve, simply scoop into individual bowls. (You may have to "rake" the granita a little bit with a fork.) Flavor granita with any of the following:

lemon juice
pureed berries (seeds strained out or left in)
pureed stone fruits
pureed watermelon (seeds discarded)
almond milk
strong espresso
melted dark chocolate (you can also add cocoa powder to the syrup)
fresh mint leaves—add these to the syrup at the start and then allow the liquid to infuse for a few hours; strain out the leaves and freeze as above
any type of wine, first boiled until reduced by half (if you don't boil the wine, the alcohol content will keep the granita from freezing)

SPUMA ALLO YOGURT
YOGURT MOUSSE

Makes 6 to 8 large servings

9 sheets leaf gelatin

2¼ cups thick (Greek-style) full-fat yogurt

2 cups heavy cream

1⅔ cups sugar

2 pints raspberries (4 cups)

You may not immediately associate yogurt with Italy, but yogurt consumption has been rising quickly in Italy for the last decade, especially in northwestern Italy, and desserts made with yogurt (including tangy yogurt gelato) are very popular. Reserve a few whole raspberries for garnish if you like.

SOAK 5 sheets of leaf gelatin in cold water to soften.

PLACE a heaping tablespoon of the yogurt in a small saucepan and scald it, then remove from the heat. Remove the gelatin from the water and stir it into the warm yogurt until dissolved. Set aside.

IN a bowl, whip the cream and ⅔ cup sugar to soft peaks. Whip in the remaining yogurt until the mixture is thick. Gently fold in the gelatin mixture.

SOAK the remaining 4 sheets leaf gelatin in cold water to soften.

PUREE about ½ cup raspberries, and then gently heat the puree in a saucepan. Remove the gelatin from the water and stir it into the warm raspberry puree until dissolved. Add the remaining 1 cup sugar and the remaining raspberries to the raspberry puree and gelatin mixture. Stir gently to combine.

ARRANGE alternating layers of the yogurt mixture and the raspberry mixture in a trifle bowl or in individual serving bowls, ending with the raspberry mixture on top. Refrigerate until serving.

PANNA COTTA CON "STREUSEL" ALLA MANDORLA

PANNA COTTA WITH ALMOND STREUSEL

Serves 6   *Piemonte*

1¾ cups granulated sugar

½ teaspoon plus
pinch fine sea salt

½ cup whole milk

3 ⅓ cups heavy cream

6 sheets leaf gelatin

1¼ cups unbleached
all-purpose flour

1¼ cups confectioners' sugar

1½ cups almond flour

Pinch ground cinnamon

10 tablespoons (1 stick plus
2 tablespoons) unsalted
butter, softened

Panna cotta translates as "cooked cream," and indeed this dessert is as simple as that. Panna cotta originated in Piemonte—though it is now enjoyed everywhere in Italy—and there it is often topped with the famed local hazelnuts to create contrast with the silky smooth texture. We've taken that idea and run with it by inventing a crunchy almond streusel, but panna cotta can also be topped with melted chocolate, berries, or cooked fruit, or reverse the order in this recipe and drizzle the caramel on top.

BRING 1 cup water to a boil, then set aside. Make a caramel by heating a small saucepan until very hot. Add 1 cup granulated sugar a little at a time, waiting for the previous addition to melt before adding the next one. When all the sugar is melted, add the ½ teaspoon salt. When the mixture has reached a rich brown color, add the hot water, turning your face away from the pan. (Be very careful, as a great deal of steam will escape when you add the water.) Divide the caramel among 6 heatproof glasses or ramekins.

IN a saucepan, combine the milk, cream, and the remaining ¾ cup sugar and scald without letting the mixture come to a boil. Add the gelatin to the warm milk mixture and stir to dissolve completely. Spoon the mixture over the caramel in the glasses or ramekins and allow to cool to room temperature.

WHEN the panna cotta is cool, cover each glass or ramekin with plastic wrap and refrigerate until cold, at least 4 hours.

WHEN you are ready to serve the panna cotta, preheat the oven to 325°F (or use a toaster oven). In a mixing bowl, combine the all-purpose flour, confectioners' sugar, almond flour, cinnamon, and pinch of salt. Stir in the softened butter with a wooden spoon.

LINE a baking sheet with parchment paper. Use your fingers to pinch off small pieces of the butter and flour mixture and drop the pieces onto the prepared baking sheet. Bake in the preheated oven until crisp and golden, about 20 minutes.

ALLOW the streusel mixture to cool slightly, then sprinkle on top of the panna cotta and serve.

BONET
PIEMONTESE TERRINE

Makes one 8- or 9-inch terrine, about 8 servings   *Piemonte*

1⅓ cups sugar

½ teaspoon fine sea salt

3 large eggs

1⅔ cups whole milk

⅓ cup cocoa powder

1 espresso made in a stovetop coffeemaker (see page 292)

1¾-ounce (50-gram) package amaretti cookies

Bonet (sometimes spelled *bunet*) is a terrine somewhat similar to the French crème caramel that was served as part of fancy banquets in Piemonte as early as the thirteenth century. A couple of hundred years later, when chocolate traveled from the New World to Europe, chefs began to include cocoa powder in bunet, along with other complementary flavorings. Eventually, crumbled almond and hazelnut cookies found their way into the mix as well—sometimes a bunet is garnished with a line of whole amaretti running vertically down the center like a row of buttons.

PREHEAT the oven to 325°F. Bring 1 cup water to a boil, then set aside.

MAKE a caramel by heating a small saucepan until very hot. Add 1 cup sugar a little at a time, waiting for the previous addition to melt before adding the next one. When all the sugar is melted, add the salt. When the mixture has reached a rich brown color, add the hot water, turning your face away from the pan. (Be very careful, as a great deal of steam will escape when you add the water.)

POUR the caramel into a loaf pan.

WHISK the eggs in a large heatproof bowl. Combine the milk and remaining ⅓ cup sugar in a saucepan and bring to a boil. Just as it begins to boil, remove from the heat. Temper the eggs by whisking in a tablespoon or so at a time of the hot milk mixture. When all the milk has been added, whisk in the cocoa powder and the espresso. Finally, crumble the amaretto cookies and add them to the mixture.

TRANSFER the mixture to the caramel-lined loaf pan. Cover the loaf pan with aluminum foil. Fill a baking pan with hot water and set the loaf pan in the baking pan so that the water comes an inch or two up the sides. Bake in the preheated oven until set but still soft, about 30 minutes.

ALLOW the bonet to cool completely. To serve, fill a pan with hot water and set the loaf pan in it for a few minutes to heat the caramel so it won't stick. Invert a serving platter over the loaf pan, then turn both the loaf pan and the platter right side up. Lift off the loaf pan.

How to
ORDER GELATO

ITALIANS DO NOT ORDER BY THE SCOOP. Gelato is so creamy and soft that it does not curl into neat balls.

1. Determine which size cone or cup you would like: piccolo, medio, or grande.

2. Ask how many flavors you may order for that size cone or cup. (There may be a sign hanging in the gelateria that indicates the number of flavors.)

3. Give some thought to a proper combination: fruit with fruit, chocolate with hazelnut, coffee with stracciatella. Vanilla is the joker of gelato and matches with almost anything.

SEMIFREDDO AL TORRONCINO
NOUGAT SEMIFREDDO

Serves 8

3 large egg yolks

⅓ cup sugar

1¼ cups heavy cream

4½ ounces hard torrone nougat

3½ ounces gianduia chocolate, chopped

A semifreddo is a kind of frozen mousse, fluffier and softer than true ice cream. At Christmastime, semifreddo is often made with the nut-studded honey-flavored nougat candy called torrone, which on its own is a Christmas tradition in Italy. Torrone comes in both hard and soft versions and is sold in rectangular bars. Because this semifreddo can be prepared in advance, it is perfect for a celebratory meal on any occasion. This can also be made in small individual molds.

LINE a loaf pan with plastic wrap, letting the plastic hang over the sides about 2 inches. Place the egg yolks in a heatproof bowl and set aside.

COMBINE the sugar with ⅓ cup water in a saucepan. Bring to a boil, then pour over the egg yolks and whisk energetically until the mixture is cool.

IN a separate bowl, whip ¾ cup cream to soft peaks. Chop the nougat into crumbs.

FOLD the whipped cream and the chopped nougat into the egg yolk mixture.

TRANSFER the mixture to the prepared loaf pan and smooth the top with an offset spatula, taking care not to deflate the mixture.

FOLD the plastic wrap over the top to cover and freeze until firm, at least 8 hours. (Semifreddo can be made up to 3 days in advance.)

TO serve, scald the remaining ½ cup cream, and then whisk in the chopped gianduia. Place about 1 tablespoon of this sauce on each of 8 individual serving plates.

TO slice the semifreddo, fold the plastic wrap back from the top. Invert a platter on top, then flip the loaf pan and platter together. Pull off the loaf pan, then gently peel off the plastic wrap. Cut the semi-freddo into 8 slices. Place 1 slice on each of the serving plates and serve immediately.

TORTE

When it comes to cakes and pastries, Italy has something of a split personality. At home, we create humble cakes that keep well. But at *pasticcerie* around the country (and Eataly stores around the world) professional bakers craft elaborate sweets of all kinds that we purchase for special occasions. Many of these—both the home-style and the more elaborate—date back to the eighteenth century, when sugar became more readily available, causing pastry making to evolve quickly, especially in the northern part of the country.

Eataly's selection of sweets comes from producers steeped in history.

SIGNS OF QUALITY

Just as with savory cooking, rely on seasonal high-quality ingredients for the best desserts.

You can still splurge on dessert if you have allergies or other health concerns. Our Golosi di Salute (Gluttons for Health) program is designed to provide options for all kinds of dietary needs. Look for the special symbol on desserts in Eataly stores.

The Italian Way with HOME-STYLE CAKES

The cakes we Italians bake at home are not too sweet, and they're not only for dessert.

PAN DI SPAGNA *Italian Sponge Cake*	Pan di Spagna is a tender plain cake that can also be used to make many other desserts, such as the Tiramisù alle Arachidi e Caramello on page 291. It can also be brushed with coffee or liqueur and then frosted with whipped cream. You can cut a pan di Spagna layer in half horizontally and include a layer of jam or gianduia spread (see page 250) in the middle. Beat 3 egg yolks with ½ cup sugar, a pinch of salt, and 1 teaspoon vanilla extract until very light yellow and airy. Separately, beat the 3 egg whites with ¼ cup sugar to stiff peaks. Fold the egg yolks into the egg whites. Sift 1½ cups unbleached all-purpose flour over the egg mixture in 3 or 4 additions and fold it in very gently. Transfer the batter to an 8-, 9-, or 10-inch round cake pan brushed with oil and lined with parchment paper and bake at 350°F until the top is golden and a toothpick inserted emerges clean, usually 25 to 35 minutes, depending on the size of the pan. Let cool in the pan for 5 minutes, then unmold to a rack to cool completely.
TORTA DI NOCCIOLE *Flourless Hazelnut Cake*	This flourless cake is made with hazelnuts in Piemonte, but in other areas of Italy a very similar cake is made with walnuts or almonds. Hazelnuts should be toasted and skinned (rub the toasted nuts in a clean flat-weave dishtowel), but use raw almonds with the skins on. The nuts and the lack of flour keep this cake moist. Finely chop 1½ cups toasted skinned hazelnuts. Separate 4 eggs. Add 1 cup sugar and a pinch of salt to the egg yolks and beat until light in color and creamy. Stir in the chopped hazelnuts. Beat the egg whites to stiff peaks. Fold the whites into the yolk mixture. Gently transfer the batter into a buttered or oiled 9- or 10-inch round cake pan or springform lined with parchment paper. Bake in a preheated 350°F oven until the top is golden brown and a tester or toothpick inserted in the center emerges clean, about 35 minutes. Cool on a rack.
CIAMBELLONE *Ring Cake*	This cake has a slightly dry crumb that makes it perfect with a glass of wine or a cup of tea or coffee. Like Pan di Spagna, ciambellone can be varied in numerous ways. You can replace some or all of the milk with yogurt for extra tenderness; incorporate lemon zest and/or citrus juice; spoon two-thirds of the batter into the pan and then arrange a thin circle of jam on top (not touching the sides of the pan) and top it with the remaining batter. Beat 1 scant cup sugar with 3 eggs until foamy. Add ¾ cup milk and 8 tablespoons (1 stick) melted butter (or ½ cup vegetable oil) and whisk to combine. Add a pinch of salt and 2½ cups unbleached all-purpose flour and beat until combined. Sprinkle 1 tablespoon baking powder over the batter and stir it in until the batter is smooth and free of lumps. Transfer the batter to a buttered and floured ring tube pan and bake in a preheated 350°F oven until the top is nicely browned and cracked and a tester or toothpick inserted in the center emerges clean, about 40 minutes. Cool in the pan.
PLUM CAKE *Pound Cake*	No one seems to know why this pound cake is always referred to by an English name in Italy, and no one knows why it's called plum cake when it doesn't have plums in it either. For a citrusy treat, when the cake has cooled slightly but is still warm and still on the rack, boil lemon juice or orange juice with some sugar until the sugar has dissolved and the juice is reduced by half. Place the rack with the cake on it over a sheet pan to catch any drips, poke the cake in several places with a skewer, and pour the syrup over the cake. Beat together 8 tablespoons (1 stick) room temperature (not hard but not overly soft either) butter with ½ cup sugar and a pinch of salt until very fluffy and light. Beat in 2 eggs, one at a time. Beat in 1 teaspoon vanilla extract and some grated lemon zest. Sift together 1 cup unbleached all-purpose flour and a pinch of salt. Sprinkle the flour mixture over the egg mixture and beat in. Transfer the batter to a buttered loaf pan lined with parchment and then buttered again. Bake in a preheated 350°F oven until the top is golden brown and a tester or toothpick inserted in the center emerges clean, about 45 minutes. Unmold and cool on a rack.

BABÀ AL LIMONCELLO
LIMONCELLO BABÀ

Makes 6 cakes   *Campania*

4 cups bread flour

3 tablespoons instant yeast

1 cup sugar

10 large eggs

14 tablespoons (1 stick plus 6 tablespoons) unsalted butter, softened, plus more for buttering pans

2 teaspoons fine sea salt

⅔ cup limoncello

The delicious little yeasted cakes known as *babà* are normally soaked in rum, but since they are a specialty of Campania, we like to soak them in one of that region's signature liqueurs—tart limoncello. If you have babà pans, which are little cups, of course use them here. If not, other pans will work fine, but you won't get the same height you would with the special pans. We like to garnish these with strips of candied lemon peel and raspberries.

BUTTER 6 babà molds (or any other mini-cake pans, or 6 indentations in a large muffin pan) and set them on a baking sheet.

PREHEAT the oven to 350°F.

PLACE the flour, yeast, and ¼ cup sugar in the mixing bowl of a stand mixer. Add 4 eggs and mix on medium speed until combined. Add 2 of the remaining eggs and mix until combined. Add 2 additional eggs and mix until combined, then add the last 2 eggs and mix until they are fully incorporated and the dough is shiny.

CUT the butter into pieces and add them, one at a time, to the dough, making sure the pieces are incorporated between additions. Add the salt and mix until combined. Place the dough in a bowl, cover with plastic wrap, and set in a warm place (about 85°F) to rise until doubled in bulk, 35 to 40 minutes.

DIVIDE the dough between the prepared molds or pans, and bake until they spring back when pressed with a finger, about 20 minutes.

SET a rack over a baking sheet. Cool the cakes in the pans on the rack for about 5 minutes, then unmold to the rack and cool completely.

IN a saucepan, combine the remaining ¾ cup sugar, the limoncello, and 1 cup water. Bring to a boil over medium heat and continue cooking, whisking frequently, until the sugar is completely dissolved, about 2 minutes. Remove from the heat.

DROP a cake into the hot syrup and allow it to be submerged completely. When there are no longer any bubbles rising to the surface, remove the cake and transfer it to the prepared rack. Repeat with the remaining cakes and syrup and serve.

BEVANDE E CAFFÈ

Life is too short not to drink well.

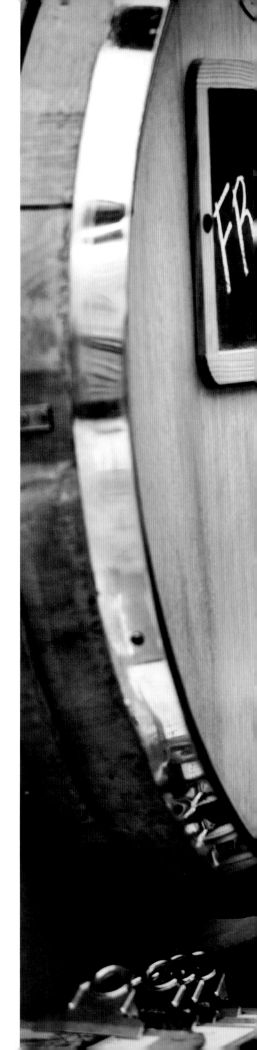

BIRRA

Though Italy is first and foremost associated with wine, Italian beer is also excellent. There are many artisanal beers produced in Italy; in addition the country has a strong history of ciders (made from fermented fruit juice—most frequently apple juice), especially in the Alpine regions of Trentino and Piemonte. In addition to those regions, the central Italian regions of Toscana, Lazio, and Abruzzo produce numerous types of beer. Winemaking requires patience, but—with some exceptions—beer is not meant to have long aging times—it lasts in kegs for up to six months and in bottles for three to four months, and a beer bottle should have a bottling date on the label. You can brew a beer and serve it in a matter of weeks.

Our first Birreria opened at the Madison Square New York City store in 2011. There are now several others, with more in the works. Not only does each Birreria serve beer and food, but each also makes its own beer in a collaboration with the American Dogfish Head and the Italians' Birra del Borgo and Baladin (see below for more on Baladin). One fascinating project that these three partners dreamed up is the Etrusca beer, which is based on archeological research. Wood, clay, and bronze vessels uncovered in a 2,800-year-old Etruscan tomb were tested and found to retain traces of ale made with pomegranate, hazelnut, myrrh, heirloom wheat, and honey. Each of the three Birreria partners then made a beer based on those ingredients in a different vessel (Dogfish in bronze, Baladin in oak, and Birra del Borgo in a custom terra-cotta fermenter). The results are as tasty as they are fascinating.

Beer should not be served ice cold, but somewhere between 42°F and 55°F. We serve beer in a special glass called a TeKu (we also sell the glasses in our housewares department) that has a stem like a wineglass, is marked like a beaker, and has a shape like a tulip with a flared lip that allows beer to retain its head.

BALADIN

In 1986, Teo Musso opened a bar specializing in beer in Piozzo in Piemonte—an area better known for wine than for beer. At the time, he was selling more than two hundred beers that other companies produced—most of them imported from Belgium—but as he became more interested in beer, he also became interested in making his own. Since 1996, Baladin has brewed its own beer (sold in bottles and in its brewpub). The first bottled beer was the super pale ale, followed by Isaac, a blanche beer modeled after those early Belgian bottles (and named for Musso's son).

By 2000, the company needed more space. Musso renovated a henhouse on his parents' farm, evicted the chickens, and created a fermentation cellar. Eventually, he would build a 330-yard "beerduct" under the main streets of the town to connect the former henhouse to the center of Piozzo.

Today, Baladin has twelve different establishments and makes not only draft and bottled beers, but also cider and all-natural soft drinks.

The Italian Way with
BEER PAIRINGS

Beers are generally divided into two categories: ales and lagers. They use different types of yeast. As a very general rule, ales are more flavorful, while lagers are more crisp and light. Because beer is carbonated, it matches especially well with spicy foods. A "hoppier" beer is pungent and sharp, lending it the ability to cut through fattier foods. And beer can be brewed with all kinds of spices and foods—the oyster stout from Birra del Borgo will match well with a seafood dish. Beers made with hazelnuts and chestnuts and others made with heirloom wheat and farro are also available. At Eataly we also like to pair beers with desserts. Ultimately, as with wine, though, any pairing that you enjoy is a good match.

TYPE OF BEER (FROM LIGHT TO DARK)	DISHES
PILSNER	Pizza Margherita (page 124) or any other pizza
WHEAT BEER	antipasto platter (salumi or seafood), Pesce alla Griglia (page 228)
PALE ALE	Arista in Porchetta (page 210), Verdure alla Piastra con Farro (page 145)
BROWN ALE	Pollo alla Diavola (page 217), roast chicken or meat
DARK ALE	Agnello alla Scottadito (page 205), game

SIGNS OF QUALITY

Never cook with a wine or beer you wouldn't drink.

Storage is important, both in our store and at home. Remember that your kitchen may be the warmest room in the house.

BRASATO DI MAIALE ALLA BIRRA
BEER AND APRICOT BRAISED PORK SHOULDER

Serves 6 to 8 as a main course   Piemonte, Lombardia, Trentino—Alto Adige, Friuli-Venezia Giulia

½ cup packed light or dark
brown sugar

1 tablespoon plus
1 teaspoon fine sea salt

1 tablespoon freshly
ground black pepper

1 tablespoon crushed
red pepper flakes

1 boneless pork shoulder (about
4 pounds), cut into large cubes

1 tablespoon sugar

¼ cup diastatic malt powder

¼ cup Italian apricot jam

2 cups apricot beer

A pork shoulder is a big hunk of meat, but keep in mind that it will shrink a fair amount during cooking. Also, any leftovers will keep nicely in the refrigerator—though this is so succulent that leftovers are rare. This dish takes time—the pork braises slowly in the oven for 3 hours—but requires little attention while it is cooking. Several breweries make tangy apricot ales and beers, including Dogfish Head Aprihop beer, which is used in this dish at Eataly in New York. Malt powder is available in baking specialty stores and brewery supply stores and in the baking sections of many grocery stores. At Eataly, this dish is accompanied by celery and apple salad with a mustard vinaigrette

IN a small bowl, combine the brown sugar, 1 tablespoon salt, black pepper, and crushed red pepper flakes. Rub this mixture onto all sides of the pork shoulder cubes and refrigerate for 4 hours.

IN a large heatproof bowl, combine the remaining 1 teaspoon salt and the sugar. Pour in 4 cups boiling water and stir until the salt and sugar are dissolved. Allow the sugar mixture to cool (add a few ice cubes if necessary). Whisk in the malt powder, apricot jam, and beer. (The beer will form a head, so be sure there's room at the top of the bowl so that the liquid doesn't overflow.)

WHEN you are ready to cook the pork, preheat the oven to 325°F. Heat a large cast-iron skillet over medium heat. Sear the pork cubes on all sides, working in batches if necessary to keep from crowding the pan. (The pork will turn almost black due to the brown sugar in the dry rub.)

TRANSFER the seared pork cubes to a large baking dish or Dutch oven. Pour the beer mixture over the pork. The liquid should cover the pork completely or almost completely. If it does not, add water just to cover. Cover the pan tightly with aluminum foil and roast in the preheated oven, checking occasionally to be sure the pan doesn't look too dry, until the meat is extremely tender, about 3 hours.

SERVE the pork with plenty of its delicious braising liquid.

*Beer is a complex art. It unites worlds, histories, and cultures.
Beer is not simply drunk; it is explored.*

VINO

Italy is one of the world's great wine powers—along with France it is the largest producer of wine in the world. Not only is the history of wine in Italy an illustrious one, but it is an ancient one as well. The ancient Romans grew vineyards and had fairly sophisticated techniques for fermenting grape juice. The art of winemaking is still practiced all over the country today. There are three official designations for wine produced in Italy, in addition to the general label of vino da tavola, or table wine. In ascending order of quality, they are:

INDICAZIONE GEOGRAFICA TIPICA (IGT): typical of a specific geographic region

DENOMINAZIONE DI ORIGINE CONTROLLATA (DOC): created according to a set of standards in a specific area

DENOMINAZIONE DI ORIGINE CONTROLLATA E GARANTITA (DOCG): created according to a set of standards (generally with lower allowable grape yields and aged longer than DOC wines) in a specific area and tasted by government inspectors before it is bottled

SIGNS OF QUALITY

If you're stuck, match the region of origin of a wine with that of the dish it's served alongside. You're never going to go wrong pairing a regional wine with a regional dish. Also consider the weight of the wine and food you are serving and try to match lighter wines with lighter dishes and vice versa so that nothing is underwhelmed or overwhelmed.

The Italian Way with
REGIONAL GRAPES

There has been a real renaissance in indigenous grapes in Italy in recent years, and Italian winemakers are constantly rediscovering new local strains. Some grapes stand alone in varietals (wines made from a single type of grape), while others are used in blends.

REGION	RED GRAPE	WINE
PIEMONTE	nebbiolo	Both Barolo and Barbaresco wines are made from nebbiolo grapes.
TRENTINO–ALTO ADIGE	lagrein	This grape is used to make dark-colored wines with strong flavors.
VENETO	corvina	Corvina (and other) grapes are dried to make intense and tannic amarone.
TOSCANA	sangiovese	Red sangiovese grapes are one of Italy's major grapes and make up much of the fruit grown in the Chianti and Montalcino areas.
UMBRIA	sagrantino	Sagrantino grapes are so dark they are almost black, and they produce intense and highly tannic red wines.
CAMPANIA	aglianico	Campania offers a rich variety of grapes. Aglianico is a red grape that grows mostly in volcanic bedrock, lending the resulting wine a smoky edge.
SICILIA	nero d'Avola	Nero d'Avola grapes make red wines that run the gamut—some are dry and light in flavor, and others pack a real punch. The results depend on aging techniques and where on the island the grapes are grown.

REGION	WHITE GRAPE	WINE
TOSCANA	vernaccia	Vernaccia is closely tied not just to the region of Toscana, but specifically to the area around charming San Gimignano, a hill town famous for its many towers.
MARCHE	verdicchio	Verdicchio grapes have been grown in the Marche since the Renaissance and are used to make two DOC verdicchio white wines: one from Matelica and one from Castelli di Jesi.
ABRUZZO	trebbiano	A workhorse white grape with a high yield by DOC standards, the trebbiano grape accounts for at least 85% of Trebbiano d'Abruzzo wine.
CAMPANIA	greco bianco, fiano, falanghina	Greco bianco (which also comes in a red variety, greco nero), fiano, and falanghina are Campania's best known white grapes.
SARDEGNA	nuragus	Nuragus is an ancient white grape grown in somewhat difficult conditions, as the island of Sardegna is exposed to the hot wind known as the scirocco. Because space is limited on the small island, grapes are often grown in conjunction with other crops, ultimately resulting in wines with hints of grassy and herbal flavors.

BRASATO AL BAROLO
BEEF BRAISED IN BAROLO

Serves 10 as a main course   *Piemonte*

2 tablespoons extra-virgin olive oil

3 pounds round steak, preferably Razza Piemontese, trussed with kitchen twine

3 cloves garlic, crushed

4 yellow onions, minced

4 carrots, minced

1 rib celery, minced

1 sprig fresh rosemary

2 bay leaves

5 whole cloves

Fine sea salt to taste

Freshly ground black pepper to taste

2 bottles (about 1½ quarts) Barolo red wine

This dish is Piemonte on a plate—simple yet refined, and infused with the flavor of one of the region's lush red wines. Indeed, Barolo is known as *il re dei vini, e il vino dei re*, meaning "the king of reds, and the wine of kings." Serve the beef and its sauce on a bed of polenta.

HEAT the olive oil, in a Dutch oven or other heavy pot large enough to contain the meat, over medium heat. Brown the meat on all sides, then remove.

ADD the garlic, onions, carrots, celery, rosemary, bay leaves, and cloves. Season with salt and pepper and cook over medium heat, stirring frequently, until the vegetables are soft, about 8 minutes.

RETURN the meat to the pan, pour in the wine, and bring to a boil. Reduce the heat to a simmer and cover the pot. Simmer, covered, turning the meat occasionally with tongs, until the meat is tender, about 2 hours.

WITH tongs, remove the meat to a carving board. Transfer all the liquid and vegetables remaining in the pot to a blender and puree to make a smooth sauce.

TO serve, remove and discard the kitchen twine. Slice the meat and pour the sauce over the slices. Serve warm.

RISOTTO ALL'AMARONE
AMARONE RISOTTO

Serves 4 as a first course   *Veneto*

4 cups beef broth

¼ cup beef marrow

4 tablespoons (½ stick) unsalted butter

2 shallots, chopped

1½ cups Vialone Nano rice or other Italian risotto rice (see page 142)

Fine sea salt to taste

1½ cups Amarone della Valpolicella

¾ cup grated aged Monte Veronese cheese, plus more for serving

This is a classic and visually striking risotto from the area in and around Verona. With the long, slow cooking required for risotto, the alcohol in the wine evaporates, so this dish has a much more mellow flavor than you might expect. If you can't locate beef marrow, substitute olive oil, and if you can't locate Monte Veronese cheese, a cow's milk cheese made in the northern part of the province of Verona, substitute Grana Padano or Parmigiano Reggiano. Amarone is a dry red wine.

PLACE the broth in a small pot, bring to a boil, then keep on a simmer.

HEAT the marrow and 2 tablespoons butter in a sauté pan over low heat until melted. Sauté the shallots until soft and transparent, about 5 minutes.

ADD the rice and toast it, stirring continuously with a wooden spoon, for about 3 minutes. Season with salt.

AS soon as the rice begins to stick to the bottom of the pan, add about ½ cup wine and cook, stirring constantly, until the liquid has been absorbed, about 5 minutes. Repeat with the remaining 1 cup wine in two additions, stirring constantly, until absorbed.

ADD about ½ cup warm broth and cook, stirring constantly, until absorbed. Continue to add the broth in small amounts, stirring continuously between additions. As the rice cooks, decrease the amount of broth in each addition. Always wait until the previous addition has been absorbed completely before adding more broth. To check, draw the spoon across the center of the pan. If liquid immediately runs in to fill the "canal," there is still too much liquid. (See page 149 for more on this technique.) Taste occasionally to check for doneness and adjust seasoning.

WHEN the rice is cooked al dente, 35 to 45 minutes total, remove it from the heat. Add the remaining 2 tablespoons butter and the grated cheese. Stir until well combined, then set aside to rest for 3 to 5 minutes. Serve hot with additional grated cheese on the side.

CODA DI ROSPO CON ZUCCHINE AL VINO BIANCO

MONKFISH WITH ZUCCHINI AND WHITE WINE

Serves 4 as a main course   *Sicilia*

2 pounds monkfish

12 baby zucchini

2 tablespoons extra-virgin olive oil

2 cloves garlic, unpeeled

2 cups white wine

Leaves of 1 sprig oregano

Fine sea salt to taste

Freshly ground black pepper to taste

The Italian name for monkfish, *coda di rospo*, translates literally as "frog's tail," presumably a reference to the unattractive appearance of this fish. But what monkfish lacks in the looks department, it makes up for with taste—it's a moist and flavorful firm fish that stands up well to cooking in wine. A dry white wine from Sicilia, especially one made with inzolia (sometimes spelled anzolia or insolia) grapes, would be great both for cooking and for drinking with this dish.

CUT the monkfish into slices and set aside. If the zucchini are on the large side (bigger in diameter than your thumb), cut them in half or in quarters the long way.

IN a large skillet, heat the olive oil over medium heat. Add the garlic and cook until very fragrant, about 5 minutes. Remove the garlic and discard it, then add the zucchini. Cook, shaking the pan occasionally, until the zucchini are browned in spots, about 5 minutes.

ADD the fish slices to the pan and sear on both sides, turning once, about 2 minutes per side.

POUR the wine into the skillet and cook at a brisk simmer until almost all of the liquid has evaporated, about 5 minutes.

ADD the oregano to the pan. Season to taste with salt and pepper. Cook until the monkfish is opaque but still moist, about 10 minutes more, and serve hot.

LINGUINE ALLE VONGOLE
LINGUINE WITH CLAMS

Serves 6 as a first course   *Campania*

3 tablespoons extra-virgin olive oil, plus more for drizzling

4 cloves garlic, thinly sliced

2 pounds small clams, such as cockles, thoroughly cleaned (see Note)

¼ cup white wine

Leaves of 4 sprigs flat-leaf parsley

Coarse sea salt for pasta cooking water

1 pound dried linguine

Freshly ground black pepper to taste

This classic primo relies on excellent-quality clams, the smaller the better. Clams cook quickly—be sure not to leave them in the pan any longer than necessary, and remove them one by one as they open. Any of Campania's three white wine superstars—greco bianco, fiano, and falanghina—would work well.

HEAT the olive oil in a large sauté pan over medium heat. Add the garlic and cook, stirring frequently, until just beginning to color. Add the clams and then the wine. Cover the pan and turn the heat to high. Cook the clams just until they open, moving them with tongs to a bowl as they do. All of the clams should be open after about 5 minutes. Discard any unopened clams.

MEANWHILE, bring a large pot of water to a boil.

CHOP the parsley and add about half of it to the pan where the clams cooked. Remove some or all of the clams from their shells and return them to the pan, along with any liquid that collected in the bowl. (If you suspect the liquid contains a little sand, either strain it through cheesecloth or a coffee filter or carefully spoon most of the liquid off the top, discarding the portion where the sand has settled to the bottom.)

WHEN the water in the large pot boils, add salt (see page 20), and then add the linguine. Cook, stirring frequently with a long-handled fork, until the linguine is al dente. (See page 74 for more on the proper cooking technique for long dried pasta.) Drain in a colander.

ADD the cooked linguine to the pan with the clams and toss vigorously over medium-high heat for 1 to 2 minutes. Sprinkle on the remaining parsley, season with pepper, drizzle with a little olive oil, and serve hot.

NOTE: *To clean clams, place the clams in a bowl filled with plenty of cold water and a little salt. Let the clams soak for about 30 minutes. They should expel any sand contained in the shells. If any of the clams are open, tap them gently. They should close up readily. If not, discard them. With your hands, lift the clams out of the water (don't dump the water and clams into a colander—you'll pour the sand back over them) and set them aside. Rinse out the bowl, fill it with clean water, then soak the clams again for about 10 minutes. Repeat a third time, or until the water is clean. Scrub the clams against each other under running water to remove any grit from the outside of the shells. Rinse thoroughly.*

ZABAIONE AL MOSCATO
MOSCATO CUSTARD

Serves 6   *Piemonte*

¾ cup Moscato d'Asti

4 large eggs

4 egg yolks

¹⁄₃ cup sugar

Mint leaves for garnish

Zabaione, sometimes spelled *zabaglione,* is a classic Italian custard traditionally made with sweet sparkling dessert wine, though sometimes fortified Marsala from Sicilia is used in its place. Zabaione can be served either warm or cool. Be sure to give it enough time to thicken and increase in volume, which will require some elbow grease.

HEAT the Moscato in a saucepan over medium heat until it is just warm enough that you cannot dip a finger into it and leave it there. Set aside.

FILL another saucepan with about 4 inches water. (To be used as the bottom of your bain-marie; when you rest the bowl on top, you'll want about an inch of space between the bowl and the water.) Bring the water to a simmer.

IN a round-bottomed stainless steel bowl, whisk together the eggs, egg yolks, and sugar until light in color and foamy. Whisk in the warm Moscato.

PLACE the bowl over the pot of simmering water and whisk constantly and energetically until the mixture has increased notably in volume, about 8 minutes. (Check occasionally to be sure the water underneath isn't boiling.) When the zabaione is ready, it will make thick ribbons on the surface when you lift the whisk up from the bowl.

REMOVE from the heat and whisk for about 30 seconds more if you want to serve the custard warm, or whisk until cool if you want to serve it cool.

DISTRIBUTE among 6 champagne glasses or other serving dishes, garnish with mint, and serve.

The Italian Way with
DESSERT AND SPARKLING WINES

WINE	REGION	DESCRIPTION
MOSCATO D'ASTI AND ASTI SPUMANTE	Piemonte	Sweet and fizzy dessert wine with fruity and floral flavors; best enjoyed young.
RECIOTO DELLA VALPOLICELLA	Veneto	Intense red dessert wine that tastes of black cherries, prunes, spice, and leather.
VIN SANTO	Toscana	Sweet, slowly fermented dark amber dessert wine with a nutty flavor made from dried trebbiano and malvasia grapes; perfect for dunking Cantucci Toscani (page 255).
MALVASIA DELLE LIPARI	Sicilia	Light dessert wine made in the Aeolian islands.
PASSITO DI PANTELLERIA	Sicilia	Robust dessert wine made with moscato grapes on the island of Pantelleria—Italy's southernmost point.
PROSECCO DI CONEGLIANO, PROSECCO DI VALDOBBIADENE, AND PROSECCO DI CONEGLIANO-VALDOBBIADENE	Veneto	Champagne's slightly less carbonated cousin.
LAMBRUSCO	Emilia-Romagna	Lightly sparkling red wines intended to be consumed young; often paired with the region's prosciutto and salami.
BRACHETTO D'ACQUI	Piemonte	Sparkling red wine with a fruity sweet-tart balance.

FONTANAFREDDA

Fontanafredda was founded in the Langhe hills—the heart of wine-growing Piemonte—in 1858. The land used to create the winery was then registered as part of the private estate of Vittorio Emanuele II, king of Sardegna at the time and later the king of Italy.

The king was in love with Rosa Vercellana, a commoner and daughter of a drum major in his majesty's service, and he gifted her the entire parcel of land. A year later he made her countess of Mirafiori and Fontanafredda.

Twenty years later, Emanuele Guerrieri, Count of Mirafiori and the son of the king and Vercellana, turned the land into vineyards and began producing wine. He was ahead of the curve when it came to both technique and ideas about business, and he was quite successful.

He was successful, too, because the land was so perfectly suited to growing grapes for wine. The vineyards of Fontanafredda lie on mostly evenly contoured, rounded hillsides at altitudes between 650 and 1,300 feet, in the municipal areas of Serralunga d'Alba, Diano d'Alba, Barolo, and Murisengo. Most of the 200 acres of land are planted with traditional nebbiolo, barbera, dolcetto, and moscato grape varieties. The soil is mainly calcareous (high in limestone)—resulting in grapes with low sugar and high acidity—but it is also very varied in composition.

Fontanafredda continues to produce both still and sparkling wines today, including DOCG Barolo and Barbaresco and DOC Barbera and Dolcetto and DOCG Brachetto d'Acqui, as well as grappa and Barolo Chinato—aromatized wine served as a *digestivo*, a drink that ends a meal.

APERITIVI E DIGESTIVI

Drinks are regimented in Italy, and that doesn't mean just pairing white wine with fish. Italy's many cocktails and liqueurs are ascribed specific properties and positions in the dining experience—they are either *aperitivi*, which whet the appetite and "open the stomach" for a meal, or *digestivi*, which end the meal and are believed to aid the digestive process. Many *digestivi* are bitter elixirs known as *amari* that were originally sold as medicine.

The Italian Way with
APERITIVI AND DIGESTIVI

AMERICANO	Equal parts red vermouth, Campari, and soda water garnished with a slice of orange.	aperitivo
APEROL SPRITZ	Aperol, prosecco, and seltzer garnished with a slice of orange.	aperitivo
BELLINI	Prosecco and peach nectar.	aperitivo
CAMPARI	Bright red bitter substance first offered at a Milan bar in 1867 and based on a secret recipe; it may be enjoyed on its own or used to make a number of classic cocktails.	aperitivo
GARIBALDI	Orange juice and bitters, such as Campari, poured over ice and garnished with a slice of orange.	aperitivo
NEGRONI	Equal parts red vermouth, Campari, and gin garnished with a strip of lemon peel.	aperitivo
AVERNA	Herbal bitter originally produced by monks in the 1800s.	digestivo
CYNAR	Dark brown and murky bitter made with several different plants, but most notably artichoke.	digestivo
FERNET-BRANCA	Herbal half-bitter that dates back to 1845; though the recipe is secret, it includes aniseseed, basil, licorice, and chamomile, among other substances.	digestivo
GRAPPA	Transparent and highly alcoholic brandy made from grape peels, seeds, and stems.	digestivo
LIMONCELLO	Bright yellow lemon liqueur made in the Campania region.	digestivo
NOCINO	Liqueur, originally from Modena, made from young green walnuts, cinnamon, and cloves.	digestivo
RAMAZZOTTI	Bitter made with gentian; sour, bitter, and sweet orange; rhubarb; cinnamon; and oregano.	digestivo
STREGA	Sweet yellow anise liqueur.	digestivo

How to
TAKE A DIGESTIVO

A DIGESTIVO IS CONSUMED AT THE END OF A MEAL. It is not combined with coffee, dessert, or anything else. In fact, a digestivo functions as an *ammazzacaffè*, literally "coffee killer," that refreshes your palate (and your breath) after an espresso.

1. Finish your meal.
2. Finish dessert.
3. Drink espresso.
4. Sip digestivo on its own.

CAFFÈ

Espresso, which to Italians is also simply *caffè*, or coffee, is right up there with pasta and pizza as one of Italy's most famous items around the world, and it deserves to be. A proper espresso is a thing of beauty. It's neither too large nor too small. It has a thick mouthfeel and enough cream on the top that when you sprinkle in sugar, it rests on the surface for a moment before sinking below it. Robusta and Arabica coffee beans, selected from the best producers with the highest standards of production, are responsible for that delicious, robust aroma and taste.

The Italian Way with
COFFEE DRINKS

Italians are a bit over the top, so we didn't stop with simply creating some of the world's best coffee. We took that rich and creamy espresso and built on it to come up with a whole list of fantastic drinks.

ESPRESSO	The ultimate coffee, good any time of day.
ESPRESSO MACCHIATO	Espresso "stained" with a dollop of hot milk.
CAPPUCCINO	Espresso with steamed and foamed milk; filling and frothy cappuccino is a breakfast classic, but not suitable for drinking after a meal.
LATTE MACCHIATO	Steamed milk "stained" with espresso; like cappuccino, latte macchiato is consumed at breakfast, not after a meal.
ESPRESSO CON PANNA	Espresso topped with whipped cream.
ESPRESSO TORINESE	Espresso and foamed milk with hot chocolate and a sprinkle of cocoa.
BICERIN	Espresso, hot chocolate, and thick cream.
PIEMONTE	Double espresso with cocoa, whipped cream, and dark chocolate flakes.
CREMESPRESSO	Espresso blended with milk and cream and frozen.
NEVE SULLA LAVA	Hot chocolate layered with cremespresso and topped with whipped cream and shaved chocolate.
ESPRESSO SHAKERATO	Espresso shaken in a cocktail shaker with ice to cool.

espresso torinese

espresso

shakerato

latte macchiato

cappuccino

How to
EAT BREAKFAST LIKE AN ITALIAN

1. Stand at the bar and peruse the newspaper of your choice. (Italy's pink *La Gazzetta dello Sport* is its highest circulation daily.) Be sure to check the soccer standings.

2. Order the coffee beverage of your choice (unless you have been eating breakfast at the same bar for years—in that case your barista will know). Please note that this is the only acceptable time of day to consume a cappuccino or a latte macchiato. Make the most of it.

3. Choose a sweet pastry. Be careful not to get confectioners' sugar on your clothes!

TIRAMISÙ ALLE ARACHIDI E CARAMELLO

TIRAMISÙ WITH SALTED PEANUTS AND CARAMEL

Serves 12 *Veneto*

10 egg yolks

2½ cups sugar

2 cups heavy cream

1 (17-ounce) container mascarpone

¾ cup to 1 cup (6 to 8 demitasses) espresso made in a stovetop coffeemaker (see page 292)

1 pan di Spagna cake (page 267)

1 teaspoon fine sea salt

¾ cup salted roasted peanuts, coarsely chopped

Tiramisù means "pick-me-up," and with its hit of espresso it does just that. Tiramisù probably originated in the city of Treviso in the Veneto (even that isn't certain), but it is now made all over Italy, and it seems as if every family has its own recipe. This version is from Eataly New York, where pastry chef Katia Delogu has incorporated a very American touch—roasted salted peanuts—into this Italian classic. You can either make the tiramisù in a pan and dish it out at the table, or divide it among individual glass dishes or drinking glasses as you're putting it together. It's great to make for a crowd or buffet because it benefits from being made in advance.

PLACE the egg yolks in a large heatproof bowl and beat by hand with a whisk until slightly thickened.

IN a saucepan, combine 1½ cups sugar with ½ cup water. Clip a candy thermometer to the side of the pan and place over medium heat, stirring occasionally until the sugar dissolves and the syrup reaches 250°F. Pour the syrup into the yolks in a thin stream, whisking constantly, and continue to whisk until the mixture is cool. Whip the cream to stiff peaks and set aside.

WHISK the mascarpone until very smooth. Stir the mascarpone into the egg yolk mixture, then use a spatula to fold in the whipped cream.

SWEETEN the espresso with sugar to taste, if desired.

CUT the sponge cake into thin strips. Brush all sides of the strips with the coffee.

BRING 1 cup water to a boil, then set aside. Make a caramel by heating a small saucepan until very hot. Add the remaining 1 cup sugar a little at a time, waiting for the previous addition to melt before adding the next one. When all the sugar is melted, add the salt. When the mixture has reached a rich brown color, add the hot water, turning your face away from the pan. (Be very careful, as a great deal of steam will escape when you add the water.)

LINE the bottom of a 14-by-9-inch baking dish or a large flat-bottomed bowl with the strips of sponge cake. Cover with half the mascarpone mixture, spreading it smooth with a spatula. Sprinkle on half the chopped peanuts. Drizzle on half the caramel. Top with the remaining mascarpone mixture, followed by the remaining peanuts and caramel. Refrigerate at least 2 hours before serving.

AFFOGATO
ICE CREAM "DROWNED" IN COFFEE

Serves 1

1 scoop vanilla or hazelnut gelato

¼ cup hot espresso made in a stovetop coffeemaker (see below) or espresso machine

You can top an affogato with lightly sweetened whipped cream or chocolate-covered espresso beans, but honestly, we're not sure why you'd want to tamper with perfection. This recipe can be increased to serve a crowd, just increase the quantities. We like to scoop the gelato in advance and store it in the freezer in pretty glass bowls. Then simply line up the bowls, pour the hot espresso over the gelato, and serve.

SCOOP the gelato into a serving bowl, glass, or coffee cup.

POUR the hot espresso over the gelato. Serve immediately.

The Italian Way with
STOVETOP COFFEEMAKERS

There are two kinds of coffee in Italy: bar coffee and home coffee. Bar coffee is made with a very large and expensive machine that becomes "seasoned" over time as the barista makes dozens of demitasses an hour. At home, Italians make a slightly different version of espresso using an octagonal stovetop coffeemaker called a *caffettiera*, often referred to as a Moka in reference to the original brand name introduced in 1933. (There is also a variation from Naples called a *napoletana* that needs to be turned over once the water begins to boil.)

A stovetop coffeemaker has three parts: the base, the top, and the filter. To make coffee in a caffettiera, fill the base with cold water; do not fill above the little valve. Set the round filter inside the bottom part and fill it with ground coffee. (While a fine grind is used for bar coffee, a home coffeemaker does best with a medium grind.) If you prefer strong coffee, tamp down the coffee with the round disk that fits on top of the filter so you can fit in more. Screw on the top, and place the entire coffeemaker over low heat on the stove. (If the burner is too wide for the coffeemaker, use a flame tamer.) The coffee will begin to burble up into the top of the coffeemaker as it brews. When all of the water has risen, the coffeemaker will sputter. Remove it from the heat and pour the coffee into a cup.

CONVERSION TABLES

LIQUID CONVERSIONS

U.S.	Metric
1 tsp	5 ml
1 tbs	15 ml
2 tbs	30 ml
3 tbs	45 ml
¼ cup	60 ml
⅓ cup	75 ml
⅓ cup + 1 tbs	90 ml
⅓ cup + 2 tbs	100 ml
½ cup	120 ml
⅔ cup	150 ml
¾ cup	180 ml
¾ cup + 2 tbs	200 ml
1 cup	240 ml
1 cup + 2 tbs	275 ml
1¼ cups	300 ml
1⅓ cups	325 ml
1½ cups	350 ml
1⅔ cups	375 ml
1¾ cups	400 ml
1¾ cups + 2 tbs	450 ml
2 cups (1 pint)	475 ml
2½ cups	600 ml
3 cups	720 ml
4 cups (1 quart)	945 ml (1,000 ml is 1 liter)

WEIGHT CONVERSIONS

U.S./U.K.	Metric
½ oz	14 g
1 oz	28 g
1½ oz	43 g
2 oz	57 g
2½ oz	71 g
3 oz	85 g
3½ oz	100 g
4 oz	113 g
5 oz	142 g
6 oz	170 g
7 oz	200 g
8 oz	227 g
9 oz	255 g
10 oz	284 g
11 oz	312 g
12 oz	340 g
13 oz	368 g
14 oz	400 g
15 oz	425 g
1 lb	454 g

OVEN TEMPERATURES

°F	°C	Gas Mark
250	120	½
275	140	1
300	150	2
325	165	3
350	180	4
375	190	5
400	200	6
425	220	7
450	230	8
475	240	9
500	260	10
550	290	Broil

INDEX